Terence Bowman, great-grandson of Alexander Bowman, was born in Bangor in 1957 and attended Bangor Grammar School. He is editor of the *Mourne Observer* in Newcastle, Co. Down, which he joined in 1976, having completed the National Council for the Training of Journalists' pre-entry course at the Belfast College of Business Studies. In 1991 he edited and published *Railway Memories*, which told the recollections of former employees of the railways in Co. Down.

G000049162

'Every possible source of information has been researched. This biography of one of the Irish labour movement's true pioneers cannot be surpassed.'
Dr John W. Boyle, author of *The Irish Labour Movement* (Washington, D.C. 1988)

Belfast Telegraph portrait of Alexander Bowman as president of the
Irish Trade Union Congress in 1901

PEOPLE'S CHAMPION

The Life of Alexander Bowman
Pioneer of Labour Politics in Ireland

TERENCE BOWMAN

ULSTER
HISTORICAL FOUNDATION

This book is dedicated to my wife Averil for her patience and understanding during many months of research, and to my late father Hugh. I regret not having had the chance to get to know him as well as I now know my great-grandfather.

First published 1997
by the Ulster Historical Foundation
12 College Square East, Belfast, BT1 6DD

ISBN 0-901905-82-8

Typeset by the Ulster Historical Foundation
Printed by ColourBooks Ltd.
Cover and Design by Dunbar Design

This book has received support from the Cultural Traditions Programme of the Community Relations Council which aims to encourage acceptance and understanding of cultural diversity.

CONTENTS

ABBREVIATIONS

B(E)T	*Belfast (Evening) Telegraph*
BNL	*Belfast News-Letter*
BPP	British Parliamentary Papers
BTC	Belfast Trades Council
BWS	*Belfast Weekly Star*
HGI	Henry George Institute
ILP	Independent Labour Party
IN	*Irish News*
IPHRA	Irish Protestant Home Rule Association
ITUC	Irish Trade Union Congress
MN	*Morning News*
MP	Member of Parliament
NW	*Northern Whig*
PRONI	Public Record Office of Northern Ireland
QUB	Queen's University, Belfast
RIC	Royal Irish Constabulary
SDF	Social Democratic Federation
TUC	Trades Union Congress
UCD	University College, Dublin
WG	*Walthamstow Guardian*
WNW	*Weekly Northern Whig*
WR	*Walthamstow Reporter*

ACKNOWLEDGMENTS

IT REQUIRED THE help of a considerable number of people and reference to numerous sources to build flesh on the few scant bones at my disposal when I undertook this biography. Special thanks go to the local studies departments in Ballynahinch (South Eastern Education and Library Board) and Armagh (Southern Education and Library Board), also to the staffs at Newcastle, Downpatrick, Newry, Bangor, Londonderry, Ballymoney, Ballymena and Carrickfergus libraries; Linen Hall Library; Belfast Central Library; Public Record Office of Northern Ireland; Belfast City Council; Queen's University, Belfast; Whiteinch (Glasgow) Library; Mitchell Library, Glasgow; Vestry House Museum, Walthamstow; National Library of Ireland; Cork City Library; Sligo Library; General Register Office, Dublin; National Archives, Dublin; University College, Dublin; TUC Library in London; British Newspaper Library at Colindale, London; Irish Labour History Society; Presbyterian Historical Society of Ireland; Church of Ireland College of Education, Dublin; Masonic Province of Down; Banbridge Heritage Development Company; Sports Council for Northern Ireland, and *Mourne Observer* colleagues.

Individuals, in no particular order, include: John W. Boyle,

Eamon Phoenix, Rayner Lysaght, Ruth McConnell, Albert Colmer, Terry Cradden, Mats Greiff, Gerry Kavanagh, Vincent McKee, Mons. Joseph Maguire, Amy Dempster, Horace Reid, Ed Kilgore, Joseph McGiverin, Peter Collins, Emmet O'Connor, David Bleakley, Nelson McCausland, Hazel Francey, the Rev. David and Mrs Maxine McConaghy, Walter Porter, Wilhelmina Pilger, Val and Anna McGann, Fr Anthony Davies, Fr Oliver Mooney, the Rev. Trevor Anderson, Victor Elliott, Christobel Sanderson, the Rev. Sidlow McFarland, Douglas Gageby, Hamish Fraser, Sidney Elliott, Donal Nevin, Joe Baker, Raymond Blaney, Malachi Curran, John Freeman, Elizabeth Belshaw, George Woodman, Jimmy Blackwood, Norman Jenkinson, Paul Clements, Michael Boyd, Jack and Mary Howard, Rosemary Graham, Robert Bowman, Helen Burland, Rosaleen Wood, Stuart Kelly, Margaret McLain, Ethel Monteath, Maureen Bowman, Margaret Bowman, Margaret McNeilly, the late Jim Hawthorne and the late Sir Ivan Ewart. Sincere apologies for any unintentional omissions.

I am also deeply grateful to the Cultural Traditions Group of the Community Relations Council, Belfast City Council, the Lipman-Miliband Trust, the Amalgamated Transport and General Workers' Union, the Enkalon Trust, Labour Northern Ireland, the Belfast and District Trades Council, UNISON and USDAW for the generous financial support they have provided for this publication.

FOREWORD

THIS BIOGRAPHY of Alexander Bowman by his descendant Terence Bowman is an excellent contribution to the local and national social history of Victorian Ireland. It is also a fitting tribute to one of the many remarkable working-class leaders who were under-valued in their day and largely ignored by traditional historians of the period. However, at long last the founders of our local trade union and labour movement are being honoured for their pioneering efforts; and, as Terence Bowman's investigations reveal, labour leaders, both North and South, made a notable contribution to the social and economic history of their time.

But breaking out of the class confines of the nineteenth century was no easy task: the situation called for radical actions by working-class men and women who were prepared to challenge the Tory/Liberal framework inside which 'the state of the nation' was decided. A 'third force,' a labour movement, was required – Bowman of Belfast made a major contribution to the radical thinking of his day.

The two-track approach employed by the author is particularly fitting: we are invited to view Alexander Bowman as a committed servant and leader of the working class while, at the same time, a family man living at the sharp end of things, enduring with his fellow workers the economic uncertainty of the industrial system and the wrath of the establishment for having had the audacity to 'get above his station' by challenging the authority of his 'betters' in his place of work and in the political institutions of his day. Alexander Bowman's life of radical witness was no easy task, but as this biography shows, in a well-combined trilogy of industry, politics and Church affairs, he set a pattern which became a model for others to follow.

But at a more practical level Bowman's life was a 'way into' the new thinking in which the working class of both Ireland and Britain was engaged in the final quarter of the nineteenth century. For example, trade union activity had made working people aware of their potential strength. Leaders like Bowman saw the need to 'agitate, educate and organise.' Such slogans led to demands for labour to have parity of esteem in the affairs of industry and Parliament. Bowman was one of the first of the few who were willing to give expression to the philosophy of action which lay behind such attitudes. So he practised and he preached the need to develop the potential for federal action across the working class. For this reason a strengthening of trades councils and the TUC became special aims in his life's work.

Even more radical, and advanced for his time, Bowman saw the link between effective trade union action and parliamentary legislation. So, once again, he led the way by standing as a candidate for the working class in employer-controlled North Belfast. Though defeated, he changed the political climate by making it normal for working men to stand for parliament in support of class interests. Nor was his vote planted in vain: North Belfast has remained ever since an area with a potentially strong Labour vote.

In this, as in many other radical respects, Alexander Bowman was a trailblazer in Victorian Belfast and particularly in the northern province. His descendant has written a life story which gives credit where credit is due.

David Bleakley

INTRODUCTION

ALEXANDER BOWMAN holds a special but generally unrecognised place in Irish political and trade union history. The product of a mixed marriage who faced a disrupted childhood following the early death of his farmer/weaver father, his formal education was curtailed and he suffered an early sacking from work for daring to speak up for colleagues in a dispute. Yet in 1885, at the age of 31, Bowman became the first working-class man in Ireland, and one of the earliest in the British Isles, to stand for Parliament – as an independent labour candidate in the newly-created North Belfast constituency.

Baptised a Catholic but raised a Presbyterian, Bowman was a pioneering trade unionist whose early political loyalties lay with William Gladstone and the Liberal Party. He was a radical for his time, advocating the nationalisation of land and an end to the landlord system, free primary and technical education, unrestricted trade between nations, a reduction in working hours, improved welfare rights, and votes for women. His election opponent in 1885 was sitting Belfast Conservative MP William Ewart, Bowman's own former linen mill employer, and while Ewart won the seat convincingly a blow had been struck on behalf of the north's developing labour movement.

Within months Bowman became embroiled in an angry disagreement with fellow trade unionists over his support for Gladstone's Home Rule bill. He did not subscribe to the widely-held view among Unionists that a parliament in Dublin, subordinate to Westminster, would ultimately lead to total independence for Ireland. During the following three years, and in the continuing fight against what he perceived as the misgovernment of Ireland, Bowman became a prominent speaker on nationalist platforms throughout the north. At the same time he opposed the use of violence as a means to obtain land reforms and legislative freedom, and never faltered in his loyalty to Queen Victoria, seeing himself as a 'real' Unionist who believed that the best way to improve Ireland's social and moral well-being lay in rewriting the Act of Union to create a more equal partnership between the two islands.

Bowman became an unequivocal supporter of Charles Stewart Parnell following the Irish Nationalist leader's endorsement of Gladstone's controversial policy. In 1887 he made it to Westminster – to give evidence to a House of Commons Select Committee on the perception among Catholics that Belfast's mainly Protestant and Conservative magistrates were biased against them. Ultimately forced by the unrelenting bitterness of many of his own co-religionists and by the resulting financial hardship to move to Glasgow, and subsequently to London, where he became closely involved with leading figures in the embryonic stages of the British Labour Party, Bowman returned to Ireland a committed socialist, free of green or orange political baggage, and gained prominence as one of six labour candidates elected to Belfast Corporation in November 1897.

To the surprise of the other, mainly Conservative, candidates, Bowman topped the poll in North Belfast's labour-conscious Duncairn ward and took his seat as the area's senior councillor. A conscientious and dedicated working-class representative in the council chamber, Bowman reached the pinnacle of his trade union career in May 1901 when he was the unanimous choice for president of the Irish Trade Union Congress. His presidential address, in which he called for the 'uniting of all sects, creeds and parties in the attempt to raise our common and beloved country to that material, moral and social position to which she is entitled,' remains one of the most powerful delivered in the history of Congress, with much of his message as relevant today as it was at the beginning of the century.

To a great extent self-educated and capable of quoting from the Bible, Shakespeare and Byron, Bowman was renowned for his speaking skills – during the period he campaigned for Home Rule he was invited to lecture in America, but declined due to his understandable fears for the welfare of his young family during an extended absence.

His is the story of an ordinary working man who, from simple beginnings as a 10-year-old part-time machine boy in a flax mill and drawing on his own natural intelligence, went on to seek election to the Westminster Parliament, then became a prominent Protestant nationalist, a socialist, a member of Belfast Corporation and, ultimately, the respected leader of many thousands of Irish trade unionists. It is also the story of politics in the north of Ireland from the 1880s to the turn of the century, and the often harsh conditions which confronted ordinary working people in Belfast, with a glimpse of the growing pains experienced by socialism on both sides of the Irish Sea.

There was a second stage to Alexander Bowman's life. Almost penniless and leading a near-nomadic existence at the dawning of the twentieth century, he gave up active politics and his involvement in trade unionism to carve a better future for his wife and six children. He rejoined Belfast Corporation as a member of its staff, serving for 21 years as the innovative superintendent of the municipal baths on the Falls Road.

Bowman lived long enough to witness the 1920 Government of Ireland Act which created parliaments in Dublin and Belfast, and, four years later, Britain's first Labour government. He derived considerable pride from the knowledge that one of his sons had been honoured with an MBE from King George V for government service during the First World War. Another son went on to become Permanent Secretary with Northern Ireland's Ministry of Labour and was awarded the CBE by King George VI, some 22 years after Bowman's death at the age of 70 in 1924.

THE McKEOWN BOY
FROM DERRY, DROMARA

ALEXANDER BOWMAN'S approach to Irish politics and trade
unionism had its roots in his growing years. More than a century
ago precise personal details about him were limited, due, it can
be assumed, to his own desire to ensure rivals were denied any
potentially damaging information about his background.
Newspaper profiles mentioned Bowman's involvement with the
Belfast Trades Council, which he had helped to found in 1881,
but none offered an insight into his ancestry or the first 20 years
of his life.[1]

Bowman died in 1924 and the last of his six children passed
away in 1970. He left no personal diaries, notes or archives of his
political and trade union life, preferring in later life to treat it as
very much a closed book. None of his children ever spoke with
any great certainty about their father's or their paternal
grandparents' background. Indeed, eldest son William, who wrote
a family history in the 1940s dealing almost exclusively with his
mother's relations, believed his father had started his working
life as a clerk with a coach-building firm.

A major problem in tracing Bowman's roots lies in the fact that
while legislation requiring the registration of civil and non-Roman

Catholic marriages in Ireland took effect from 1845, the registration of all births, deaths and Catholic marriages was required by law only from 1864. Prior to those dates a researcher must rely to a large extent on church records and these are often incomplete. Many Church of Ireland records were lost during the Irish Civil War, with the bombardment and destruction of Dublin's Four Courts at the end of June 1922. The keeping of Catholic records was not permitted under the Penal Laws, which were not substantially repealed until 1829 with Catholic Emancipation.

To begin unravelling the Bowman family mystery it can be established, by way of Alexander's 1880 marriage certificate, that his father was a farmer named William McKeown.[2] Furthermore, when filling in the 1911 census return in Belfast, Bowman gave the place of his birth as Co. Down.[3] It is also known that he had a younger brother called Hugh. When Hugh married in 1885, he stated that his father was a farmer, but he supplied the name William Bowman. Illegitimacy as far as Alexander was concerned is an obvious conclusion, yet the truth is more complex.

Clues can be found in a brief obituary report published after Hugh's death in March 1954,[4] his descendants' understanding that his mother's maiden name was Elizabeth Rogers, and, most crucially of all, a frank addition to Alexander Bowman's marriage certificate by the officiating clergyman. That revealing explanation, which remained hidden from most if not all of Alexander Bowman's descendants for more than a century, was penned by the Rev. Lamont Hutchinson, minister of Belfast's Argyle Place Presbyterian Church from the time of its opening in April 1864.[5] Clearly implying he had known Bowman for a number of years, Hutchinson wrote:

> His mother was married first to a man called Bowman to whom she had a number of children. After his death she married McKeown to whom she had Alexander and some other children. He also died when his children were very young. These children began to be called by people Bowman, but without any wish on the part of their mother that it should be so. It went on nevertheless and soon their own name was lost and so it remains lost.

Alexander and Hugh, therefore, had no Bowman blood – both being children from the marriage between their mother, only carrying the Bowman name through her first marriage, and William McKeown. Indeed, it is also clear that the older boy was christened Patrick, but from an early age was known by the name Alexander.

Trying to establish which of the many farming McKeowns in Co. Down was Alexander's father was assisted by the revelation in Hugh's obituary report that he was 'born in Dromara district and came to the city at an early age.' Attention therefore must turn to Dromara, close to the source of the River Lagan and some 20 miles from Belfast. In the mid-nineteenth century the village, with an immediate population of 230, was described as 'much improved during the past few years, the cause of which is attributable to the prosperous state of the linen trade.'[6]

Griffith's valuation records, compiled in the years leading up to 1861 and published in 1863,[7] identify Patrick and William McKeon (sic) as tenants of adjoining holdings of ten acres and five acres respectively at Derry, a 631-acre townland comprising 65 farmhouses on the Ballynahinch side of Dromara and located within the Barony of Lower Iveagh. Derry's population in 1861 was 305, having fallen from 319 a decade earlier.[8] There was one landlord for the whole townland, James Forde Graham, of Ballymaglave, Ballynahinch, Co. Down, to whom the rents were paid.[9] The acreages point to a sub-division of one larger holding, with Patrick and William McKeown being father and son respectively.[10] They alone bore the McKeown surname among the tenant-farmers in Derry, although their roots were in the adjoining 1,231-acre Burren townland.[11]

As a pointer to the McKeowns' origins, a weather-beaten gravestone in Dromara's parish cemetery bears the inscription 'Patk. McKown of Burrin,' as well as a carved face, most likely of the deceased. He died in January 1816 at the age of 72, leaving a number of descendants, including, it is believed, James, Bernard and Patrick McKeown. The latter named, who by the late 1820s rented a six-acre farm at Derry, was the father of William McKeown.[12]

Records for the Church of St Michael at Finnis, just over a mile from Dromara on the road to Rathfriland, show that on 26 November 1853, William McKeown and Elizabeth Bowman were married by the Rev. John Irwin.[13] On the same day the couple also underwent a civil marriage at the Lisburn Registry Office. The bride, described as a widow, was 31, while the groom, a bachelor, was 26. Both lived in Derry townland. The civil record confirmed that William McKeown's father was named Patrick and that both men were farm labourers. Elizabeth's father was a weaver called William Rogers.[14]

No other McKeown-Bowman marriages were recorded for that period anywhere in Ireland. St Michael's was a Catholic church and William McKeown was the Catholic partner in a mixed marriage to a Presbyterian.[15] The double wedding, with Catholic witnesses at the church service and Presbyterian witnesses at the registry office, implies a desire on the couple's part to show any objectors that their marriage had been copper-fastened by both the Catholic Church and the State.

And critics there surely would have been, for Elizabeth was pregnant at the time of the marriage. On 17 March 1854, just four months later, the couple's son Patrick was baptised at St Michael's. A daughter, Mary, was baptised on 25 September 1856, and a second daughter, Elizabeth, followed on 4 February 1859. For both Patrick and Mary, their mother's name was recorded as Elizabeth Bowman, while for daughter Elizabeth her maiden name of Rogers was used. The couple's fourth and final child, Hugh, was born on 8 July 1860, but he was not baptised at St Michael's. Nor do the baptismal records mention Alexander, leading to the conclusion that he had been named Patrick after his grandfather.[16]

Aware of the date of his mother's marriage to William McKeown, and in order to protect her from the accusing finger of Victorian morality, Alexander Bowman claimed repeatedly he was born in 1855. When filling in the family's census form in Glasgow in May 1891,[17] and again in Belfast in April 1911, he gave his age 'at last birthday' as 36 and 56 respectively. However, when cross-examined under oath by a panel of MPs at Westminster in 1887, he said he was then 'only 33' – thereby confirming 1854 as the year of his birth.[18]

His children were certainly kept in the dark, for when Bowman died in November 1924 the age given on his death certificate was 68,[19] while two newspaper obituaries stated he was 72.[20] The actual day of his birth was never in doubt for the family always celebrated it on 16 March.[21] In an era of high infant mortality it was normal for a first-born child, particularly a son, to be baptised the day after birth, and in Patrick/Alexander's case that was clearly on 17 March 1854. Indeed, it is possible that Alexander Bowman, while aware of his McKeown parentage, never knew about his baptismal name, which appeared just once, in the far-from-public church records at Finnis, Dromara.

William McKeown was 37 when he died from tuberculosis of the liver on 5 January 1865. His death certificate revealed that, as well as being a farmer, McKeown supplemented his income as a weaver.[22] No longer able to run the farm, something she would have come to accept during her husband's lengthy illness, Elizabeth journeyed to Belfast with her children to find work.[23] The move represented a final break from Dromara, where she had lost two husbands and her father-in-law and both her parents were almost certainly dead.[24]

That leaves the matter of Elizabeth's first marriage, along with Lamont Hutchinson's revelation that it too had produced 'a number of children.' Records for Loughaghery Presbyterian Church, between Ballynahinch and Hillsborough, near the village of Annahilt,[25] show that the Rev. Robert Moorhead officiated at the marriage of Elizabeth Rogers, of Burren, to John A. Bowman on 9 April 1844.[26] Even older records for Loughaghery church give the date of Elizabeth's baptism as 25 May 1823, and confirm her father's name as William,[27] while her husband, a son of John Bowman of Derry townland, was baptised on 25 April 1819. The marriage produced three children: William, baptised on 5 March 1845; Nancy Jane, baptised on 7 May 1848, and James, baptised on 6 April 1851. The baptismal register shows the Bowmans lived in Derry townland. While no mid nineteenth-century burial records survive for Loughaghery church or the parish graveyard at nearby Annahilt, it can be accepted, given the wording of Mr Hutchinson's addendum, that Elizabeth's husband died in his early 30s within months of James's birth.

There is every likelihood that Elizabeth's decision to marry a neighbouring Catholic more than four years her junior, whose child she was carrying, and so soon after her first husband's death, led to her alienation not only from the Rogers family, but also from any surviving Bowmans. It is also possible that intense bitterness had been sparked by the expansion of the McKeown farmland to include those acres previously rented by the Bowmans in Derry.[28]

Following McKeown's death Elizabeth, with no-one to turn to and at a time when tenants unable to pay the rent faced ejection and the threat of the Lisburn workhouse, decided to move to Belfast. There were Bowmans already living in the Shankill area, as well as several Rogers from the Dromara area,[29] who might have been unaware of the second marriage in an era of limited communications. Eldest son William, by then almost 20, was the main breadwinner and, in time, the householder.[30] That would help to explain why people mistakenly called Elizabeth's other children by the Bowman surname.

The evidence confirms Alexander Bowman's Co. Down roots and serves to show why, as the product himself of a mixed marriage, he always fought against religious intolerance. Furthermore, after spending his first 10 years on a farm, he held an abiding interest in tenants' rights and the welfare of rural people. However, in the stricter Victorian age, and in light of his political aspirations, it is hardly surprising that Bowman chose to avoid any direct references to his complicated family background. Brother Hugh clearly felt when he married in 1885, two years after Mr Hutchinson's death, that identifying his father as William Bowman to a new clergyman was a private matter.[31] If his mother had retained the McKeown surname he would doubtless have explained, quite truthfully, that she had remarried and that her second husband had also died.

The ultimate fate of the Bowman half-brothers and half-sister from the first marriage, as well as the two other children from the second, remains a mystery. There is evidence to suggest that William Bowman moved with his mother to London where, in the 1890s, he would link up again with half-brother Alexander. With emigration and premature death among possible answers for the others, Hugh was surely remembering his own sisters, as well as his mother, when he had his twin daughters christened Mary and Elizabeth in 1893.[32] The latter also bore Rogers as her middle name, as did Alexander's fourth son Thomas, although his was spelt Rodgers.[33]

More than a century later, it is hard to know just how many people were ever aware of the truth. It is quite possible that Alexander Bowman's own children were kept largely in the dark about their father's parentage and the manner in which they had acquired a surname not truly their own. If some of the older ones did have an inkling, they never shared the knowledge with their own families. Later in life, when he was no longer involved in politics and trade unionism, Bowman would mention links with Carrickfergus, and indeed both he and Hugh and members of their respective families are buried close together in its Victoria cemetery. However, the answer to that aspect of the mystery lies with Hugh's wife Lizzie, who, although born in Belfast, had family roots in the Co. Antrim coastal town.[34] As far as the Bowman brothers were concerned, the Dromara family link seemingly ended the day their mother set off for Belfast.

Another hint about Alexander Bowman's childhood was contained in a speech he gave at Belfast's Foyle Street in the run-up to the 1885 general election, when he told supporters how, as a 10-year-old boy, he had served as a part-timer in a nearby mill – attending school for half the day and then working in the machine room in the afternoon.[35] His previous schooling would have been at the Burren National School or else at Derry's own small schoolhouse. The latter was run by the Church of Ireland's Church Education Society, and was not exclusively for children of the episcopalian faith.

In later life, when speaking on Nationalist platforms, Bowman would describe the leading figures in the United Irishmen movement as 'men willing to suffer in the cause of Ireland.' Henry Monro, the United Irish general executed after the Battle of Ballynahinch in 1798, was arrested near the area which would be Bowman's childhood home. Folk memories of the incident persist in the district to this day, and Bowman might well have been aware of them.[36]

The evidence points to a difficult, although not unhappy childhood in Dromara, where he watched and in time picked up his father's skills as a weaver, and then Belfast, where the boy had to put those talents to use in order to supplement the family's limited income.[37] Indeed, as employment laws stood in the 1860s children could have been working from the age of eight.[38] It is also very likely that the 'mill' he mentioned in his pre-election speech was the Agnes Street-based Brookfield powerloom linen weaving factory. Later renamed the Agnes Street Weaving Co.,[39] it was the only linen factory close enough to the Foyle Street meeting place to match Bowman's description.

The flaxdresser's job the young Alexander had his heart set on was a skilled one, offering the hope of higher wages.[40] The seven-year apprenticeships were not taken lightly – with just one apprentice being taken on for every seven qualified flaxdressers. Their work involved pulling lengths of flax fibre through hackles – tools which consisted mainly of rows of sharp pins set into a board – in preparation for spinning. Fine yarn was created by combing the flax through as many as three hackles. Apprentices like Alexander, taken on when he was barely into his teens, began with the coarsest grades, graduating to higher quality materials. Flaxdressers were viewed as the 'elite,' with many believing they were the mainstay of the industry. As far as Bowman was concerned, he was determined to show his mother that her sacrifices had not been in vain.

Positioned well away from the noisy machinery, there was plenty of opportunity for the flaxdressers to talk quietly as they worked. And the better educated among their numbers – including those, like Bowman, who felt continually driven to improve their knowledge of current and general affairs – also took full advantage of the factory's reading area during breaks.[41] Conditions were often far from healthy and lung disease was prevalent owing to the hot and steamy atmosphere and the 'stoor' – fine flax particles – in the air. Many of the men, Bowman included, would experience health problems and few ever reached an advanced age.

It is also known from the same Foyle Street political meeting that in 1874, when Bowman was barely 20, he joined a workers' deputation which approached the factory's manager to have a 'work grievance removed' – most likely in connection with a major dispute affecting the linen industry at that time. For his efforts he was dismissed but he had little difficulty finding a new flaxdressing position with William Ewart and Son at its Crumlin Road factory.[42] The Crumlin Road mill, opened in 1865, was the mainstay of the company's Belfast empire, which included the Mountain Flax Spinning Mill at Ligoniel and the Glenbank Bleachworks.[43] By the time Bowman joined Ewarts it was already one of Belfast's major employers, processing flax in all the stages of its manufacture, through spinning, weaving, bleaching, dyeing and finishing, to the creation of a range of finished linen articles.[44]

Around the same time Bowman met near-neighbour Rose Ritchie. Rose, some 18 months his senior, was the daughter of Co. Antrim-born farmer's son James Ritchie and his wife, the former Isabella Boomer from Dundrod, Co. Antrim.[45] Upon their marriage the Ritchies had moved to Dundonald, Co. Down, where he helped to run a farm at Ballybeen.[46] Rose was born at Dundonald on 3 October 1852, and baptised at the local Presbyterian church.[47] In time Ritchie rented his own land but subsequently set himself up in business as a dairyman and grocer in Belfast, at the junction of the New Lodge Road and the Antrim Road. Almost bankrupted by his debtors, Ritchie first moved to premises in Nassau Street and then to nearby Crimea Street where he continued for a time in the dairy business. He then worked there as a cooper, ultimately moving to 125 Agnes Street where he had a workshop at the rear of his home.

Ritchie and his wife had seven daughters and a son, with three of the girls dying young. Rose, eldest of the children, was doubtless aware that flaxdressers offered a fair prospect for financial security, despite the health risks involved in their work. It is possible, too, that she was drawn to Alexander as a relative of an established labour militant to a potential activist. Printer Robert Ritchie had been active in forming a short-lived trades council in Belfast in 1872, and in the major linen strike in 1874 into which Bowman had found himself drawn. Ritchie was an obvious candidate for the role of personal stimulus for the young flaxdresser's militancy.[48]

Alexander and Rose were married on Monday 30 August 1880, by Mr Hutchinson at Belfast's Eglinton Street Presbyterian Church, rather than the minister's own Argyle Place church which had closed for renovations.[49] Bowman's best man was 21-year-old teacher James Mitchell Lee, who was on the staff of the Argyle

Place National School.[50] Rose's sister Martha was the other witness. The newly-weds moved into 101 Crimea Street, which for a period from 1876 had been the Ritchie family home. The couple would be together for 44 years and have six children, five sons and a daughter. Their first child, born in August 1881, was christened William James – after Alexander's two older half-brothers and the couple's respective fathers, William McKeown and James Ritchie.

THE EMERGENCE OF A
TRADE UNION LEADER

BELFAST'S POPULATION had grown from just 22,000 in 1807 to around 230,000 by 1880.[1] The harbours had been extended, the shipyard had been established, banks and numerous other businesses had been opened, and horse-drawn trams and railways had arrived. The expansion of the cotton, linen and allied industries, largely due to the introduction of steam-driven machinery, played a major role in the town's rapid growth.[2] The period also witnessed the rise of a new industrial working class and an accompanying movement to improve conditions in those industries and beyond.

Most of the workers lived in tiny terraced kitchen houses, built in their thousands by the mills. Bowman and his new wife had their first marital home in the heart of the staunchly Protestant Shankill, paying a weekly rent of about 3/6d (17°p) which was deducted from his wages.[3]

During his time at the Agnes Street factory and later at Ewarts, Bowman witnessed at first hand the grim conditions faced by many of his fellow workers. At first he was inclined to blame excessive drinking for many of society's ills and took an active interest in temperance work.[4] He joined the theologically-based Bible

Temperance Association – a report in the *Northern Whig* on its sixth annual meeting, held on 30 March 1881, in the Mercantile College at Glenravel Street, is the earliest-known newspaper reference to Bowman.[5]

In time, however, Bowman came to the conclusion that over-indulgence in drink was as much a consequence as a cause of the poverty which confronted so many working-class people, and he concentrated his efforts on trade union work.[6] Another factor was the first-hand experience of financial hardship he and Rose faced in the early months of their marriage. From the beginning of October 1880, the Spinners' Association, which represented the owners of Belfast's linen mills and factories, cut the 56-hour working week to 40 hours because of a fall in demand for its products, with wages being proportionately reduced.[7]

By then Bowman, emerging from anonymity, had joined the Flaxdressers' Trade and Benevolent Union, which was one of the first to represent workers involved in the production of Irish linen. The union had been formed in 1872, and by the 1880s its membership averaged 1,360. Yet on its own one union could do little to sway an implacable employer.[8] A solution lay in co-ordination. The Belfast Trades Council was born out of a committee of trades, set up in May 1881 to support linen tenters striking against a 10 per cent reduction in their wages, which then averaged about 30 shillings a week.[9]

In March of the previous year a meeting of Belfast's trades societies had been held in the Painters' Hall at Curtis Street to support the creation of a board of arbitration in the town.[10] Organised by the Housepainters' Society, the meeting sought an amicable way of settling disputes between employers and employees. No outcome of the meeting was ever reported, suggesting that it had ended in failure. However, the dispute involving the tenters – or power loom mechanics – brought matters to a head.

The 40-hour working week affected most employees in the linen industry, with only a few factories maintaining full hours during the winter of 1880/81.[11] Hopes were raised that normal hours would be restored from Monday 4 April 1881. However, a condition was attached that a 10 per cent increase in wages, which had been awarded in November 1879 during a period of growth, was to be rescinded.[12] Disgruntled tenters, all members of the Belfast and North of Ireland Power Loom Tenters' Trade Union, called a meeting at which it was resolved they would accept a reduction not exceeding five per cent.[13]

The employers rejected the compromise offer and a strike began within days, hitting nine of Belfast's linen factories and involving a total of 79 tenters. The owners of another 12 factories chose not to impose the wage reduction.[14] Since the tenter's job involved not only supervising the work of the weavers but also looking after around 40 looms, thousands of women and girls soon found themselves out of work.[15]

The flaxdressers, having failed to have the wage cut delayed by two months, submitted an identical proposal to that of the tenters.[16] Within a short time four of the nine factory owners had accepted the five per cent compromise.[17] Of the five still affected two had closed their doors and three were continuing to work without tenters or by relying on apprentices.[18] The Agnes Street weaving factory was one of the two to shut while Ewarts, initially hit by closure, reopened in the middle of April with the majority of employees returning to their work.[19] Between 800 and 900 female employees later walked out at the York Street weaving factory after a non-union tenter was brought over from England.[20]

The dispute dragged on into the next month with employers holding firm over the 10 per cent reduction, or making their own deals with the tenters. The last hope for the striking tenters was the May 1881 meeting, held in the Painters' Hall.[21] Samuel Monro, a member of the Belfast Typographical Society, chaired the proceedings which were attended by dozens of delegates representing such trades as the brassfounders, painters, yarndressers, printers, bookbinders, flaxdressers, joiners and shoemakers. It was the first known occasion when Bowman's views on trade union matters were published in the press, although his name was misspelt 'Beauman.'[22]

Bowman voiced regret that the strike had continued for so long and pointed out that, unlike the flaxdressers, the tenters had made no approaches to the Spinners' Association with a view to having the matter settled by arbitration. He also felt they should have contacted the other trade unions before embarking on a strike which had led to 'thousands of girls being thrown out of work.' There were angry retorts that thousands of female workers had previously lost their jobs because of the activities of the flaxdressers.

Block printer William Shirrah proposed that the tenters, while justified in resisting the arbitrary demands of the employers, should approach them with a view to reaching an agreed settlement. Robert Ritchie, still on the scene following the 1874 dispute, seconded the proposal with the hope that one outcome of the strike would be the formation of a trades council in Belfast.

The submission cut little ice with the employers, who still believed that as each day passed the strike was weakening. Michael Andrews, secretary to the Spinners' Association, wrote back:

> I have submitted your letter to the employers affected by the tenters' strike and I am desired to say that, owing to the arrangements which have been made in their respective factories, they do not consider there is any question now in dispute with their former tenters, and they would therefore have no points to lay before the arbitrators.[23]

It was not until 29 October 1881, long after the tenters' dispute had ended with the employers refusing to give any more ground, that the Belfast Trades Council held its first exploratory meeting.[24] It was attended by many of the same delegates who had gathered five months earlier in the Painters' Hall. The few absentees included the still-aggrieved tenters who did not affiliate to the trades council until August 1883.[25] Trades councils had existed intermittently in Ireland from the 1820s, but it was not until the 1880s that they were formed on a permanent basis, with Cork and Belfast leading the revival.[26]

The new council's avowed aim was to promote 'the moral and social elevation of the operative class, and the consideration of all such questions as affect the political and social interests of labour.'[27] Monro, a typographer with the *Northern Whig*, was elected the first president, with Joseph Mitchell of the Ironmoulders' Union as his deputy, and Bowman as secretary. The trio would be the backbone of the council in its early years. Affiliates paid a yearly fee of 2d. per member and were permitted to send two delegates to the fortnightly meetings in the

Typographical Institute at 20 College Street.[28]

Brief but informative accounts of trades council meetings,[29] written by Bowman, appeared in the *Northern Whig* from 10 January 1882 onwards, when the report of the 'first bi-monthly meeting proper' noted a 'good attendance.' The second meeting, a fortnight later,[30] attracted 40 delegates representing some 7,000 working men. The scheduled debate on 'the causes of depression in trade and how best to meet the evils resulting therefrom,' spilled over to the third meeting, with members generally agreeing that 'commercial dishonesty is to a large extent the cause of the depression in trade and that emigration would be, in some measure at least, a cure for the evils resulting therefrom.'[31] The initial reports refrained from naming council members to avoid victimisation by employers. Yet the Belfast Trades Council remained very much against strike action, believing it should be retained as a last resort course of action.

Around this time Bowman's name began to feature in press reports as an enthusiastic member of the Belfast Debating Society. It had been formed in October 1881, just five days before the first exploratory meeting of the trades council, and often attracted attendances of 200 or more. It met under the chairmanship of James Flinn each Monday evening in the Lombard Hall at Lombard Street. Representatives of all shades of religious and political opinion paid an annual subscription of three shillings, their objective being 'the mutual improvement of the members by the discussion of questions of public interest.'[32] Several early reports mentioned Bowman's surname but it was not until February that his Christian name also appeared.[33] It was for a debate on a subject which within four years would have a profound impact on his life: 'Is Ireland entitled to Home Rule, or the right of making her own laws?' Few details were given of his contribution, except that he spoke in favour of the motion which was defeated.

The earliest trades council press report to carry Bowman's name was published two weeks after the Phoenix Park murders – when the 'Invincibles' assassinated newly-appointed Irish Chief Secretary Lord Frederick Cavendish and Permanent Under-Secretary the Hon. Thomas Henry Burke. The killings had taken place as the council was holding its meeting on the evening of 6

May 1882, with the condemnations being voiced at their next meeting.[34] Bowman, emphasising that first and foremost he was an Irishman, expressed his 'most entire repudiation of any sympathy with such an atrocity.'

The trades council also took a leading role in urging Belfast Town Council to provide a free rate-supported public library for the rapidly expanding population. Monro and Bowman, along with leading businessmen and merchants, attended a meeting of the town council with the request that the authority should 'proceed at an early date to ascertain whether the ratepayers of Belfast were prepared to avail themselves of the provisions of the Library Act.'[35]

Although Monro was president of the trades council, it was Bowman who addressed Mayor Edward Porter Cowan and town councillors, pointing out that the delegation represented 10,000 working men:

> We feel handicapped in the race with other nations to maintain supremacy as a manufacturing centre. I know that in Belfast comparatively little has been done to advance the mental and moral interests of the working men, while in the countries of the continent, chemical schools and other educational institutions are supplied for the benefits of the working classes.[36]

Bowman also argued that the provision of a public library would help to improve relations between employer and employee:

> Working men as they become educated are far less dangerous to the interests of social order and of material progress, and they soon recognise that their welfare is identical with the interests of the employer, and they are less likely to take rash or foolish steps on their own behalf which might be fraught with effects ruinous to the industry of the town.

Their efforts contributed considerably towards an extensive campaign, but the demand for a library was still resisted.[37] Further pressure forced the town council to relent and a ballot was conducted among all the ratepayers. Of the 10,200 voting papers issued, 5,200 voted for and 1,400 were against.[38]

* * *

Indicating the Belfast Trades Council's growing stature, Bowman was accorded the honour in 1882 of becoming its first delegate to attend a British Trades Union Congress, the council having opened affiliation talks with the TUC's parliamentary committee that February.[39] Bowman, who was still living at 101 Crimea Street[40] – the following year he would move to no. 79[41] – travelled by ferry to Liverpool to attend the fifteenth annual Congress which met in Manchester's Co-Operative Hall from 18 to 23 September. He represented both the trades council and the Flaxdressers' Trade and Benevolent Union.[42]

Bowman was among the early speakers, declaring his support for the Payment of Wages in Public Houses Prevention Bill.[43] He claimed that people were 'sometimes driven to intemperance owing to receiving their wages in public houses.' Congress president Robert Austin backed Bowman's claim that one of their own affiliated bodies, the Amalgamated Society of Engineers, paid benefits to out-of-work members 'at such establishments' in Belfast. During another debate Bowman voiced support for a motion – later carried unanimously – calling for the employment of additional factory inspectors to ensure workplaces were run to the standards required by law.[44]

At the Manchester Congress Bowman also launched a stinging attack on the judiciary in Ireland, claiming that county court judges were 'pre-eminently hostile to the labouring classes.' He made the comment when demanding that the Employers' Liability Act should be mandatory, thereby protecting the rights of working people who sought to bring compensation actions in the county courts.[45] A judge in Belfast, he said, had 'stigmatised trade unions as Communism and Nihilism,' and he asked: 'How can we expect to have justice meted out by one who regards our organisations with such feelings?'

He returned to the subject of the judiciary when delegates debated a call for the Summary Jurisdiction Act of 1879 to be extended to Ireland.[46] Bowman declared that the Irish stipendiaries and magistrates, then trying defendants on disturbance charges arising from the land war of the previous three years:

> ... are absolutely hostile to the masses, and have no sympathy whatever with the people who appear before them. Unless the working men of England and Scotland stand by their brethren across the Channel, and enable them to see that their rights are respected by the administrators of the law, Ireland must still continue to be a weak spot in the Empire. It is certainly deplorable that outrages so often occur and that the law is so often violated, but there is a point beyond

which submission ceases to be a virtue. Ireland has submitted to indignity, to insult, and to wrong from the hands not so much of her legislators as of the administrators of the law, and we want the provisions of the Summary Jurisdiction Act extended to Ireland so that the Irish might enjoy those elements of the Magna Carta which members of other parts of the Empire already enjoy.[47]

Bowman successfully moved a motion before the Manchester Congress on the Irish parliamentary and municipal franchise.[48] He pointed out that in Ireland the parliamentary voting qualification was a rating of £4 a year, while for municipal voting it was £10 – 'the effect being that almost four-fifths of the entire working class are excluded from participating in municipal elections, to their great detriment.'

Bowman also sought election to the TUC's parliamentary committee, which conducted the affairs of the organisation and scrutinised relevant legislation coming before parliament. With delegates permitted to vote for up to 10 candidates, he polled 25 and finished 17th in a list of 25 contenders – with the first 10 being elected to the committee.[49]

The following months witnessed a more settled period in terms of industrial disputes, but considerable concern was still being voiced about health and safety standards. At a meeting of the trades council in May 1883, a resolution was passed:

... that in the opinion of this council, representing the artisans of Belfast, there should be a more efficient inspection of factories and workshops in the North of Ireland and throughout the Kingdom generally, and that to this end deputy inspectors ought to be appointed, selected from the working classes.[50]

Bowman reported a fortnight later that he had received a letter from Henry Cameron, Belfast's inspector of factories, expressing his 'anxiety to co-operate with the council in such a way as should be likely to prevent violations of the Factory and Workshops Acts taking place.'[51] The council resolved that their secretary should take 'such steps as may be necessary to have the attention of the Government directed to the fact that it is impossible to efficiently discharge the duties devolving on the inspector in connection with the Belfast district.'

Considerable effort was devoted during the early summer of

1883 to supporting a major all-Ireland exhibition of industry to be staged in Cork, where the MP for the Cork City constituency was Nationalist leader Charles Stewart Parnell. Michael McCarthy, general secretary of the Cork Trades Association, attended a meeting of its Belfast counterpart and reported that the Mayor of Belfast, Alderman David Taylor, and several leading merchants had 'thrown themselves heartily into the work of raising a fund for the purpose of defraying the expense of a deputation attending the opening of the exhibition.'[52] The Conservative mayor headed the list with a personal subscription of ten guineas and consented to act as treasurer.[53]

Thanks largely to Taylor's efforts, 44 delegates representing 20 different trades travelled south to take part in the opening parade on 3 July 1883.[54] The Belfast party, carrying a special banner and wearing silver badges bearing the Ulster coat of arms, included three representatives of the Flaxdressers' Society: Alexander Bowman, James Workman, later to be his election agent, and Robert Gageby, who would be elected with Bowman to Belfast Corporation in 1897.

When it was all over Bowman and several members of the trades council delegation travelled to Alderman Taylor's home, where council president Joseph Mitchell – who had succeeded Monro – presented the Mayor with a framed photograph of the party taken in Cork.[55] Bowman told Taylor of the respect held for him by the working-class people. He also hoped Taylor 'should be again elected to fill our civic chair,' a wish endorsed by councillors a few weeks later when they gathered for their annual meeting.[56] Such a harmonious link with the Mayor, knighted by Queen Victoria two years later, indicated a growing acceptance in Belfast of the trade union movement.

In the meantime Bowman had attended his second Trades Union Congress, held in Nottingham's Mechanics' Hall from 10 to 15 September. Once again he was sole nominee of Belfast Trades Council.[57]

Bowman spoke on government efforts to complete the codification of the criminal law and its Criminal Procedure bill – several sections of which prompted fears that they would subvert people's rights.[58] In particular, they included a proposal to give power to magistrates to hold, in the words of delegate Henry Crompton, 'secret enquiries without the presence of the prisoner and to commit to prison for eight days any contumacious [disobedient] witness.'[59] Bowman, still critical of the judiciary, declared that what was being objected to had 'already been tried in Ireland and we know with what result.' He also proposed that Congress's parliamentary committee should seek the inclusion of a clause conceding to small debtors in Ireland, with liabilities under £50, the same protection afforded in England. His resolution was adopted.

Bowman again raised the linking of municipal to parliamentary voting rights in Ireland.[60] He won unanimous support for a motion which viewed 'with deep concern the continued exclusion from electoral rights in municipal affairs of the mass of parliamentary voters.' He told delegates: 'Many of you would be surprised to learn that in Belfast, with a population of almost 250,000, there are only 9,000 municipal voters, while there are 23,000 parliamentary voters – so that 14,000 voters are precluded from municipal action.' The voting system would in time be changed, one important result being the election 14 years later of Bowman and five working-class colleagues to Belfast Corporation.[61]

His final initiative was to again seek election to the parliamentary committee.[62] As in 1882 his votes fell short of the required number – he polled 21 to finish 18th out of 23.

GLADSTONE AND
THE LIBERAL CAUSE

As 1884 DAWNED seeking public office was probably the last thing on Bowman's mind. Having quit his job as a flaxdresser to become a traveller for long-established Belfast clothiers Black & Co., of Royal Avenue,[1] he attempted in March to resign as secretary of the trades council.[2] He cited the state of his health and the change of employment as reasons why he could not 'give such constant attention to the duties of the office in the future as had been required in the past.' Members pleaded with Bowman to change his mind, and won him over by agreeing to appoint bookbinder Robert Meharg as assistant secretary to ease his workload.[3]

A month later, and in a rehearsal of future events, Bowman faced an accusation that he was mixing party politics with his trade union role. At a meeting of the trades council, vice-president Thomas Johnston drew attention to newspaper reports that their secretary had seconded a vote of thanks to a speaker at a lecture held under the auspices of the Belfast Liberal Association.[4] 'Did he do this in his official capacity?' asked Johnston. 'And is it right that our secretary should take part in political meetings?' Bowman replied that he had not been acting as secretary of the trades council, and members agreed 'that, having heard Mr Bowman's explanation, the council is of the opinion that it is quite satisfactory.'

The source of the row was the first indication of Bowman's involvement with the Liberals. He went a stage further in June 1884, addressing the subject of extended voting rights when he proposed a motion at an important conference of local Liberals in the Assembly Hall at Independent Street, off Short Strand.[5] The proposal welcomed the government's decision to introduce a new franchise bill,[6] which would further extend voting rights.

Bowman declared that no-one who viewed the history of Ireland could believe that the 'exclusion of one section of the community from participating in the advantages of any measure of reform could be conducive to the well-being of the State.' He continued:

> During several centuries, indeed from the time of the Norman Conquest, there has been a nation existing within a nation – a nation whose interests and rights and privileges are to some extent antagonistic to the interests, rights and privileges of the great masses of the people. That elite section of the community, which during all those centuries has possessed these exclusive privileges, has been desirous of preventing the common people from enjoying like privileges. The Irish question has almost been incapable of solution. It has been an excitingly crude problem, and has excited the anxiety of statesmen during these many years. I believe the reason for this is because the people of Ireland have been largely treated on different lines to the people of England, Scotland and Wales. We have heard a great many people expressing fear that if the franchise were extended to Ireland the power of Mr Parnell would be largely increased. I confess that I do not share that fear.

Having taken such a strong political stand, it was not surprising that Bowman should rebuke the *Northern Whig* for referring to his trades council position in its report.[7]

* * *

While Gladstone knew he could command support for the franchise bill in the House of Commons, he hit problems in the House of Lords where the Conservative majority feared it would ultimately lead to the loss of their power of veto over legislation they did not like. Conservative leader Lord Salisbury refused to support the bill without an accompanying redistribution of parliamentary seats.[8] Liberals were incensed and in Belfast a meeting was called that October. The platform party included three Liberal MPs: Samuel Walker QC, MP for Co. Londonderry and Solicitor-General for Ireland, Thomas A. Dickson (Tyrone) and William Findlater (Monaghan). Bowman was invited to second a resolution proposed by Randalstown tenant farmer Samuel Black that 'we regard the action of the House of Lords with reference to the franchise bill as unconstitutional, disrespectful to the representatives of the people, and subversive of responsible government.'[9]

In arguably his most important speech to date, Bowman claimed that householders in Ireland deserved to be treated in the same way as their counterparts in the boroughs of England, Wales and Scotland, where all householders enjoyed the right to vote. In Belfast, he said, there were 50,000 householders, yet only 30,000 names on the parliamentary roll.[10]

In these circumstances it is imperative for Irishmen, and especially Irish artisans, to support to the utmost of our power the government that is endeavouring to do us justice. The Lords are never weary of telling us that when the Irish are contented and prosperous, like the English and Scots, they will give us this boon, but, as a matter of fact, the refusal to give Irish people their rights is the cause of the entire dissatisfaction that exists. Is it not a great shame for noble and honourable gentlemen and members of the two Houses of Parliament to stand up and tell us that we are an integral part of the Empire, when this, the very fundamental principle of popular government, is different in Ireland? But on what principle of justice or reason can they assume the Irish to be an integral part of the Empire, and yet if one expresses a contrary view to this he is branded as a traitor?

Having drawn together King Alfred, the Norman Conquest, King John and the Magna Carta, Oliver Cromwell and the French Revolution in a single line of argument, Bowman accused the House of Lords of never caring for the people, but, rather, 'legislating with a view to propping up their own privileges, rights and principles at the expense of the interests, rights and well-being of the people. Let us approve of this resolution and when we have found the culprits guilty, we will leave the judge to pronounce the sentence which their bad deeds merits,' Bowman concluded with cheers and clapping ringing in his ears.

Gladstone and Lord Salisbury eventually agreed to enact the bill along with an accompanying parliamentary seats redistribution bill. The new franchise bill met little opposition in the House of Lords on 4 December and the royal assent was given two days later. The deal struck by Gladstone and Salisbury increased from three million to five million the number of parliamentary voters throughout the United Kingdom, including Ireland where the increase was 230 per cent. Under the terms of the redistribution bill the total number of MPs would increase from 652 to 670, with Irish representation remaining unchanged at 103.[11] However, Belfast, through the creation of new electoral divisions, would have four seats instead of two.

For Alexander Bowman, the changes, coupled with the previous year's alteration to the law concerning candidates' expenses,[12] would prove a crucial factor in his willingness to stand for parliament.

Despite his growing political profile, Bowman remained secretary of the Belfast Trades Council. The infrequency of newspaper reports from that period onwards reflected the demands being placed on Bowman by a considerable list of outside interests, as well as his own work and his young family. Away from his trade union efforts Bowman continued to extend his knowledge of national and international affairs through regular attendance at meetings of the Belfast Debating Society. He was also a member of the temperance organisation known as the Independent Order of Good Templars.[13]

His other key role was as secretary of the Irish Land Restoration Society. It had been founded in Belfast in the spring of 1875 by a group of mostly young men who met in Robinson's Temperance Hotel at Donegall Street. The foundation members issued a brief manifesto in which, without suggesting any method, they promoted the view that land belonged equally to all the people and ought somehow to be restored to its 'rightful owners.'[14] The public's growing interest in radical politics was reflected in the sizeable audience which attended a meeting organised by the society in the Secession Church at Belfast's Botanic Avenue in December 1884.[15] The key speaker was the body's chairman, the Rev. John Bruce Wallace, minister of Clifton Park Congregational Church.

During that winter Wallace had been staging a series of Saturday 'social and industrial conferences' at the Mercantile College, with Bowman among the enthusiastic attenders. At the December 1884 meeting Bowman reiterated the Society's policy, saying the members were opposed to the 'exclusive possession by the few of land designed by the Creator for the support of all.' The land, he continued, was 'God's free gift to each successive generation. Our ancestors might have granted away their own rights, but they could not grant away the rights of their descendants.' Referring to the action of a landlord in Donegal who had evicted 300 families, Bowman said it illustrated the power of 'unrestrained landlordism.' He went on to point out that landlords were supposed to pay a tax of four shillings in the pound based on the rental value of their land, 'but they are paying on a 200-year-old valuation, and thus robbing the nation of something like £20 million a year.'

Bowman also helped to organise a visit by American land reformer Henry George to Belfast in January 1885. George had published his book *Poverty and Progress* in 1879 in San Francisco. An English edition appeared before the end of 1880 and within another two years worldwide sales had exceeded one million copies. George argued that since economic progress entailed a growing scarcity of land, the idle landowner reaped even greater returns at the expense of the productive factors of labour and capital. Such unearned economic rent, he held, should be taxed away by the State. George envisaged that the government's annual income from the 'single tax' would be so large that there would be a surplus for the expansion of public works.

Speaking at the Ulster Hall, George offered workers a simple remedy for their social problems. 'All over the civilised world,' he declared, 'the great social problem presses harder and harder, demanding solution or bringing destruction. This civilisation cannot stand unless we find some means for quieting social discontent.' Industrial depression, said George, was caused by private landlords, who made no contribution to production, taking for themselves in rent a large proportion of the wealth produced by society. He concluded that property rights had to be based on labour.[16]

According to the unsympathetic and pro-Conservative *Belfast*

News-Letter, the proceedings ended in uproar as many members of the audience were totally opposed to George's views.[17] Also present that night was Belfast Presbyterian fundamentalist and prominent Orangeman the Rev. Dr Hugh Hanna, but his efforts to debunk George's arguments were blocked by chairman the Rev. Bruce Wallace. 'Roaring Hugh,' as he was nicknamed, was afforded the opportunity to debate the subject with Wallace at an equally well-attended meeting in the Ulster Hall the following month, with Bowman serving on the organising committee.[18]

Also in January Bowman helped to organise a public meeting called by the trades council at the St George's Hall in Hill Street to protest against Belfast Town Council's decision to award the plastering contract for the new public library to the Glasgow firm of Caird and Co., whose tender was £600 more than the figure submitted by a local company.[19]

After a resolution urging Belfast Town Council to rescind its decision had been passed, Bowman proposed a second motion, calling for similar municipal franchise rights in Ireland to those which already applied in Britain. If that happened, he said, they would have the remedy to the problem with the town council 'in our own hands.' He was interrupted by a member of the audience who accused him of raising a political issue which was not relevant to the meeting. No-one could be heard amid the resulting confusion – until the objector, joiner John Donaldson, was lifted from his seat to the platform to make his point. Bowman's motion was seconded by borough cashier Edward de Cobain,[20] who said it was a matter of justice since they were only asking for what had already been conceded in England and Scotland. The resolution was carried by a large majority, along with a prophetic call to form a joint committee with a view to 'returning eligible men to represent the working men and artisans at the Corporation of Belfast.'

Councillors did reconsider the plastering issue after receiving a delegation representative of the public meeting, and the contract was eventually given to a local company.

As for the Belfast Debating Society, Bowman lent his weight to supporting such motions as: 'Should the municipal and parliamentary franchise be assimilated in Ireland?', 'Should the manufacture and sale of intoxicating drinks be prohibited?', 'The need for new laws in Ireland,' 'Would Home Rule be beneficial to Ireland?','The Lords, the people and the franchise bill,' 'Is the Irish policy of the government unworthy of the confidence of the people of Ireland?', and 'Was the conduct of Oliver Cromwell patriotic?'[21] Speaking on the need for new laws in Ireland, Bowman went on record as favouring a degree of Home Rule when he called for the abolition of the office of Lord Lieutenant and the creation of a council consisting of Ministers for Agriculture, Commerce and Education, all as members of the Cabinet, along with the Lord Chief Justice and the Lord Chancellor. They would be empowered, he proposed, to make Orders in Council on local matters and to hold inquiries 'regarding all railway, harbour, borough and other bills for local improvement, and report to the imperial parliament.'[22]

But it was the Liberal Party which commanded much of his time during the early months of 1885. Following the Belfast Liberal Association's annual general meeting on 28 January, his name appeared in press reports alongside the president, John Shaw Brown, and the secretary, Dr Hugh Hyndman – the latter reporting a 'year of great activities with the energies of the committee being put forth in new directions with most encouraging results.'[23] Bowman might not have been thinking of his own political ambitions, but his mind was clearly on future elections. As well as seconding a resolution calling for the new Franchise Act to be expanded to include women householders, he also proposed that their executive committee should 'take such steps as are necessary to have central and representative bodies appointed in the several electoral divisions, so that all matters municipal and parliamentary may be properly attended to.'

Gladstone's government was heading out of office and a general election was on the horizon. With Bowman's bid for a seat at Westminster drawing nearer, he found himself serving on a committee alongside rival-to-be and former employer William Ewart. While plans for an exhibition in Belfast along the lines of the one held in Cork in 1883 had foundered, there was considerable enthusiasm for an 'Artisans' Exhibition' in Dublin during the summer months. Earlier that year a delegation from the central organising committee had paid a visit to Belfast to seek support for the exhibition, the staging of which, it was estimated, would cost around £5,000.[24] It was agreed on the proposal of John Shaw Brown, who was also president of the Linen Merchants' Association, seconded by Bowman, that the project deserved 'hearty and cordial support' and, accordingly, a local executive committee should be established. Bowman further expressed the view that 'we should show that we in the North of Ireland desire the well-being of the country as much as any of the other provinces.' With an office at 3 College Street, the Belfast executive committee included William Ewart MP, Sir David Taylor, John Shaw Brown and Edward de Cobain, as well as trades council members Mitchell, Bowman and George McIntosh.[25] There was also support from trade unions.

Yet, despite the best intentions of the Belfast committee, there was little Ulster representation when the Artisans' Exhibition opened on 24 June. 'Having regard to the efforts made by the committee to encourage the trades of the North of Ireland to take part, the result is not a little disappointing,' commented the *Northern Whig's* Dublin correspondent.[26]

* * *

During those summer months of 1885 Bowman maintained the twin-track approach to his politics – continuing to speak and act on behalf of the trades council in his capacity as secretary and involving himself in Liberal Party activities in Belfast. In August he was delegated to represent the trades council at a meeting convened by the Mayor, Sir Edward Harland, to consider amendments to the Criminal Law Amendment bill, with particular reference to the protection of young women.'[27] The meeting was prompted by the previous month's revelations of criminal vice in England. William Stead, editor of London's influential *Pall Mall Gazette*, mingled with prostitutes to hear their stories and then intentionally 'bought' a 13-year-old girl for £5. His aim was to expose the unsavoury practice among some parents of selling their young daughters for immoral purposes.[28]

Bowman argued in favour of the age of consent for women being raised to 21. He asserted that the punishment of penal servitude for committing such offences against young women was 'too good and flogging not bad enough.' It was agreed that resolutions relating to setting the age of protection at 21, stricter penalties

and rights of search be forwarded to new Prime Minister Lord
Salisbury and Home Secretary Sir Richard Cross and to Belfast's
two Conservative MPs, William Ewart and Sir James Corry.[29]
When Stead and leading members of the Salvation Army were
subsequently summoned for trial for the abduction of the girl,
Eliza Armstrong, Bowman spoke at a public meeting in their
support.[30]

Eight days later the Belfast Liberal Club staged a banquet in
honour of John Shaw Brown.[31] All the leading figures in Ulster
Liberalism were there with Bowman being accorded the honour
of proposing the toast to the evening's chairman, Arthur Sharman
Crawford.

For Bowman there would be one final opportunity to expound
his views before the election was called. The subject was the right
of women householders to vote and the venue was the Ulster Minor
Hall.[32] Bowman was billed as one of the speakers, along with
Stoke-on-Trent Liberal MP William Woodall who, having
introduced a Women's Suffrage Bill in parliament that year,[33] was
recognised as the parliamentary leader of the movement; Miss
Isabella Tod, from the North of Ireland Committee for Women's
Suffrage; former Belfast Conservative MP William Johnston of
Ballykilbeg, who was also a leading member of the Orange Order;
and another prominent Belfast Liberal, Finlay McCance.

Johnston proposed a resolution stating that the passing of the
Franchise Act, 'by admitting all men who are householders,
supplies the strongest reason for the inclusion of all women who
are householders at the earliest possible moment.' Bowman,
seconding the resolution, praised the proposer for his 'cogent
arguments,' saying it had been accepted 'as a recognised fact that
women who discharge the duties of citizenship ought to be invested
with the privileges appertaining to that state.' He added:

> By the enfranchisement of women a grand and glorious impetus
> and help will be given to every social reform, and not only will
> social reforms be advanced by extending the franchise to women,
> but truth, morality and temperance will have valuable workers in
> their persons.

Election fever was in the air and Alexander Bowman was ready
to play his part.

THE WORKING
MEN'S CANDIDATE

S EEKING A SEAT in parliament during the late Victorian era was usually limited to the well-off or those with financial backing since candidates had to pay their own election expenses and contribute towards those of the returning officer, as well as maintaining themselves once elected. Bowman, therefore, was breaking the mould when he allowed his name to go forward as the working men's candidate for North Belfast.

The request, on 9 October 1885, that Bowman should stand for Westminster was backed by a petition signed by some 400 to 500 voters and delivered by an 'influential and representative' deputation to his new home at 61 Berlin Street, off the Shankill Road.[1]

Meanwhile, Bowman visited Lurgan to address local power-loom weavers on the advantages of trade union organisation and membership.[2] The meeting in the town hall at Union Street had been prompted by unrest in the power-loom factories and in the handkerchief industry. A union had already been formed that year for Lurgan's female hemmers and veiners and a move followed to organise the male weavers.[3] Bowman, invited as secretary of Belfast Trades Council, was accorded an attentive hearing by the packed attendance. He made a case for trade unionism as being necessary for workers, but beneficial too for employers:

> Trades' unionism is also of immense advantage to employers – for it tends to minimise strikes and to substitute for them the rational and efficient system of arbitration. In a place where party feeling runs so high as it unfortunately does in the Province of Ulster, it would be difficult to over-estimate the value of an organisation capable of producing so very satisfactory a result.[4]

It was agreed that the men would form themselves into a trade union. However, the resolution was not pursued and no trade union was formed by the Lurgan power-loom weavers at that time.[5]

For the North Belfast election campaign Bowman refused on principle to canvass for votes or financial subscriptions,[6] preferring to put forward his views at three public meetings in the constituency – with one being abandoned because of disruption by flour-throwing supporters of his Conservative opponent. At the first rally, held on 30 October in the Clifton Park Congregational Church Sunday School rooms in Foyle Street, Bowman set out his conditions for standing and his policies.[7] James Workman, from Bann Street, Bowman's election agent, was in the chair and offered the audience an insight into the candidate:

> He is a comparatively young man, aged about 30 years,[8] and yet some 11 years ago he was one of a deputation appointed by the men of the shop in which he then worked to go to the manager of the firm to have a grievance removed. He got discharged from his employment because of his pluck yet he has often figured in a similar capacity since then. Outside his own trade he has not been idle. Some four years ago he conceived the idea of more closely uniting the working men of Belfast. To accomplish that object he, assisted by a few other trade unionists, waited on all the trade societies in town, numbering about 40, with the result that in six weeks from the commencement of the movement a meeting of delegates from almost all the societies was held and the trades council was there and then established.

Workman also pointed out that Bowman had sought to end striking, with arbitration the favoured option in the event of a dispute. Bowman, he said, had obtained the consent of almost all the trade societies to the scheme, but could make no progress with the employers. During a dispute involving Belfast's bakers one of the strikers was arrested and jailed for two months for intimidation, he continued. According to Workman an approach was made by Bowman to Henry Broadhurst MP who had the matter raised at parliament. The end result was a reprimand for the stipendiary magistrate involved. Workman also pointed out that just two Westminster MPs were representatives of labour, while no fewer than 270 represented landed interests, 120 the law and some 150 were manufacturers, merchants and other company owners.[9] 'We want representatives who will be independent of any party in the State,' he declared, 'people who will not be dragged after any party for mere party purposes, but who will sit in the interest of a class which has not received that recognition from legislation it deserves.'

Accepting that there were financial obstacles in the way of any working man seeking to take part in an election campaign, Workman added: 'All our candidate desires is sufficient to defray his election expenses. He will be able to support himself afterwards without any monetary assistance.'

Bowman was clearly moved by the warm reception he received from the packed meeting. The request that he should stand, he said, had come from 'Whig, Tory and Nationalist without distinction of religious creed,' and he was 'pleased to see them united in the cause of labour, but pained to imagine that no more suitable person can be found to represent your interests.' He continued: 'Since I commenced work, when scarcely 10 years of age, as a machine boy in a mill not 200 yards from this room, I have not shrunk from doing my duty by my fellows and endeavouring as far as lies in my powers to promote the well-being of the industrious people among whom I have lived.'

Referring to Workman's point about election expenses, Bowman said the Corrupt Practices Act prevented Ewart from spending more than £700 and he knew his own supporters would not require a quarter of that amount. Given that the returning officer's expenses would not exceed £150, he estimated that 3,000 workmen in the North Belfast area each contributing one shilling would 'abundantly supply all our requirements.' And he added: 'If you pay those expenses and return me to parliament I guarantee to support myself while there – I can do much with tongue and pen – and I would never require you to contribute one penny towards my expenses in attending to your legislative interests.'

He then set out the two conditions upon which his candidature rested, firstly that there was no other *bona fide* working man wishing to stand in his place. If such a person stepped forward, said Bowman, 'then I will labour in his interest, in order to secure his return, as heartily and with as much vigour as I shall work in support of my own candidature.' Secondly, it was his wish:

> ... that the people of the constituency by themselves, and those friends in other parts of Belfast, who while they are not so situated as to be able to vote for a labour representative, are not only willing, but even anxious, to have an opportunity to do something to assist in securing the full recognition of the right of the working-class element to direct representation in the Councils of the Empire.

Moving to political issues, Bowman contended that there were many important questions awaiting the attention of parliament, 'in which the working classes have the most supreme interest.' His first target was a recent amendment to the Employers' Liability Act of 1880 which had been 'so emasculated by employers of labour, or their friends and sympathisers,' before becoming law:

> No matter how great the sufferings of a family whose breadwinner had been carried home a ghastly corpse, owing to an accident traceable to the negligence of employers, the Act allows no more than three years of wages as compensation for that valuable life. And even that small sum of money is almost impossible for the family to secure. The Act has been so hedged around in its provisions that it presents the most serious obstacles to the carrying out of its authors' intentions.

Bowman also pointed out that many seamen lost their lives each year and it was 'only fair that the meagre protection afforded to the industrial population on land by the Employers' Liability Act ought to be extended to the shipping trade.'

Harking back to a subject first covered in his 1882 TUC speech, Bowman said another matter was the need to increase the number of factory, workshop and mines safety inspectors – of which there were still just three for the whole of Ireland.

He then repeated his call for the assimilation of the municipal franchise in Ireland to the parliamentary franchise, as was already the case in England, and demanded the abolition of all property qualifications for service on local boards. 'We, as an integral part of the British Empire, have a right to expect and demand the equalisation of our laws to those of England and Scotland,' he said. Turning to education, he contended that it was the duty of the State – and in its interests – to provide for the elementary, technical and general education of the people. 'Under the existing system,' he said, 'the cost of providing education for his children is in many cases an utter impossibility for a hard-worked and poorly-paid toiler.'

Bowman went on to promote his views on temperance. 'All who have studied this question feel how intimately the social and physical well-being of the people is associated with the promotion of the temperance reform,' Bowman declared. 'As all power ought to abide in the people, they ought to possess the power of veto.' And turning to the existence of 'frightful criminality in our midst,' he stated, in a reference to the Stead case:

> We have learnt that crimes which are mainly the result of the deep poverty and dense ignorance which prevail – crimes of a nature too horrid to mention – have been unearthed. It is the duty of the people to hear and attend to that cry for justice and protection which has arisen from the throbbing heart of our centres of population and industry, and has penetrated to places to which the cry for justice has seldom reached; and to return men to parliament who will seek to stamp out this hideous and almost unmentionable vice which is rampant in our midst – men who will give effect to the principle that righteousness exalteth a nation, and that vice is a disgrace to any people.

Turning his attention to his opponent, he claimed that Ewart had participated in just 208 parliamentary divisions out of 1,450 since the 1880 general election. 'I hold,' said Bowman, 'that when a man undertakes to perform a certain duty, and when the electors commission him to do it, he is, in honour, bound to comply with his promise.' He added:

> During my contest in the North division I, for my part, will not utter one word calculated to give offence to my opponents. We can afford to conduct the contest in a spirit which will enable us to say at the close, whether we win or whether we lose, that we have nothing to regret. We are fighting for a principle and we can afford to fight without indulging in personal abuse.

With a rallying cry which echoed almost word for word a speech by Henry Broadhurst at the TUC two months earlier, Bowman closed by declaring: 'The forthcoming election will be to the people what the Springtime is to the farmer. If you neglect the duty of seed-sowing you cannot possibly expect a rich harvest of legislation.'[10]

Among those to support Bowman was the Rev. George Magill, minister of Donegall Street Presbyterian Church, which Bowman had been attending since the death of the Rev. Lamont Hutchinson in October 1883.[11] Magill said he was not there to advocate any political party, but 'the right of the working man to be heard in the Imperial Parliament.' The formal resolution of support for Bowman, 'to secure his return to Parliament as the labour representative of the North division of Belfast,' was proposed by mechanic Sinclair Watson and seconded by flaxdresser William Halliday. Just two would stand for the seat.[12] Bowman, described on his nomination paper as a former flaxdresser who was a draper's traveller, and merchant William Ewart, who had been a Belfast MP since 1878.

The Liberals would contest only two local seats, East Belfast and South Belfast, being soundly beaten in both.[13] While Bowman remained a member of the Belfast Liberal Association and enjoyed the support of the Liberal press, he declined to attend Liberal Club functions during the elections.[14] Nor is there any evidence of Bowman having been formally selected or even endorsed by Belfast Trades Council, quite possibly for fear that his known Liberal sympathies would tend towards politicising the body. The working men's candidate was, however, formally nominated by trades council president Joseph Mitchell and fellow member James Melville.[15]

Two nomination papers submitted for Ewart showed, quite purposefully, that he could draw support not only from the gentry, the church, and the business community, but also from ordinary working men. Among his working-class supporters were a stonecutter, a tenter, a brass moulder, a painter and a linen mill winding master.[16]

Despite the pro-Conservative *Belfast Evening Telegraph's* summary dismissal of the labour nomination as 'Mr Bowman and his friends... having a little joke,'[17] Bowman's pioneering place in Irish political history was recognised by other newspaper editorials. Mindful that the Liberals were still showing no signs of selecting their own candidate and, indeed, that the party had not won a Belfast parliamentary seat since 1868,[18] the *Northern Whig* all but endorsed the working men's representative at that early stage in the campaign. An editorial published three days after the Foyle Street meeting put Bowman's decision to stand for parliament in context:

> ... Mr Bowman does not come forward as the opponent of Mr Ewart in the ordinary party sense. He does not appeal to the Liberal electors against the Conservative, nor to the Nationalists against both. What his convictions are on ordinary party questions we do not know, and we scarcely care to inquire. Whatever they are, they have not been very prominent. But in questions between masters and working men Mr Bowman has taken an active part on the side of the latter; though he has never used his influence in an extreme and aggressive spirit against the employers. That he has the confidence of a large body of Belfast artisans is manifest from the position he holds as secretary of the trades council.
>
> In this position Mr Bowman has not, we believe, encouraged strikes, but he has done the best he could to prevent them without sacrificing the interests of those whom he especially represents. He has been especially favourable to arbitration in disputes which have arisen between workmen and employers.[19]

The Nationalist *Morning News* said from the outset of Bowman's campaign that it had nothing against the representative of the 'democratic working men' seeking election to Westminister.[20] It added: 'His programme is to some extent non-political, and he appeals to the elector of North Belfast in the interests of the people rather than in the interests of any party.'

Bowman's second meeting, held on 13 November, broke up in uproar and mob violence with Bowman having to leave the Foyle Street schoolroom after an attempt had been made to drag him off the platform by members of the largely Conservative audience. While Ewart himself distanced himself from the violence, those responsible were very likely his own employees, and there was a strong suspicion that the culprits were paid or otherwise induced to mount the attack on his rival.

'Mr Workman, finding that the abandonment of the intention to hold the meeting was not sufficient to check the violence of those who were in the hall, made his way into the centre of the hall at very great personal risk to at least let them know they would not be permitted unseen to destroy valuable property,' reported the *Northern Whig*.[21] It described those responsible for the disruption as a 'coarse and reckless crowd of Conservative camp-followers, prepared, to all appearances, to take any course, however scandalous, that might be necessary to prevent Mr Bowman's supporters from holding their meeting.' The *Whig's* account continued:

> The scene in the interior of the school was indescribably disagreeable and no doubt in many respects it was a sad reflection on the poor creatures who could be so utilised by their enemies. Not being able to discover in the school – a place, by the way, to which some of the rowdies were probably paying their first visit – any of the supporters of Mr Bowman, the roughs proceeded to exercise their wantonness by throwing here and there small well-prepared handbags of bakers' flour. Probably they aimed the bags at the heads of those whom they may have supposed to be the friends of Mr Bowman, but they had so completely taken possession of the building that they did not even retain sufficient room to admit those on whom they intended to practise their violence. This was, of course, their mistake and it is not surprising that in that portion of the scheme which devolved upon themselves, the helpless dupes should have overdone their cowardly work.

> It seems, indeed, that those who were equipped with flour bags were so anxious to cover the supporters of Mr Bowman with an article which free trade makes plentiful that they took any individual in the room who might be found not acting as the others were for an opponent, and discharged the flour bag on his head or on his face. In this way the undiscerning creatures beat themselves with their own weapons and lost the satisfaction which it would have brought to have known that they were offending the friends of the candidate.

Windows were broken, the school's harmonium was smashed, furniture was damaged and a gas bracket was wrenched out of its socket 'with the double object of letting the gas escape and using the bracket as a weapon of assault.' The police eventually gained entry to the schoolroom and 'only after prolonged exertions by the constables were they able to effect a clearance of the building.' Workman was one of several Bowman supporters who sustained injuries, none serious, and the candidate, before quitting the scene, indicated to friends that the meeting would be held at a place and a time 'to be notified by advertisement.'

The *Northern Whig* added: 'For a considerable time after the school had been cleared Foyle Street, Clifton Park Avenue and the Crumlin Road were obstructed by knots of the disturbers, who appeared to be exuberant over the disgraceful scenes which, fortunately for them, the intervention of the police had brought to a termination.'

The *Morning News* saw a humorous side to the story, reporting that 'some half dozen of the constabulary were present but their efforts were of no avail – indeed they got their own share from the Ewartites, principally in the shape of flour lavishly showered over their faces and helmets. The constables were hardly to be recognised with the flour over their black tunics, and they themselves were, perforce, obliged to laugh at their own comical appearance.'[22] The reality, however, was that a serious threat of violence existed, further manifesting itself in an attack on Bowman's home in Berlin Street. Trade unionist Robert McClung, recalling the incident some 44 years later, said the house had been wrecked and Bowman with his wife and family had escaped out the back to safety.[23]

Ewart referred to the unseemly episode at Foyle Street when he addressed a Conservative campaign meeting three nights later in Clifton Street Orange Hall. He offered an assurance to Bowman and his supporters that he was in no way involved and that he very much regretted what had happened. 'I am an advocate of free speech and I would wish every man to get a fair hearing,' he declared. 'Mr Bowman has conducted his candidature in a creditable manner and I hope this unfortunate little incident will be forgotten. I have no doubt – and I trust sincerely – that no friend of mine would ever do anything to disturb any meeting of Mr Bowman's.'

Despite the apology Ewart was clearly aware that Foyle Street had cast a shadow over his own campaign. He targeted Bowman's already well-publicised Liberal sympathies and asked his audience:

Will the electors of North Belfast send to parliament a supporter of Mr Gladstone and Mr Chamberlain? If they want such a man, they have the candidate in Mr Bowman. Or will they send a supporter of Lord Salisbury – such as I have declared myself to be? Mr Bowman wishes this to be a non-political contest. I have read over his speech and the comments of his supporters and I must say he very carefully avoids the question of politics. Are you content with Mr Bowman as a politician? I have no accurate knowledge of Mr Bowman's politics, but I have heard he is a disciple of Henry George and that he is in favour of the nationalisation of the land. He is prepared to go, I might say, to revolutionary measures. As I would be very sorry to bring any wrong accusations against him, I would hope that on this question of politics Mr Bowman will enlighten the electors.

Such a blatant challenge to Bowman served to stir up further bitterness towards the labour candidate, as well as producing an example of Victorian humour. The Rev. Dr Hugh Hanna, who evidently had a clear memory of the labour candidate from the Henry George debate earlier in the year, stepped forward and declared:

The Conservatives of North Belfast are not likely to be afraid of any of those spectres of the nursery who are sometimes invoked to frighten ill-behaved children. We are not in the slightest bit afraid of a bo-man. I am rather glad such a spectre has appeared as we will have the opportunity of dealing with him in such a manner at this election as will prevent him ever attempting to scare anyone again.[24]

Choosing to ignore the challenge over his politics, Bowman held his rearranged meeting – the third and final rally of his campaign – in St. George's Hall on 18 November.[25] Supporters well outnumbered opponents, but a number of Ewart's men had managed to gain entry thanks to the ready availability of forged admission tickets.[26] 'In addition,' reported the following day's *Northern Whig*, 'large crowds outside in High Street kept cheering for Ewart. Until the meeting concluded they completely obstructed the thoroughfare and blocked the entrance to the hall.'

Benjamin Hobson, a fellow Liberal and, like Bowman, a commercial traveller,[27] took the chair as James Workman had problems making his way through the crowd outside. He directed his opening remarks at the hecklers, noting that as many were Protestant working men he would appeal to them to accord 'civil and religious liberty' to the labour candidate. 'Surely a working man deserves as much at your hands as any moneyed capitalist?' he declared.

Bowman, who also called for a fair hearing, pointed out that the position he occupied was 'not of my seeking.' He continued:

I never pulled a wire or asked a single individual to promote my candidature, and I challenge any man in the house to say that I have canvassed for a vote. I am strongly of the opinion that canvassing ought to be made an illegal practice.

He then broadened the scope of his address, taking in such issues as the price of sugar and the high standard of machinery in Belfast linen mills. As far as the production of linen was concerned, he said workers in Belfast were better equipped than their counterparts in France or Belgium where they did not have two-sided spinners. And although the workers in those countries faced longer hours, they actually performed less work:

That is my reply to Mr Ewart as to whether it is fair that we should be put into competition with nations working 72 or 78, or in rare cases, 144 hours weekly.[28] Does Mr Ewart think that the workers of Belfast will put themselves on the same level as those on the continent?

Asked for his views on breaking the union with Great Britain, Bowman replied that he had not put himself forward as a politician and therefore he had nothing to say on such issues. However, Bowman's election manifesto, read out at the meeting,[29] indicated that he was in favour of maintaining the link, but 'as we can only have a satisfactory and abiding union on the basis of justice, I will oppose every movement in the direction of injustice and wrong.' The manifesto also indicated his support for an amendment to the Employers' Liability Act and its extension to cover seamen; free primary and technical education; free trade with other nations; a reduction in working hours; a more just system of levying local rates; assimilation of the franchises; female suffrage; settlement of international disputes by arbitration, and the appointment of extra factory inspectors from the working classes.

Bowman went on to claim he was fighting the election in alliance with:

...almost 40 candidates throughout the United Kingdom who are seeking the suffrages of the electors on purely working men's principles, and these men will not permit themselves to be absorbed into any of the great political parties, but will continue in the House of Commons, as many of them have done outside it, to stand up for the rights of their fellows.

After a vote of confidence in Bowman had been formally proposed by election agent Workman and seconded by James Melville, the motion was supported by James Cumming.[30] They had before them, said Cumming, a man who would work honestly in the interests of the working classes. Bowman was a man 'from whose eyes I have seen the light of Irish eloquence flash' and he would 'support the cause of purity in national life.' That support, said Cumming, was necessary following the revelations in the *Pall Mall Gazette*. Stead, he declared had 'sacrificed his all in life for the preservation of purity. He went down into the very hell of London, saw it under the gaslight, and found in its dens princes of the blood Royal.'

Cumming's remarks prompted hecklers to shout out: 'That is not true' and 'He got three months for it.' The latter portion of his speech was drowned by rival supporters noisily leaving the building and an attempt to put Workman's motion to the meeting was interrupted by jeers. Hobson declared that it had been carried and brought the meeting to a close with the customary votes of thanks.

The *Morning News* offered Bowman a degree of support in an editorial the following day,[31] interpreting his manifesto as stating that the union with Great Britain was being conducted 'without due regard to justice.' The paper suggested that the 'finest efforts' of the Irish Party had been made for the working classes 'and the members only wait for the augmented strength they will possess in the coming parliament to renew their exertions on behalf of labour.' It added:

> The Irish Party is the party of progress, and consequently its members are the special friends and advocates of those who earn their bread in the sweat of their brow. Should Mr Bowman be returned to parliament, he will find there a powerful party devoted to every item, or almost every item, in his circulated address.

Despite such potentially provocative words from its nationalist rival, the *Northern Whig* maintained its support.[32]

There was also a special campaign song, author unknown, for the labour candidate:

Brave workmen, all true men, no few men are ye,
To the poll, then, up roll them, and strike to be free
Too long, men, ye strong men, as slaves ye have toiled,
And others, though brothers, your labours have spoiled.

William Ewart, we're assured, to himself has been kind
And you, men, though true men, for yourselves have been blind.
That great giant, defiant, Goliath-like he,
Our David despises, purse proud man is he.

In schoolroom, in Foyle Street, great victory had he;
But we'll reach him, and teach him, in the poll booth he'll see.
To the poll, men, then roll, men, and soon he shall see
Who's the right man to fight, man, and win victory!

Three cheers for the vote, men, now we workmen are free,
And we all, men, though small men, victorious shall be;
And Bowman, stout foeman, is our man today,
And let no man e'er go, man, his mates to betray!

If a low man should go, man, his mates to betray,
Let him go, man; he's no man, a traitor is he!
Come then all men, great and small men, a great pull today,
A strong pull, and a long pull, and a cheer all the way.

CHORUS: But Bowman, brave foeman, no slow man is he,
So for Bowman we'll go, man, and strike to be free![33]

Ewart held his final campaign meeting on 24 November in the dining room of his company's mill at Crumlin Road.[34] Mindful of the growing level of sympathy his opponent was attracting, he went on the offensive, attacking Bowman for not keeping to his earlier promise to avoid 'uttering a single word or doing a single deed unworthy of him.' He went on:

> Too much personality has been introduced into the contest and absolutely false statements have been made about myself, particularly with regard to the Employers' Liability Act. My workmen are possessed of intelligence and it is for them to say if I acted in a manner adverse to their interests.

Thomas Johnston, vice-chairman of Belfast Trades Council, said they 'all should be up and doing something for the Conservative cause, the cause which has shown itself to be well worthy of our support.' Johnston went somewhat further than Ewart probably would have wished at a public meeting by raising the Home Rule issue to its highest level yet. He branded Bowman a Republican 'and one of the deepest dye' and claimed that he had expressed the wish to see 'the last thread binding England and Ireland severed.' Johnston added:

> If he would cease to pose as a labour candidate and come out as a Radical or Republican, we would be able to understand him; but, as a working man's candidate, except that he is a working man himself, he has little or no claim to represent us. I believe Mr Ewart will be in the future, as he has been in the past, a faithful and efficient guardian of the interests of the working men in Belfast.[35]

Workman hit back at the charges, declaring in a letter to the *Northern Whig*: 'Mr Bowman desires me to say that the statements are absolutely false, especially regarding his wish to sever the last thread that binds England and Ireland together. Indeed, these statements were so false that even the *Belfast News-Letter* would not give credence to them.'[36]

While the *Belfast News-Letter* poured scorn on Liberals and Nationalists standing elsewhere, it was quite reserved in its final comments on the fight in North Belfast, adopting the view that Bowman did not represent a threat: 'The opposition to Mr Ewart can be understood, but Mr Ewart is as sure of being returned as that the sun will rise tomorrow morning.'[37]

The *Belfast News-Letter* might have been more critical and the *Morning News* even more forthcoming in its support, had word come through earlier that Parnell was backing Bowman. However, his tactical endorsement came in a statement issued after the newspaper election editorials had appeared and after the candidates had held their final campaign meetings.[38] Parnell's message was simple and direct: 'Mr Bowman is opposing Mr Ewart, Conservative, on purely labour lines, apart from any political organisation, and he should have the thorough support of the Nationalist voters.' In adopting such an approach Parnell was also hoping to attract Protestant working-class votes for Nationalist candidate Thomas Sexton in the marginal West Belfast constituency.[39]

Voting on 26 November, eight days after the formal dissolution of parliament, went smoothly with, according to the *Belfast News-Letter*:

> ...a large number of volunteers on both sides, who worked assiduously during the day for their respective candidates, and in all the polling

districts there was an entire absence of anything like faction. There was not even as much as the ordinary electioneering banter to enliven the proceedings.[40]

The counting of votes took place in the solicitors' room at the county courthouse and lasted some three and a half hours. William Ewart polled 3,915 votes to Alexander Bowman's 1,330, giving the sitting MP a majority of 2,585 in an 87 per cent poll. The population of North Belfast was 53,427 while the total number of voters on the register was 6,810 and there were 27 spoiled votes. Ewart proposed a vote of thanks to the returning officer and also referred to the 'good feeling' that had prevailed during the contest. Seconding the motion, the defeated candidate thanked all those who had 'wrought so vigorously for myself; and, although I have been beaten, I am not deterred.'[41]

The *Belfast News-Letter* reported that Ewart found on reaching his carriage that the horses had been unharnessed:

He took a seat on the box and the crowd, cheering enthusiastically, dragged the vehicle away towards Mr Ewart's mill... There is no power in Belfast could impair Mr Ewart's popularity, and those who despatched the labour candidate on a forlorn hope were well aware of the fact. Mr Ewart is the real labour candidate...[42]

Ewart's election expenses amounted to £455 6s. 1d., while Bowman's team spent £366 18s. 4d. The *Northern Whig* reported that the entire expenses bill for the four Belfast seats added up to £4,250 13s. 7d., excluding unpaid and disputed charges.[43]

To put Bowman's achievement at the polls in context, in the July 1886 general election, held following the defeat of Gladstone's Home Rule bill and using the same electoral registers, Nationalist candidate James Dempsey polled 732 votes to William Ewart's increased total of 4,522.[44] With just nine more votes cast in the July 1886 election, it becomes clear that Bowman attracted the votes of some 600 Liberals, while the remainder were Nationalists who had followed Parnell's instruction.[45]

The *Northern Whig*, acknowledging the significance of the result, commented: 'As a matter of fact, Mr Bowman has been universally congratulated on the excellent fight he made. The numbers recorded for Mr Bowman show a desire among a large body of the artisans to have some representation at Westminster independent of the great political parties.'[46]

HOME RULER

BOWMAN'S FORTHRIGHT backing for Home Rule stemmed not only from his unwavering faith in Gladstone, but also his long-held belief that London cared little for the interests of working-class people and a growing feeling that those interests would be better served through a legislative government based in Dublin but still linked to the imperial parliament. It was also an extension of the viewpoint he had articulated to members of the Belfast Debating Society as far back as February 1882.

The idea of Home Rule had been put forward in 1870 by Isaac Butt, through the Dublin-based Home Government Association of Ireland, a body comprising Conservatives and Liberals, Protestants and Catholics.[1] Reconstituted as the Home Rule League in 1873, the organisation wanted an Irish parliament which would manage the country's internal affairs and have control over its resources and revenues but, at the same time, contribute towards imperial expenditure and be represented on imperial matters at Westminster.[2]

While Protestants gradually became less involved in the movement, the mood changed perceptibly after the November 1885 election. It had resulted in the Liberals winning 335 seats, the

Conservatives 249 and Nationalists the balance of 86. In Ireland itself there was a setback for Gladstone with the Liberals – who had won 15 seats in 1880 – being wiped out completely, with 85 Nationalist MPs and 18 Conservatives being returned to Westminster. In Leinster, Munster and Connaught the Nationalists won all the seats with the exception of the two for the University of Dublin. In Ulster there was a Nationalist majority of 17 to 16 over the Conservatives, compared to the 18 Conservatives, nine Liberals and two Home Rule MPs returned at the general election of 1880.

Bowman retained his position with the Belfast Trades Council and reconfirmed his Liberal sympathies after the non-party approach to the November election. It was the Liberal Party which was commanding much of his attention, for Bowman believed that Gladstone, with another ministry in the offing, was preparing to right a number of the perceived wrongs in Ireland. On 14 January 1886, Bowman delivered a lecture on 'The Present Crisis: Political Industrial and Economical' to the Mountpottinger Liberal Club[3] – which he had no problem visiting with the election campaign now in the past. Declaring that with the Conservatives the country had a government which was 'in office but not in power,' he felt that when it came to a vote Parnell's MPs would side with the Liberals, not from any love of Gladstone's party but from the political benefits which could be derived from such support. 'The Irish Party has been in determined opposition to whatever government is in power since it came into existence,' said Bowman. 'And Lord Salisbury need not hope for more favourable treatment at its hands than was accorded to Mr Gladstone, who had done so much and laboured so hard to strike the shackles from their limbs.'[4]

Having cited examples of beneficial Liberal legislation adopted in previous decades, Bowman welcomed the election to Westminster of 12 labour-minded candidates, 'men who are in sympathy and touch with their fellow workers,' and suggested that it augured well for the future.

Two weeks later Bowman took part in a public meeting called to protest at the high salaries being paid to the town clerk and other Belfast Town Council officials at a time when ratepayers were facing increasing financial pressures, with the previous 20 years having seen average rents rising from 1/6d a week to 2/6d but without matching wage rises.[5] There was standing room only in St George's Hall as speaker after speaker condemned the council's decision to award town clerk Samuel Black an increase of £75 a year, taking his annual salary to £2,000 – especially as the Chief Secretary for Ireland was paid £2,500 and the Prime Minister £5,000.[6] Bowman seconded a motion branding the increases as 'unjustifiable,' and said trade in Belfast was 'so depressed that it is impossible for the toiler to receive such reward for his labours as would enable him to live in even tolerable comfort; and not only that, thousands who are anxious to have work cannot find it.'

He also addressed a well-attended but disrupted meeting organised by the Irish Land Restoration Society at the Botanic Avenue Exhibition Hall.[7] Titling his lecture 'The Land for the People,' he set out the society's thinking and declared:

> Surely there must be something wrong in the social state which compels the really industrious, the wealth-producing class, to live unnatural existences, to enjoy none of the good things which their muscular force and creative skill called into being; while the idle, spendthrift, supercilious knaves who would not descend to engage in trade or perform a single day's work of a useful nature have their eyes standing out with fatness?

Bowman was interrupted repeatedly during his lecture and the accompanying disorder ultimately broke up the meeting. The controversial content of his address also led to a series of critical letters in the press,[8] prompting a response from Bowman who declared that 'David-like, I shall go forth to the fray depending on the omnipotency of truth rather than in the weakness of my puny arm.' Describing Henry George as a 'true prophet,' he added: 'It would be difficult to over-estimate the effect produced on English political life during the years since his book was published. It would be strange if a theory having no bottom could produce these results.'[9]

Appealing though Bowman's increasingly socialist views may have sounded to the Liberals' working-class element in Belfast, it was, however, Home Rule which dominated public attention.

Gladstone had been invited to form a government after the Conservatives were defeated in the first critical division of the new session at Westminster. Although the vote had been on an amendment in favour of giving local bodies the compulsory power to obtain land for allotments – prompted, according to Bowman, by the teachings of Henry George,[10] – in effect it represented a test of confidence in the government. The division on 26 January saw 257 Liberals and 74 Irish Nationalists siding with Gladstone, while 234 Conservatives and 18 Liberals sided with Lord Salisbury.

Rumours had been rife of Gladstone's impending support for Home Rule. They had a particularly strong impact in Belfast where the Liberals, still reeling from election failure, were unwilling to make any firm pronouncements until they had heard the proposals from Gladstone himself. In the early weeks of 1886 they resisted moves by the local Conservatives to form a united front, preferring to maintain a 'wait and see' approach.[11]

Belfast Liberals sought to calm mounting fears by declaring that 'the maintenance of the authority of the Imperial Parliament over Ireland, as an integral part of the United Kingdom, is essential to the security and well-being of this country.' They also protested against 'any legislation calculated to endanger or impair the unity of the Empire,' and warned that the establishment of an Irish parliament would be 'inconsistent with the maintenance of the Union and fraught with danger to the Empire.' The statement concluded with confirmation of their 'unabated confidence in Mr Gladstone and the leaders of the Liberal Party.'[12]

However, with Gladstone back at 10 Downing Street from February, the general committee of the Liberals' Ulster Reform Club decided to ascertain thinking on Home Rule, with a delegates' convention being announced for 19 March at St George's Hall. Ostensibly the idea behind the conference was to discuss various resolutions aimed at providing a response to Gladstone's request for the 'free communication of views from the various classes and sections most likely to supply full and authentic knowledge of the wants and wishes of the Irish people.'[13] Gladstone's statement singled out 'social order, the settlement of the land question and a widely-prevalent desire for self-government beyond what is felt in Great Britain, but necessarily subject in all respects to the law of imperial unity.'

In fact, the meeting served to emphasise the ever-widening gulf between the pro-Union Liberals, who feared that any Dublin parliament would give added impetus to the separatist movement, and a small but vociferous minority of Gladstone supporters, who favoured at least a degree of devolution for Ireland. The convention, chaired by linen merchant Finlay McCance, attracted delegates from most parts of the north, including tenant-farmers' associations, the Ulster Liberal Society, the Belfast Liberal Association and the Ulster Reform Club. It was also infiltrated by a considerable number of Parnell's followers who voiced loud approval for any indications of support among Liberals for Home Rule.[14]

The first of three resolutions assured the new government of their support in maintaining law and order in the country, but added:

> We believe the true policy as regards the conservation of order in Ireland is to proceed as early as possible with remedial legislation, and that we disapprove of any exceptional coercive legislation for this country, believing that Ireland should not be asked to submit to any restraints on liberty other than may from time to time be adopted for the whole of the United Kingdom.

While that resolution was passed with little dissent, the second, despite gaining majority support, revealed clear signs of division. Former Tyrone Liberal MP Thomas Dickson, renowned as an uncompromising friend of the tenant-farmer,[15] declared there was:

> ... urgent and immediate need of a measure for the final settlement of the land question on the basis of the compulsory extinction of dual ownership, by purchase from the landlords, upon such terms as will secure substantial reductions of the present rents, leasehold, judicial, or otherwise; that pending such a settlement, we advise that wide powers should at once be given to some tribunal to stay evictions in cases where they can be shown to involve injustice or hardship.

Farmer Robert Carlisle, with Bowman lending support, opposed the resolution in terms previously espoused by the Irish Land Restoration Society. Their amendment declared:

> ... the conflict between occupiers and owners of land in Ireland, being the cause of distress, discontent and disorder, we are convinced that

no settlement of the land question would be satisfactory that would not cause an immediate reduction of the fair rents fixed, and also bring leaseholders within the jurisdiction of the land courts; that we are of the opinion that land has not contributed its fair proportion of taxation to the State, and that an Irish Land Bill, to be of a final and satisfactory character, should provide to the State a revenue from the land of a 20 per cent valuation, ... and that tenants wishing to purchase their holdings should get two-thirds of the purchase money from the State, to be repaid in 50 years.

Bowman, saying he personally would have worded the amendment in 'more drastic terms,' was vehemently opposed to the implication contained in the original resolution that the government would pay a huge sum – estimated at £50m or the equivalent of half the annual Irish budget – to buy out the landlords.

In the case of nine-tenths of the landlords of the United Kingdom the land was obtained by spoilation and robbery. Not one-tenth was obtained by purchase. Nine-tenths of the estates are held by reason of some ancestor of the present holder having been able to dupe some of the weak rulers who guided the destinies of these countries in the past.

He also pointed out that if the government did borrow the money to buy out the landlords' interest, the 'industrial classes will end up paying the interest on the loan for the purpose of creating a peasant ownership.' Bowman continued:

The time has come when we must have our laws framed on the basis of justice and equity – equity to every man of the entire community – and not conceived in the spirit of a class. The time has come when the land must be restored to the position it occupied before the period when spoilation and robbery gave to many of the landlords of the United Kingdom their present titles.

When the Carlisle/Bowman amendment was put to the meeting it received only limited support. Bowman called in vain for a second vote, while Carlisle claimed the discussion had been stifled. Tensions became more apparent with the third resolution, put forward by delegate Thomas Sinclair, which 'respectfully' urged Gladstone not to combine the land question with the National question. While accepting that the election results had pointed towards support for extended powers of local self-government, the resolution voiced the 'determined opposition' of Ulster Liberals to the establishment of a separate Irish parliament, as being:

> ... certain to result in disastrous collisions between sections of the people holding conflicting views on social, economic, and religious subjects, and likely to create such a feeling of insecurity as would jeopardise all industrial and commercial pursuits, and we are satisfied that the maintenance of the Union with Great Britain is the best safeguard for the peace, prosperity and liberty of all classes in Ireland.

Sinclair added a personal view that 'there must be no Home Rule plank in the Ulster Liberal platform.' He further stated that:

> ... a Dublin parliament would not be a constitutional government at all. It would be far better to live under the undisguised autocracy of the Russian Czar, than of a parliament whose members would today surrender their judgment to one leader, the next day to a more frenzied successor, and the next to an ecclesiastical tyranny more frenzied than both. The time has come when we must all appear in our true colours. The prince of statesmen has asked us to declare our side – we owe it to him, to ourselves, and to our country, to give him an emphatic and unmistakable answer.

Opposition to the resolution was led by Thomas Dickson, whose amendment, while falling short of seeking an Irish parliament, demanded 'the largest possible scheme of local self-government.' It offered 'unabated confidence' in Gladstone and urged him:

> ... when dealing with the pressing question of local self-government in Ireland, to make full provision to safeguard the rights of minorities, to maintain the supremacy of the Imperial Parliament, and to draw close the bonds of political union between the people of Great Britain and Ireland.

While he objected to Sinclair's resolution because he felt it would close the door to remedial legislation in Ireland, his seconder, Thomas Shillington (jun.), from Portadown, was quite prepared to speak in favour of a parliament sitting in Dublin. He also described as a 'slander and a calumny' the inference in the resolution that it was impossible for people in Ireland to live at peace with one-another. Shillington, chairman of the Ulster Land Committee, put the blame for 'disastrous conflicts' in Ireland on 'the ascendancy of one party amongst them, whose business is to create those dissensions.'

He attacked the term 'separate Irish parliament' in the resolution, describing a parliament as a place for talking. Shillington said he would have strongly supported the resolution if it had referred to a 'separate and independent' parliament or one 'endowed with powers to legislate for us on all questions affecting imperial matters.'

Bowman, backing the amendment, declared that the majority of MPs returned for Ireland were 'devoid of honest principle.' By removing the grievance which weighed upon the Irish people, they would 'remove the cause which has led to the existence of the National League.' Bowman said they needed a measure which would 'go to the root of the problem and settle it once and for all.' He also doubted whether 'mere county government reform will rid us of the domineering power of English ignorance.'

His views were drowned in a growing uproar which ended with the Dickson/Shillington proposal being declared lost. Accusations were levelled that a number of Belfast Liberals had crowded into the hall just in time for the vote, which involved the two sets of supporters moving to either side of the hall. The resolution's supporters countered by claiming that the presence of many Nationalists from Armagh and Tyrone had falsely inflated support for the amendment.

Either way, it was agreed on the proposal of Thomas Andrews, seconded by James Lee,[16] that copies of the three resolutions should be forwarded to the leaders of the Liberal Party for their consideration and that a committee be appointed 'to take such action as they may think best calculated to promote the objects of the resolutions.'

While the *Northern Whig* had no doubt that the wording of the amendment to the third resolution did not actually advocate Home Rule and that it was defeated by a 'considerable majority,' the *Morning News* took a contrary view, declaring that the convention had backed Gladstone on Home Rule and, further, had 'opened a new chapter in Ulster history, one which will no doubt finish most agreeably – by seeing the Irish nation, North and South, united in one happy and prosperous family.'[17]

Those who had hoped the convention would end the matter and that Gladstone would heed the Ulster Liberal viewpoint, were proved wrong, for just under three weeks later, on Thursday 8

April 1886, Gladstone detailed to parliament his Home Rule plans for Ireland. The controversial announcement had been preceded two weeks earlier by confirmation of the resignations of Joseph Chamberlain, President of the Local Government Board, and George Trevelyan, Chief Secretary for Scotland, who joined other opposing Liberal Unionists.[18]

The Prime Minister's bill proposed a parliament to take control of internal Irish matters, including the Irish civil service, general taxation, the judiciary and the police, while Westminster would keep control of customs and excise duties, defence and foreign affairs. The position of Lord Lieutenant would be retained but the requirement that he should be a Protestant would no longer apply. Financially, Ireland would remain fiscally linked to Great Britain and would contribute one-fifteenth of the United Kingdom's general expenditure.

The bill's provisions included the withdrawal of the 28 Irish representative peers from the House of Lords and the 103 Irish members from the House of Commons, but Gladstone would later agree to reconsider that element. The number of Irish representatives at the new Dublin parliament would double to 206 under the same franchise conditions and electoral boundaries. However, with a view to protecting minorities, particularly the Protestants, Gladstone also proposed a 'first order' of 75 members, including, if they wished to serve on it, the 28 peers. Those seeking election for a 10-year term on the 75-strong body would face a £200 a year property franchise – thus ensuring the exclusion of the less well-off. Gladstone's idea was that the two orders would deliberate together but, in the event of a contentious issue, there was provision for a separate vote. Each order would have the power of veto.[19]

Gladstone, by then 76 and knowing his time was limited, hoped the measure of Home Rule he was proposing would keep Ireland part of a strengthened United Kingdom and thereby avoid the possibility of unlawful secession. He followed the Home Rule bill – or Bill for the Better Government of Ireland – with a linked Irish Land Purchase bill, along the lines debated at the Liberal convention. It proposed the issue of £50m. of new three-per-cent stock for the purpose of buying up the estates of landlords who were willing to sell their lands.[20]

The *Northern Whig*, which until then had clung to the hope that Gladstone would change his mind, removed itself from the fence and declared:

> It is a grave thing that a Prime Minister of the British or Imperial Government should make such a speech, still graver that it should be introductory of such proposals. There can be no further disputing about what Mr Gladstone's intentions are, or about what confidence he may now deserve. All who approve of his plan must be prepared to admit that an Irish parliament in College Green is desirable. Everyone, indeed, must be ready to say Yes or No on this question.

The only point the *Northern Whig* felt could be greeted with 'unmixed satisfaction' was the initial proposal to exclude Irish members from the London parliament:

> To allow them to make laws for Ireland and then to pass over to London to obstruct legislation in order to obtain other Nationalist concessions from the Ministers there, would have been most absurd, indefensible, and preposterous. ...The plan is even more thorough-going than was expected. It affords no protection to the large and respected Ulster minority whatever. The government of the country would merge in the supremacy of the Irish Nationalist majority, such as we have known it to be at the best, and it might very soon become worse.[21]

The *Morning News* welcomed the bill but added that it was 'clearly framed with the utmost conceivable anxiety to satisfy the Loyalist minority in every possible respect, and to give them more guarantees than they possibly could be entitled to.'[22]

For Protestant Home Rulers, Gladstone's conversion afforded them an opportunity to step into the daylight and challenge more openly the Unionist contention that all Protestants in Ireland opposed self-government.[23]

THE RESIGNATION FROM
BELFAST TRADES COUNCIL

GIVEN THE GROWING hostility towards Gladstone within the loyalist community, the Liberals decided to call a second convention for the end of April 1886. Whereas the first had attracted the various shades of party thinking, for the second, in the Ulster Hall, the mood was altogether different, with a large number of Conservatives gaining entry to swell the anti-Gladstone ranks.[1] The audience included 100 men from the Sirocco Works who had been led to the hall via Ballymacarrett and the Queen's Bridge by a rider carrying the royal standard. Unbowed, Bowman and others in the embryonic Home Rule wing took their places in the hall. He would later claim they were not permitted to speak.

Under the chairmanship of Thomas Sinclair, the delegates, through four resolutions, all adopted without dissent or amendment, expressed their opposition to Home Rule. They repeated their conviction that the unsatisfactory land tenure system could be blamed for Irish discontent but deplored it being linked to the Home Rule bill, and maintained the 'necessity for giving the Irish people, by extension of representative institutions, a larger control over purely local affairs.'

A week after the second convention the *Belfast News-Letter* reported that, with a view to putting forward the anti-Home Rule message, a deputation 'representing the feelings of the trade unions in Ireland' had left for London the previous evening with the intention of meeting John Bright, Joseph Chamberlain, Henry Broadhurst 'and other Members of Parliament supposed to be identified with the interests of the artisans and working classes.' The members of the deputation were identified as being Samuel McComb and William Johnston, from Londonderry, John McKee, William Thompson and William Currie, from Belfast, and Hugh Scott and James Kirk, from Donegal.[2]

The newspaper, pointing out that Gladstone in his recently-issued manifesto had stated that the upper classes only were opposed to Home Rule, declared that the London-bound delegates 'will be able to show him that his scheme has no favour with the bone and sinew of Irish society.'

Bowman, acting on the instructions of Belfast Trades Council's parliamentary committee, denied in a telegram to the House of Commons that the deputation had been appointed by the trades council or any other trade unions in the town.[3] He added that 'some members of the deputation are not trade unionists at all.' Bowman followed that up with a letter to Broadhurst – by then Under-Secretary at the Home Office – again with the aim of minimising the importance of the delegation. The Press Association in London reported that:

... a deputation of workmen, representatives of the recent Belfast Liberal meeting, as well as other parts of Ulster, had an interview with Messrs. Thomas Burt and George Howell and other Liberal and Radical Members of Parliament, to enter a protest against Mr Gladstone's Irish policy, the adoption of which would, in their opinion, be ruinous to the interests of the working classes in Ireland.

The Press Association is requested to state that Mr Broadhurst has received from Mr Alexander Bowman, secretary of the United Trades Council of Belfast, a letter informing him that the deputation from the North of Ireland, purporting to represent the Protestant working men of Ulster, which has proceeded to London for the purpose of interviewing various Members of Parliament with regard to Home Rule, is not appointed by either the trades council or any individual society. It is added that the members of the deputation have authority only to speak for themselves and for those who have employed them, and that they include some uncompromising enemies of the principle of trade unionism. The question of Home Rule, it is said, has not been considered by any of the Belfast trades union organisations. Mr Bowman, who is a Protestant, adds that personally he is in favour of the Home Rule scheme, but that he considers the land purchase proposals dangerous.[4]

William Currie, a linenlapper by trade and spokesman for the delegation, wired an immediate response from London to the Belfast press, branding Bowman's actions as 'unwarranted interference.'[5]

The controversy was also raised at the trades council with painters' representative Charles Dargan proposing, and assistant secretary Robert Meharg seconding, that the body 'repudiates the opinions expressed ... by our secretary, Mr Bowman, with regard to a deputation of workmen sent to London.' The motion, including a call for the result to be published in the press, was put to the meeting with little debate and was defeated by 14 votes to 11.[6]

Nor was that the end of the matter, for Joseph Mitchell, president of the trades council, weighed in with a statement to the Belfast press which indicated along the way that he, unlike Bowman, strongly opposed Home Rule:

> As the communication sent to Mr Broadhurst by Mr Alexander Bowman has spread abroad the impression that the Belfast United Trades Council is opposed to the mission of the working men's deputation now in London, I think it is right to state that no expression of opinion on this matter has been issued by this body. This being the case, I think Mr Currie has just cause for complaint against Mr Bowman for having in any way identified the Council with opposition to the views which are now being laid before the English working man with so much honesty and ability.[7]

Mitchell, clearly stung by people reminding him that he had proposed Bowman as a candidate for the previous year's North Belfast election, added:

> During the past few days considerable fault has been found with me in this matter. My reply is, had I known Mr Bowman's views were such as he expressed in his letter to Mr Broadhurst, I would not have been connected with his candidature in any way whatsoever. Though differing politically from Mr Ewart, I am glad to see that through him North Belfast will be found in opposition to a measure which, I am convinced, would be injurious not only to the best interests of

Belfast, but to those of Ireland.

Bowman took not only William Currie but also the *Northern Whig* to task in letters carried by the paper on 20 and 21 May. The response to Currie took the form of a letter to Broadhurst and was signed 'Alexander Bowman, secretary of the Belfast Trades Council.' Referring to Currie's claim that the initial exchange had been unauthorised, Bowman wrote:

> This statement is untrue for I was directed by the parliamentary committee of the trades council to write it, and a resolution condemning the action of the parliamentary committee, which was submitted to the council, was negatived by a large majority. But even if my letter had been unauthorised it would still have been a simple statement of fact. From Mr Currie's letter I observe that the pretension to represent the trade unions of Belfast has been abandoned. Therefore, the parliamentary committee has no further concern with the deputation.
>
> Mr Currie now alleges that they were appointed at the Liberal meeting held in Belfast on 30 April. Perhaps you will permit me as a Liberal, who has also the honour to be a member of both the general council and the executive committee of the Belfast Liberal Association, to say that the meeting to which Mr Currie refers was not a Liberal meeting at all, as fully two-thirds of the audience were not Liberals but Conservatives... I did attend the meeting and requested the promoters to permit me to move an amendment expressing continuing confidence in the leadership of Mr Gladstone. This they firmly refused to allow.[8]

It was clear, however, that Bowman was gaining little if any public sympathy for his stance. A letter published in the *Northern Whig* and signed 'A Radical Workman,' described Bowman's message to Broadhurst as 'a tissue of misrepresentations almost from beginning to end' and protested:

> ... in the strongest possible manner against Mr Bowman dragging the trades council into the Home Rule controversy and, further, his implied sympathy of the Belfast trades unionists with the Home Rule measure now before parliament. No one knows better than Mr Bowman that there are not a dozen Protestant trades unionists in Belfast in favour of Home Rule, but he has not the manliness to tell Mr Broadhurst that. He must find some way of blowing his horn and his position as secretary to the trades council furnished him with ample means. He declares himself a Home Ruler. Why did he not do so as a

parliamentary candidate at the general election? He has not the excuse of the English and Scotch people that the question was not before the constituencies because it was fully discussed in Belfast.

The letter closed with a stinging personal attack on Bowman, challenging him to indicate which trade he represented: 'So far as is known, he is neither a trades unionist nor does he represent any trade. When elected secretary of the trades council he was a flaxdresser, but he has long since quitted that employment.'[9]

Undaunted, Bowman's next move was to help to launch the Irish Protestant Home Rule Association in Belfast – largely in response to those Unionist claims that there were few if any Protestant Home Rulers in Ireland. It also followed the appearance in Belfast of a petition addressed to Gladstone, which sought the signatures of Ulster Protestants who were generally in favour of the measures contained in the Home Rule bill as the best means of establishing a 'real' union of Great Britain and Ireland.[10]

The petition, which hoped that some degree of Irish representation would be retained at Westminster for imperial matters, also declared:

> We believe that an Irish parliament, constructed by the wisdom of the parliament of the United Kingdom on the basis of the government scheme, can be entrusted with the home legislation for our country, without any risk of retaliatory measures against the minority, however conscious that minority may be of deserving some retribution for the ungovernment of past generations.

The association's inaugural meeting, held on 21 May 1886, in the Castle Restaurant at Donegall Place, attracted as many as 100 Protestant and Liberal Home Rule sympathisers from various parts of Ulster.[11] The organisation's chief support came from Presbyterian tenant-farmers, led by members of the business and commercial classes, who usually had a background in the struggle for land reform. They were also, in the main, the leaders of the minority pro-Home Rule wing of the Ulster Liberals. Thomas Shillington from Portadown was elected president,[12] while Belfast collar and cuff manufacturer David Briggs took on the duties of acting secretary. It was Briggs who, in an earlier letter to the *Morning News*, had suggested the establishment of a Home Rule organisation.[13]

A resolution setting out the new body's intentions was proposed by Belfast solicitor Thomas McClelland,[14] and seconded by Bowman who described himself as 'the representative of the Liberal working men of Belfast.' Passed unanimously, it pledged support for Home Rule:

FIRSTLY, on national grounds. The opinions of the Irish people do not obtain adequate expression in the legislature for their country and are altogether ignored in its administration.

SECONDLY, on religious grounds. Because the practical exclusion of our Roman Catholic fellow countrymen from positions of official authority... creates feelings of sectarian distrust and animosity which are really subversive of the cause of true religion.

THIRDLY, on social and commercial grounds. In consequence of the unequal distribution of positions of trust among the various religious sections of the community, bad feelings are engendered, personal intercourse is strained and society is disorganised.

FOURTHLY, on Imperial grounds. The provision of Legislative and Administrative autonomy to Ireland is not only demanded by a sense of justice to the Irish people, but is dictated by wisdom and prudence in the interests of the Empire of Great Britain and Ireland.

Bowman, praising Gladstone as 'the greatest leader of Liberal thought in England and perhaps the world,' stressed that one of their aims was to remove from Protestants 'suspicion and distrust of our Roman Catholic brethren.' He also emphasised the Protestant Home Rulers' contention that legislative independence did not mean separation from the United Kingdom.[15]

Although the new association would tend towards grossly exaggerating its support among rank and file Protestants, with its business meetings being held behind closed doors and public meetings around the province attracting sizeable Catholic attendances, its main significance would lie in the fact that Gladstone, Liberal supporters and the Nationalists would place much faith in the body.[16] Indeed, the Prime Minister saw it as being more representative of true Protestant thinking on Home Rule than was being articulated by his own party dissidents, the Conservatives and the Orange Order.[17]

The only newspaper in Belfast fully to report the IPHRA's inaugural meeting was the *Morning News*.[18] The *Northern Whig*, which declared that the group's formation had been received 'with a good deal of surprise amongst the Protestant residents of this town,' repeated a claim from the *Belfast Evening Telegraph* that no more than 20 people had been present. 'It might safely be added that a large percentage of these were juveniles, and it would have been difficult to say to which religious denomination the majority of the others belonged,' the *Northern Whig* added. Responding to the hostile report, Briggs said there were at least 90, if not 100, present with 'our warmest sympathisers including several ardent, consistent Tories.' The various Protestant denominations were represented, with 'not a single Catholic' taking part in the proceedings.[19]

Despite the scepticism and the invective of the Unionist newspapers, the association did attract a degree of support, with plans for the establishment of branches from Antrim to Cork being announced within days of the parent body's formation.[20]

At the end of May 1886, Thomas Dickson, whose amendment at the first Liberal convention had exposed the divisions among local party members, met Gladstone in London and presented him with the pro-Home Rule petition which, he claimed, had been signed by 500 Liberal Protestants from Belfast, Antrim and Down. He also claimed they had been collected in just a few days and 'more than a thousand additions will follow shortly.' Gladstone told Dickson he was 'much pleased to receive this expression of Liberal Protestant opinion from Ireland.'[21] The Prime Minister also forwarded a personally-signed message to the IPHRA in Belfast, thanking them for the 'admirable set of resolutions passed at your meeting on 21 May.'[22]

Given such dramatic and public developments it was hardly surprising that there followed a determined bid to remove Bowman from his position as secretary of Belfast Trades Council when it met on 5 June. President Joseph Mitchell sought to establish what steps the council intended to take about their secretary's 'misleading' information in the letter to Broadhurst. He also read a letter from the No. 2 branch of the Amalgamated Society of Carpenters and Joiners warning that they intended withdrawing their delegates from the council 'until such times as Mr Bowman be removed from office.'[23]

Bowman defended his actions at length, saying he had written to the MP 'only as a trade unionist and a working man.' No further action was taken at that meeting, but on the proposal of vice-president Thomas Johnston, seconded by Samuel Monro, it was agreed that a special meeting should be convened to discuss Bowman's conduct in writing to Broadhurst. Monro handed in a notice of motion to be discussed at the special meeting. It recalled the council's avoidance of 'political questions of a party and contentious nature' and accused Bowman of violating the principle by taking an active part in party politics, most notably his support for Home Rule.

> The secretary's action in this particular case has by implication committed the council to approve of that measure and, as a protest against such an assumption, and in justice to the great majority of Belfast trade unionists thus dragged unwillingly into a false position, we call upon Mr Bowman to resign forthwith his position as secretary.

The meeting was held a week later at the usual venue, the hall at 20 College Street, with 31 delegates in attendance.[24] There was one notable absentee at the outset – Bowman himself. It was twice agreed that they should wait for him and when he did arrive, half-an-hour late, he explained that he had been delayed 'owing to the disturbed state of the town.'

Before Monro's proposal could be put to the meeting Bowman asked that the 'house should not be divided nor any discussion take place on the motion now before us.' He went on to explain that: 'Under any circumstances I cannot hold office in the council longer than our next meeting owing to circumstances which have arisen.' This was a clear reference to his evolving link with the IPHRA. Newspaper compositor Robert McIntosh proposed and printer William Goyer seconded that they accept his resignation as secretary. The resolution was passed unanimously and Monro then withdrew his notice of motion, explaining he had proposed it 'simply for the good of the council.' A further debate took place on the advisability of submitting a report of the meeting to the Press, the members voting 18 to 13 in favour of publication. The members elected Meharg as their new secretary with Goyer as his deputy.[25] Despite Bowman's activities with the Protestant Home Rulers, his resignation as secretary of the trades council did not end his membership of the body which he continued to attend until early the following year.[26]

As the drama was unfolding in Belfast, Gladstone's Home Rule bill was defeated by 343 votes to 313 at its second reading during the early hours of 8 June.[27] Ninety-three Liberals voted against the bill. The *Northern Whig* was less than jubilant in view of the obvious repercussions facing the Liberal Party, including Gladstone's likely resignation, the dissolution of parliament and the prospect of another election.

While Bowman and a number of the minority pro-Gladstone faction were determined to maintain their support for the Prime Minister through the IPHRA, members of the much larger pro-Union element in the party were already re-identifying themselves as Liberal Unionists.[28]

Commenting favourably on the new formation, the *Northern Whig* declared:

> It was never expected that a Liberal government would introduce such a measure as the one just defeated. It never could have been imagined in the wildest dreams that a Liberal government, six months after the last election, would appeal to the country in favour of such a measure and against a hundred Liberal members.[29]

The IPHRA refused to die along with Gladstone's bill, believing that the latter could be resurrected with the return of Gladstone to power. Even before the vote was taken, advertisements had been placed in the *Northern Whig* inviting interested members of the public to forward their names to Briggs so they could receive circulars regarding future association meetings.[30] Briggs and another member, commercial traveller William Hammond, had already been elected as joint honorary secretaries of the central executive with a third, solicitor James J. Johnston, soon to follow. They also indicated that a full-time paid secretary would be appointed to deal with the anticipated business.[31]

In an address to Protestants published on 25 June, the day which marked the formal dissolution of parliament, the association sought to counter the 'gross misrepresentations which allege that the Protestants of Ireland are unanimously opposed to the Irish policy of Mr Gladstone.' It also called on Irish Protestants to make a 'united effort to close the dreary chapter of our country's misgovernment and render possible a new era of peace, contentment and prosperity.' It was signed by officials from Belfast, Portadown, Antrim, Dublin, Limerick, Cork and Waterford.[32]

Given the high profile achieved by the IPHRA and the impact it was having on British Liberal thinking – much to the annoyance of local Liberal Unionists – rumours began to circulate that the organisation would be putting forward candidates in its own name in the approaching general election. That proved not to be the case, with Briggs vehemently denying a report carried in the *Northern Whig* that he planned to stand for the Ossory division of Queen's County.[33] Instead, the IPHRA willingly lent its support to Nationalist candidate Thomas Sexton in the knife-edge West Belfast constituency. Sexton, a Dublin-based journalist, had won the Sligo South seat the previous November and had also come within 37 votes of capturing West Belfast in the same general election.[34]

Sexton and members of the National League met the executive committee of the IPHRA at its office in the Queen's Building on the corner of Royal Avenue and Berry Street.[35] He told them he had consulted a number of Protestants in West Belfast that afternoon and had received considerable encouragement for his campaign.[36] Sexton, who was invited to address an IPHRA meeting in St. George's Hall in early July, acknowledged at that gathering the 'great service rendered by the Irish Protestant Home Rule Association in the present struggle' and trusted that with their co-operation there would be 'an emphatic victory at the polls in favour of Irish self-government.'[37]

With the attendance boosted by a large number of West Belfast Nationalists, there was endorsement for Sexton's candidature, with members adopting a resolution in which they pledged themselves to 'support to the best of our power all parliamentary candidates who are in favour of the establishment of a parliament in Ireland with legislative and administrative authority for Irish affairs, and to oppose all other candidates hostile to that policy.'

Sexton argued that under Gladstone's Home Rule proposals the 28 peers who would sit in the proposed Dublin parliament would be able to resist any measure directed against Protestants 'if such a thing were attempted.' He added:

If it be a fact, as it has been often asserted, that all the wealth and intelligence of Ireland is to be found with the Protestants, then the Protestant people will be able to return a strong and protective representation. The truth is, however, that this cry of religious intolerance is a phantom. The question now is this, is Ireland to be allowed to manage her own affairs?

Sexton's winning margin over Conservative James Haslett on 6 July 1886 was 103 and while the involvement of the IPHRA was, in consequence, less crucial, the victorious candidate was still happy to acknowledge their presence in the campaign, declaring: 'The association is a formidable physical fact which no argument can get rid of.'[38] Even the *Northern Whig* accepted that the 'puny efforts of the so-called Protestant Home Rule Association may have had some influence, though a very slight influence, on the result.'[39]

Their influence would prove more tangible in the Londonderry City constituency. Journalist and author Justin McCarthy, standing as a Nationalist, beat Conservative Charles E. Lewis, who had the support of the Liberal Unionists, by just four votes after a successful election petition. Since Lewis had won the seat the previous November with a slender 32-vote majority, the revised July result in McCarthy's favour pointed to the importance of even a small number of Protestant Home Rulers.

Four Protestant supporters of Home Rule failed to gain seats as Gladstonian Liberals in North Antrim, Mid Antrim, East Belfast and North Tyrone. The association actively lent its support to the successful Nationalist candidates in South Londonderry (Timothy Healy) and South Tyrone (William O'Brien), while Protestants James Williamson and Robert Gardner stood unsuccessfully as Nationalists in North Armagh and Mid Armagh respectively. IPHRA member and tenant-farmer John Pinkerton was returned unopposed as Nationalist MP for Galway City, a seat he would hold until 1900. It was estimated that 9,000 votes had been cast for Protestant Home Rulers, with some 2,500 Protestants in the north of Ireland who had previously voted Liberal, supporting Home Rule candidates.[40]

The 1886 general election saw the return of Lord Salisbury as Prime Minister. The Conservatives held 315 out of the 670 seats, their new allies the Liberal Unionists 78, the Gladstonian Liberals 191, and the Irish Nationalists 86. In Ulster the Nationalists retained their 17 to 16-seat majority over pro-Union MPs and throughout Ireland as a whole they again led by 85 seats to 18.[41]

Bowman was not openly involved in the summer 1886 election activities involving the IPHRA, although by then he had been appointed paid secretary and most likely would have been working behind the scenes.[42] The first public indication of his appointment came in a newspaper advertisement at the end of July urging Liberals who were entitled to vote in West Belfast, and who were not on the previous year's register, to contact him at the association's office in Royal Avenue.[43]

One reason for his low-key approach to the early work of the association was the very real problem of anti-Home Rule sentiment which was running high in Belfast. Bowman lost his job as a commercial traveller because of his Home Rule sympathies, while Briggs was forced to step down as an honorary secretary because members of his family were intimidated and threats were made that his business would be boycotted. Dublin branch secretary Hubert Oldham, while not actually naming Bowman and Briggs, described the harassment they faced for agreeing to be publicly identified with the movement, when he addressed the branch's first general meeting at the Central Lecture Hall in Dublin's Westmoreland Street that September:

> There is a gentleman [Bowman] in Belfast who is a most active member of the executive committee, a married man with a family. He had an important situation but, when he took the position of an executive officer of the association, he was immediately deprived of it, and his family and himself were left without the means of support. The committee in Belfast at once appointed him their assistant secretary for they considered that a blow struck at one of their members was also a blow struck at themselves.

> Another gentleman [Briggs], a manufacturer in Belfast, had lent important services in establishing the Protestant Home Rule Association there. When that became known pressure of one kind or another was brought upon him in the way of business, and it was pointed out to him that certain people had it in their power to ruin him financially if he did not withdraw from membership of the association. He did not withdraw from it, but he had duties besides

those of a politician and it was necessary for him to resign the prominent office he held in the association, although he is still a member of the executive committee. Through the tyranny of men he was connected with in business, he was obliged to beat that half retreat.[44]

The Home Rule crisis, before and after the vote, had been marked by some of the worst sectarian rioting ever witnessed in Belfast, with some 50 deaths and many injuries, including those sustained by 371 police officers, resulting from gunfire and other acts of violence during the period June to September 1886.[45] It is not difficult to imagine how a Presbyterian from the Shankill Road area, who was still supporting Gladstone, would have felt concern for his family's safety if not his own. With that in mind Bowman moved his wife and three young children to yet another address, 32 Greenmount Street, which, while still in North Belfast, was some distance from the Shankill and cost him £13 per year in rent and rates.[46] Sons William and Robert would in time be enrolled in the infants' class of St Paul's School at York Street, a short distance on foot from their new home.[47]

His re-emergence into the public spotlight came as a result of the Belfast riots and the arrest of one of his wife's relatives for allegedly stoning police on the Shankill Road at the beginning of September. Bowman took the stand at the Crumlin Road courthouse to give character evidence on behalf of Samuel Officer – one of Rose Bowman's cousins[48] – who was accused of being a member of a riotous mob. Officer, from Aberdeen Street, who was acquitted of the charge, convinced the court that he had been going on a message because his wife was in poor health. There had been no disturbance where he was arrested and he would not have heard the Riot Act being read at nearby Agnes Street.[49]

The episode gave Bowman an opportunity to emphasise his Dissenter heritage and to express his disgust at the treatment of fellow Presbyterians by the still-dominant Church of Ireland establishment in Ireland. Since he had avoided the issue of religion prior to the introduction of Gladstone's Home Rule bill, it is very likely his actions amounted to a political tactic to stress the aims of the IPHRA.

No sooner had he returned home from the courthouse than

Bowman was putting pen to paper to criticise court officials for being insulting towards Presbyterians. He explained that legislation allowed Presbyterians to raise their right hand instead of kissing the leather-bound Bible when being sworn in to give evidence.

> I, of course, exercised my right to refrain from kissing the book. However, when I raised my hand the clerk of the court asked me, did I consider that form of oath binding on my conscience. I replied, 'I am a Presbyterian,' but that did not satisfy his scruples. He repeated his question. Well, sir, rather than make a scene I said I did consider it binding. But I would like to know if officials are within their rights to thus insult Presbyterians by asking them if that form of oath which the legislature has provided for their especial use is binding upon their consciences?[50]

Warming to the theme of discrimination against Presbyterians and justifying his own Home Rule stance, Bowman pointed out that, despite the disestablishment and disendowment of the Church of Ireland by Gladstone in 1869, Ireland still had no Presbyterian peers in the House of Lords and of 622 government offices and appointments throughout the island, members of his church held just 24, despite constituting one-eleventh of the population.

> To my mind, it certainly appears strange that after all our fulsome professions of loyalty, we, as a Church, should still be treated as we are. It is not surprising that the members of the Protestant Episcopal Church should desire to maintain the status quo. The curious feature in the whole case is the fact that, although we boast of our civil and religious liberty and freedom – and I have no doubt that many people believe we have it – the profession of any religious belief except one is a bar to employment in governmental office in Ireland. It is passing strange that Presbyterian representative bodies, presbyterial and synodical, as well as the General Assembly, should pass resolutions approving of the existing system, under which they are practically precluded from participating in either the profit or honour of sharing in the government of the country. Surely this is not such treatment as should satisfy men having a sense of right and justice, even if they themselves are not the aggrieved?

A fortnight later, and in response to a Liberal Unionist correspondent who had predicted that Home Rule would result in Catholic domination, Bowman claimed that Protestants living in the mainly Catholic areas of south and west Ireland were not excluded from 'those positions and offices which are in the gift of the people.' He went on to assert that no fewer than 33 Protestant Members of Parliament had been elected in overwhelmingly Catholic constituencies.

We find in municipal matters the same liberality, the same ignoring of religious differences. At this hour, in the Catholic city of Galway, the chairman of the Town Commissioners is a Protestant, the chairman of the Harbour Board is a Protestant, the chairman of the Board of Guardians is a Protestant. The Mayors of Waterford for the years 1884 and 1885 were both Protestants and I might multiply instances such as these almost indefinitely. With such facts as these before me I think I am justified in refusing to believe that, when justice should be done to the majority of our fellow countrymen, they would be less generous than they are at present.

Bowman closed with an insight into his contemporary political thinking:

If power is distributed among all, the conflict of supposed interests results in a general compromise roughly identical with the common good. It is in order that effect may be given to this general principle – by admitting the whole people to the full functions of government – that I desire to see the present system swept away.[51]

NATIONALISTS,
NOT SEPARATISTS

IN OCTOBER 1886 Bowman represented the Irish Protestant Home
Rule Association at a meeting of the Belfast Young Ireland Society,[1]
held to mark the completion of a memorial to the poet and writer
Francis Davis, 'The Belfastman,' who had died the previous year.[2]
The platform party at St Mary's Hall included Nationalist MPs
Thomas Sexton, West Belfast, and Michael McCartan, South Down.

Bowman was being drawn more deeply into nationalist culture
and politics, coupled with a growing concern for the land question.
At the outset the IPHRA had voiced no firm views on the issue
but, towards the end of 1886, with Home Rule hopes temporarily
fading, the organisation was becoming increasingly identified with
land agitation.[3] To emphasise both points, Bowman travelled to
Annaclone, in Co. Down – not too far from his place of birth –
that November to address a meeting of Protestant and Catholic
tenant-farmers and labourers on the land question. The gathering
was chaired by Katesbridge farmer Uriah McClinchy, secretary of
the local Gladstone branch of the IPHRA, which, with some 200
members, was one of the most active northern groups.[4]

The tone of the meeting was established when a letter was read
out from Thomas Shillington who, in expressing his regrets at

being unable to attend, declared:

> The Down and Armagh farmers will doubtless pay thousands of
> pounds in the present winter in excess of the rent their lands have
> earned during the past year, and thus their poverty will be intensified
> and the natural resources of the country drained as a consequence of
> the folly of the farmers and labourers allowing themselves to be
> diverted from pursuing their own interests. I trust they will no longer
> allow the landlords and their followers to befool them by playing
> upon old religious and racial animosities.

A series of resolutions passed by loud acclaim included a
declaration that 'the smallest measure of local government which
can be accepted by the Irish people is that contained in Mr
Gladstone's Bill for the Better Government of Ireland.' In addition,
there was full backing for Parnell's party 'and their sleepless
struggle on behalf of the lives and liberties of our people,' a demand
for lower rents and better housing for labourers, and a call for the
abolition of the landlord system in Ireland. Bowman proclaimed:

> We are Irishmen as well as Protestants and we have come to the
> conclusion that our people are not governed as they ought to be. We
> have no freedom to consider our own affairs, but we have the right to
> contribute to the expenses of the government. Have we any right in
> county matters? Have we any control over the grand jury? Have we
> anything to do with the police force? Have we anything to do with
> the education system? No – along with the whole list we have no
> rights, except the right to pay, and some people say we ought to be
> satisfied with things as they are. The man who says that must have a
> low idea of the rights of humanity or the rights of society.

> For how much longer will large tracts of land go out of cultivation?
> For how much longer will people be driven away from our shores?
> The landlords will have to be got rid of by hook or by crook. I do not
> mean I would deal very harshly with them, and I would not treat
> them the same way as they have treated the people. Many emigrants
> had to leave in pestilent, rotten ships for homes across the ocean; and
> many of them never reached their destinations, and when they did
> they very often had not a penny to begin life with. I would give the
> landlords cabin passages across the sea along with £1,000 which
> they ought to be well-satisfied with, and it would be a good thing to
> get rid of them.

Referring to the 'enormous rack-rents' imposed on rural
dwellers, despite farm produce falling by 20 per cent, Bowman

said that on his way to Annaclone from Banbridge that day he had passed 'cabins which labourers live in, and I am sure the landlords would not put their horses or dogs there.' He continued:

> I am sorry to see little children and women having to live in such places. It is a travesty on our civilisation and a disgrace on the landlords' humanity. If I were the landlord of such places and saw the consequences of my dealings, I would go home and cut my throat.

He voiced confidence in Parnell's party and closed by quoting Byron: 'For freedom's battle once begun, Bequeathed from bleeding sire to son, Though baffled oft is ever won.'

The local MP, Michael McCartan, singled out Bowman for special mention in his speech, referring to him as 'the Joseph Arch of Belfast, and more, a man who always speaks out regardless of what anyone might think. He is the life and soul of the Protestant Home Rule Association in Belfast.'[5]

Bowman saw out the year by attending the 14th annual meeting of the North of Ireland branch of the National Society for Women's Suffrage at the Ulster Minor Hall,[6] and an IPHRA meeting at which Dublin secretary Hubert Oldham spoke on the Liberal Party in Ireland.[7]

By the beginning of 1887 the IPHRA was claiming, more than a little optimistically, that its Belfast executive had 1,000 members, with between 5,000 and 10,000 supporters throughout Ulster, another 1,200 members in Dublin, and at least another 1,000 in the south and west counties of Ireland.[8]

Bowman, again representing the IPHRA, was guest lecturer that January in Co. Antrim, attending a meeting in Toomebridge's Temple of Liberty in aid of a new National League hall at nearby Creagh townland.[9] His topic was 'The Act of Union: how it was obtained, its results and the remedy.' Contending that the cause of Irish liberty had not been aided by the Act of Union, Bowman declared:

> The Act of Union in 1800 was secured by the exercise of force, fraud and corruption. One hundred and thirty-eight thousand armed men represented the physical force employed by Lord Castlereagh in carrying out his nefarious designs. All who ventured to oppose his project were intimidated into acquiescence. The most fradulent

promises were made to the Catholic hierarchy. They were wooed into supporting the design by a promise that Catholic Emancipation would be conceded but this promise appears – like a pie-crust – to have been made in order to be broken.[10]

While there had been substantial industrial growth in Britain and around the world during the nineteenth century, argued Bowman, trades in many parts of Ireland had been 'annihilated.' He continued: 'Since 1800 Ireland has scarcely for a single year been permitted to enjoy the full liberty which in theory is secured by the British Constitution. Such are the direct results of the Union.' He added:

This country has been oppressed, harassed and wounded by the operation of harsh laws and by the corrupt administration of such other laws as would not pass muster in other countries. Nevertheless, since the passing of the ill-starred Act of Union the fire of patriotism has not ceased for a single instant to glow on the altar of Irish Nationality. English government in Ireland may be summed up in one ominous word – disaster.

As a result, Gladstone's generous soul is weary of the eternal, repressive expedients to which succeeding generations of British statesmen have resorted. He knows that a Union preserved and maintained by the exercise of force on one side and through the influence of fear on the other, cannot be a satisfactory arrangement and he seeks to conciliate rather than coerce. He hopes to found a Union upon mutual interest, upon affection, and upon the inherent wisdom and justice of the cause he recommends.

Bowman concluded by stressing that far from being separatists, as their enemies claimed, the members of the IPHRA were 'the true friends of the real and abiding Union which might be attained when Mr Gladstone's Plan for the Better Government of Ireland has been enshrined on the statute book of the realm.'

To further emphasise the point that the loyalty of Home Rulers to Queen Victoria was beyond reproach, Bowman proposed in a letter to the *Morning News* that the monarch's forthcoming golden jubilee should be commemorated by way of public and commercial backing for the proposed Forster Green Hospital in Belfast and with the particular target of tackling the disease known as consumption.[11] Noting that 'various proposals have been made as to how we may best express our gratitude for the blessings which have been enjoyed by us within that fifty year period,' Bowman pointed out that consumption was rife in the ever-expanding Belfast:

> Our humid atmosphere and variable temperature, together with the unwholesome and unnatural surroundings amid which our artisans and operatives in mill, factory and workshop are compelled to live, move and have their being have caused the physical health of our people to degenerate. Many fearful diseases, practically unknown in agricultural or pastoral districts, take root and flourish abundantly in a densely crowded community like Belfast. One form of disease, consumption, is dreadfully prevalent amongst the young men and women who are engaged in our staple manufacture.

> Who can gauge the feelings of anguish with which an aged mother marks the silent but steady progress of the insidious disease which is persistently sapping the vitals of the staff whereon she hoped to lean in her declining years? I have heard the hollow, wracking cough and seen the hectic flush overspread the cheek when any extra exertion was required. I have watched the generally silent sufferer until some morning there was a vacant berth, frame or loom. The disease had gained the mastery over its victim. The place that had known him in the hive of industry would know him no more.[12]

St. Patrick's Day, 17 March, saw Bowman travelling to Aughagallon, close to Lough Neagh, to address a large gathering of Catholic and Protestant tenant-farmers from Co. Antrim.[13] Four resolutions were passed, demanding a parliament in Dublin, supporting Parnell and the Irish Party at Westminster, condemning land-grabbers as 'a very great evil and the main prop of tottering landlordism,' and describing the National League as 'the saviour of the Irish people.'[14]

Bowman said it was only through union and combination that Ireland would be triumphant in the 'long struggle against the Saxon.' He went on to describe Westminster as 'an alien parliament' and said even the best efforts of statesmen had failed because they could not 'enter into the aspirations and feelings of the Irish people.'

* * *

Early in April, and separate from his IPHRA activities, Bowman attended a conference in the Belfast YMCA hall at Wellington Place, conducted by William Jones of the London-based Peace Society. Numbering clergymen and many middle-class men and women among its membership, the scripturally-based society's aim was to promote the idea of international arbitration to avoid war. A resolution was passed stating their desire to form a Belfast Peace Society and Bowman, the seconder, was elected to serve on the committee.[15]

That same month the IPHRA joined a series of nationalist meetings organised in opposition to a further revision of the Irish criminal law which Lord Salisbury's Conservative government had promised in the Queen's speech that January. The resulting Crimes Bill, aimed at suppressing the National League in any district where the government felt it was necessary, was introduced in parliament on 28 March by Arthur Balfour, the newly-appointed Chief Secretary for Ireland.[16] The legislation, intended to be perpetual rather than of limited duration, would empower magistrates to question, either privately or on oath, any individual they thought capable of providing information of any nature. It would also allow magistrates to deal summarily with conspiracies against the payment of rent, boycotting, intimidation, unlawful assembly, resistance to eviction and the incitement of others to commit any of those offences – the maximum penalty being six months' imprisonment with hard labour.[17]

Protest rallies were organised by the National League throughout Ireland but it was the involvement of Protestants in the campaign in the north that guaranteed widespread press coverage and considerable hostility from Loyalists. Within a fortnight of the introduction of the Crimes Bill northern meetings were held at Draperstown, Ballycastle, Ballymoney and Annaclone. The latter, organised by the IPHRA, was addressed by East Mayo Nationalist MP John Dillon.[18] The previous year Dillon, fellow MP William O'Brien and others had instigated the 'Plan of Campaign' aimed at forcing landlords to reduce exorbitant rents. The idea was that tenants should pledge themselves to offer to the landlord what they considered a fair rent and, if he refused to accept it, to then lodge the money in a mutual defence fund for the benefit of evicted tenants.[19] The new Crimes Bill was Balfour's response.

By addressing the Annaclone meeting Dillon became the first leading member of the National League to speak on an IPHRA platform, outside an election campaign, and thus boosted the organisation's standing.[20]

Bowman wound up the speeches, claiming that even the promoters of the Crimes Bill accepted there was not an unacceptable level of lawlessness in Ireland. 'And even if it were necessary,' he declared, 'it would be useless as crime is only the ulcer on the surface of the body politic, indicating the presence of an irritating cause and who, having the ordinary amount of common sense, would think of curing smallpox by driving under the surface of the skin the evidences of the disease?'

Anger over the Crimes Bill prompted the IPHRA to meet in the Round Room of the Rotunda in Dublin, where it was decided to stage their own complementary series of protest rallies. Bowman, disagreeing with the subsequent *Northern Whig* tally of 'probably not 50 Protestants' in attendance, claimed in a letter to the paper that the meeting had attracted 1,000 Protestants, the crowd being so large that it had filled the concert room in addition to the Round Room.[21]

On 18 April 1887, the day the Crimes Bill passed its second reading in parliament by 370 votes to 269, the association was represented by McClelland, Briggs and Bowman at a meeting in St Mary's Hall to launch its campaign. Fr Patrick Convery, president of the Belfast branch of the National League, welcomed 'so many supporters of Mr Gladstone, both Protestant and Catholic, united in one bond, carrying forward and falling into line with the enlightened people of the three kingdoms to protest against the bill – the most iniquitous, brutal and unjust since the days of the Penal Laws.' Bowman, speaking in support, described the Crimes Bill as 'one of the most drastic and barbarous ever submitted to the intelligence of any Senate in the world.'[22]

However, as the Protestant Home Rulers would soon learn, sharing platforms with Nationalists and enjoying Gladstone's support also meant their association had to contend with fierce opposition from the Unionists, including the rival Ulster Loyalist Anti-Repeal Union which had vowed to support the government's efforts to 'repress crime and outrage in the south and west of Ireland, and to strengthen their hands in passing the Crimes Bill through parliament.'[23]

The first of the IPHRA's provincial meetings was held on 7

May 1887, at Pharis, eight miles from Ballymoney, Co. Antrim. It passed off without incident, although there was a heavy police presence and a Royal Irish Constabulary shorthand notetaker kept a record of the speeches.[24]

Speaking in favour of a resolution which condemned the Crimes Bill as 'a violation of our civil liberties and calculated to embitter the relations between England and this country,' Bowman told the audience, mainly comprising Presbyterian farmers and Catholic labourers, that they were involved in a struggle to remove the causes that were preventing peace, prosperity and progress in Ireland.

Bowman believed that a new day was dawning and Protestants and Catholics living in rural areas were beginning to realise how much they had in common.

> They are all forced to live in unwholesome houses, to take bad food, and to do with wretched clothing in order that they may swell the rent roll of the landlords who spend the money on debauchery in Paris or Vienna. Ireland had been practically left for dead by the landlord robbers until Mr Gladstone bound up her wounds, and what was the result? The heart of Ireland went out in response to the great statesman's noble exertions. As sure as the sun will rise again, so the Grand Old Man [Gladstone] will lead the Irish people to the consummation of the greatest of modern reforms – our right to legislate for ourselves.

The second meeting, scheduled for Armagh's Market Square on 10 May, was the first to face a counter-demonstration, prompting magistrates to ban both groups from gathering at the Square because it was 'likely to result in serious disturbances to public peace.' Undeterred, the Loyalists went ahead with their meeting in the Tontine Rooms at English Street, while the Home Rulers met in the National League Rooms at Ogle Street. Fifty extra policemen were drafted in to support the Armagh constabulary but there were no disturbances.[25]

Two public meetings were held the following day at Toomebridge, Co. Antrim, and at Kilrea, Co. Londonderry, with Bowman managing to attend both.[26] He strongly defended Parnell, prompted by the publication in *The Times* the previous month of a forged letter in which the Nationalist leader appeared to apologise for his 'tactical' condemnation of the Phoenix Park murders of

1882.[27] It formed part of a series of articles the London newspaper published alleging a link between Parnell and crime in Ireland, aimed at undermining the Nationalist leader's position. Bowman declared:

> The government is afraid to bring Mr Parnell before a jury on a charge of having written that letter. Yet they have been circulating these infamous lies throughout the length and breadth of Ireland for the purpose of affecting the minds of the mob against the noblest patriot who lives today. There is one thing we can look to with hope and that is how, at no period in the history of Ireland, dark as it is, has our country been without advocates, without friends, without men willing to raise their voices on her behalf, without men willing to suffer in the cause of Ireland – Robert Emmet, Wolfe Tone, John Mitchel, John Martin, Thomas Meagher, Daniel O'Connell and Isaac Butt, and their mantle has now fallen on the shoulders of Charles Stewart Parnell.

Magherafelt, Co. Londonderry, venue for the next meeting, was also targeted for a proposed loyalist counter-demonstration.[28] However, local magistrates, finding no clear authority behind the rival meeting, decided against imposing a ban. Instead, adopting a different tactic, they ordered the closure of all public houses in Magherafelt during the day. And, as an added precaution, 50 extra police officers were drafted into the town. The organisers of the Home Rule meeting, having been made aware of the financial loss facing the local publicans on the town's market day, agreed to postpone it on the understanding that the ban would be revoked. Bowman and the other speakers, who had arrived early in the morning, headed back to Belfast on the midday train. There was no rival loyalist gathering and the closure order on the public houses was lifted two hours later. During the afternoon sporadic fighting broke out between supporters of the two sides but the police were able quickly to restore order.

Bowman headed north again to speak at Ringsend, six miles from Coleraine, Co. Londonderry.[29] There was a heavy police presence and the customary official notetaker but no loyalist counter-demonstration. Bowman admitted that he could himself fall foul of the coercion legislation and find himself in Kilmainham Prison. 'But a great teacher once said, "Blessed are ye when men persecute you for righteousness' sake." It is for righteousness' sake that the leaders of the Irish people are taking up their present position,' said Bowman. 'They are prepared to risk death itself to secure the rights of the people.' And again to stress that his aspirations were not separatist, Bowman added: 'I do not for a moment mean that a parliament in Dublin should impair the imperial parliament. It is evident that the creature is not greater than the creator. The supremacy of Great Britain would remain.'

At Caledon, Co. Armagh, on 16 May the threat of a counter-demonstration saw 60 extra policemen being drafted into the village and a ban being imposed on both meetings.[30] Orders also went out to close the local pubs. The Protestant Home Rulers did, however, attempt to hold a meeting, attended by about 60 sympathisers, in a meadow a short distance from Caledon – until the police arrived in force with batons drawn and the proceedings were quickly brought to an end.

Bowman was not in Caledon but he was one of the scheduled speakers for a meeting in Cookstown, Co. Tyrone, that same day.[31] Despite the intervention of local loyalists a ban was viewed as unnecessary – instead an order was issued requiring the closure of the public houses but only in the event of either meeting taking place. The IPHRA officials, following an approach from local traders, agreed to abandon their demonstration. However, a group of angry Nationalists, clearly dissatisfied at such ready acquiescence, passed their own resolution: 'If the regeneration of Ireland depends on the Irish Protestant Home Rulers, a very long time will elapse before it is realised.'

The banning of a meeting in Dungannon, Co. Tyrone, scheduled for 19 May and with Bowman as one of the advertised speakers, was subsequently raised in parliament by John Dillon, who demanded to know from Chief Secretary Balfour how such an order could be justified. The IPHRA members, having again faced the prospect of a loyalist counter-demonstration, had moved their meeting to the home of local sympathiser William Moffett, of Dungannon House.[32] It was their contention that the gathering, because it was on private property, was therefore lawful and the police had no right to interfere. RIC District Inspector William Kelly had other ideas and led a contingent of officers up to the crowd which numbered several hundred. The meeting was dispersed after a brief but peaceful confrontation and the passing of a series of resolutions.

Replying to Dillon in the House of Commons, Balfour claimed that in the opinion of the local authorities the original meeting could not have been held without endangering public safety – including the risk of loss of life – because of a threatened counter-demonstration involving loyalists from Dungannon and other parts of Co. Tyrone. Dillon retorted that it was 'the deliberate and avowed policy in Ulster to call rival meetings in every instance where an anti-coercion meeting is called.'[33]

The *Northern Whig*, in an editorial on the Dungannon episode, claimed that rallies called by the IPHRA were attended almost exclusively by Catholics and Nationalists, with only a 'sprinkling' of Protestants.[34] Referring to Bowman's presence at virtually every meeting organised by the association, the paper launched a further bitter attack on the figure whose labour cause it had so willingly supported 18 months earlier:

> Mr Bowman and certain other prominent Home Rule advocates are seldom what they profess to be and are represented to be by the Nationalist journals. Mr Bowman, when he contested the North Belfast division a year and a half ago, did not avow himself to be a Protestant Home Ruler. If he had done so he well knew that his prospects with the working classes and as a professed working men's candidate would have been quite hopeless. Under such circumstances he could never have faced the constituency at all. Most of those who promoted his electioneering objectives, and this journal which supported him as a labour candidate, would not have done so had he then declared himself to be what he is now.

Garvagh, Co. Londonderry, was the venue for the next meeting but there was no loyalist protest. The *Belfast News-Letter* scornfully declared that those in the area who could be designated Protestant Home Rulers were 'so few and very far between, that the Loyalists did not deem it necessary to assemble in public for the purpose of protecting the reputation of the district from the utterances of one or two individuals hankering after notoriety.' A crowd estimated at 200 gathered opposite the Commercial Hotel at Main Street and, according to the *Belfast News-Letter*, was 'as anti-Protestant as it could well be. Some considerable hissing and cheering took place during the progress of the proceedings and towards their close the crowd had dwindled away to one-half its original size.' Bowman was again on the platform and various anti-Crimes Bill resolutions were passed by acclaim.[35]

Next on the itinerary was the Co. Down fishing port of Kilkeel, where a call from the Home Rulers to the people to 'attend in their thousands to protest against landlord tyranny and the Crimes Bill' on the local market day, was countered by posters urging local Protestants and Orangemen to gather in similar numbers to 'protest against the movers of sedition and disloyalty who are lifting up their cursed heads in our midst.' The posters declared:

> The National League, assisted by a few misguided Protestants, are endeavouring to pollute the sacred soil of Mourne, a place hitherto peace-loving and law-abiding. Fellow-men, will you, whose forefathers have bled and died for religion and for loyalty, stand by and behold that glorious heritage being torn from you without striking a blow in its defence? Rise, sons of William, rise, and show your determination to maintain the integrity of this grand Empire, and, to aid the government in their resolution to re-establish the Queen's authority in Ireland by their passing of the Crimes Bill, assemble in your thousands in Kilkeel.

The message carried the signatures of District Master Samuel McMurray and District Secretary William Sloan. Kilkeel thus joined the lengthening list of towns and villages where the authorities felt they had to act to prevent an outbreak of violence, although without a doubt the attendance figures subsequently claimed by both sides were wildly exaggerated. An additional 50 policemen were drafted in from various local towns.[36]

In the case of the Home Rulers' meeting, scheduled for 1.30pm, the handwritten proclamation, signed by Francis Charles Needham, third Earl of Kilmorey and a former MP for Newry, and his agent, John Quinn Henry, of Mourne Abbey, was presented to Alexander Bowman, as its main organiser. The order referred to the likelihood of serious public disturbance and warned the two sides 'at their peril to refrain from so assembling, or they will be dispersed by force.'

An identically-worded notice was presented to the loyalist leaders for their meeting which was scheduled for noon. The publicans and spirits dealers in the town had also been served with an order to close their premises.

Bowman immediately walked to the town's Market Square where a large platform had been erected. Anticipating that the meeting would be dispersed by force, he said he did not blame the police, accepting they were duty-bound to execute the order signed by the 'lord of the soil and his servile agent.' He continued:

> As soon as they come to disperse us we shall retire from this place into the yard of Morgan Bros. on the Shore Road. There we will talk to you of the way we are treated by British rule – no, not British rule. We are ruled here by the autocrat Kilmorey and his sycophant Henry. We are told that one of the birthrights of Englishmen is the right of public meeting and free speech, but, rather than enjoying those rights, we are at the command of Kilmorey, Henry and a pack of hirelings compelled to disperse...

At that point Henry arrived at the head of a body of policemen and one of their number, Sgt Patrick Dowds, called on the meeting to disperse. Local curate Fr Daniel McAllister, after telling Henry they would leave quietly, added that Balfour would fail in the same way as previous Conservative Irish ministers had failed.

The Morgans ran a grocery business and the crowd in their yard could hardly have numbered more than 100.[37] The platform party included 10 Catholic priests. The resolutions attacked the Crimes Bill as being 'completely uncalled for and unnecessary,' described rents as 'unfair and unjust,' and declared that 'no solution of the Irish land difficulty can be final and satisfactory except such as provides for the extinction of dual ownership of land.'

On 26 May Bowman and the Home Rulers returned to Magherafelt, venue for the cancelled meeting a fortnight earlier.[38] Once again the authorities felt it was unnecessary to proclaim the gathering, despite the announcement of a counter-demonstration, and the public houses were allowed to remain open. One hundred extra RIC men were drafted into the town but there was no trouble. The IPHRA meeting was held in the pork market at Rainey Street with the several hundred-strong crowd enlarged by the police presence, while a Conservative meeting attracted a like attendance in the town's old courthouse building at Broad Street. There was a similar return to Cookstown, the aim being to ensure none of the original venues was missed.[39] No rival meeting was held and the proceedings passed off without incident.

Bowman attended one more provincial meeting, staged in a field outside Omagh on 30 May, although it was organised by National League supporters with backing from the IPHRA.[40] It was preceded by a two hour-long parade through the Co. Tyrone town involving up to 10,000 banner-carrying protestors and led by Catholic clergy and bands. Two hundred extra police officers and one hundred members of the Highland Light Infantry were brought in from Belfast to keep the peace. There was no counter-demonstration, one explanation being that Nationalists had put up orange-coloured posters indicating that the intended rival gathering had been postponed.

The IPHRA held its own final rally of the campaign four days later, drawing the same speakers together at Belfast's St George's Hall, along with one new face, West Cavan Nationalist MP Joseph Biggar.[41] While the speakers were Protestants, the audience, claimed the *Northern Whig*, was 'almost exclusively Catholic, including a large proportion of the working class, and decidedly rough in character.' The meeting, chaired by Thomas Shillington, was interrupted by a few minor disturbances but finished with a standing ovation for the speakers. The Crimes Bill was passed into law, despite strong opposition, on July 19.[42] Hot on its heels came the new Land Act.[43]

The Protestant Home Rulers remained quiet in the weeks immediately before and after the final vote, one reason being that the period coincided with the main celebrations to mark the golden jubilee of Queen Victoria's reign. Belfast, in common with towns and cities throughout the Empire, played its part and the festivities, principally marked on June 21, were colourful, enthusiastic and widely enjoyed.[44] The Home Rulers did not want their actions to be misconstrued as insulting to the sovereign, but they did not remain silent for long.

TESTIMONY AT WESTMINSTER;
DEFIANCE IN ULSTER

Emphasising Bowman's standing, as a Presbyterian, in the nationalist community, he travelled to Westminster in the middle of August 1887 to give evidence to a House of Commons Select Committee on policing in Belfast and the allegedly anti-Catholic borough magistrates system in the wake of the previous year's post-Home Rule bill riots.[1]

His comments to a seven-strong panel of MPs were particularly significant since they provided an all-too-rare insight into Bowman's own background, including the year he moved to Belfast (1865), the amount of rent he paid for his home at Greenmount Street (£13 a year, including rates), and his record of employment – as a flaxdresser (he used the term 'heckler'), then a draper's traveller and, at that time, as secretary of the Irish Protestant Home Rule Association.

Bowman, who received £6. 6s. expenses and a £5 travel allowance for the six days he was away from home, also revealed that he had read the *Northern Whig* practically every day for nine-tenths of his life, and that he had worked in 'a very large number of large workshops in Belfast where Protestants and Catholics work together.'

The Select Committee comprised Belfast MPs Sir James Corry and Thomas Sexton; Col Edward King-Harmon, Conservative MP for the Isle of Thanet division of Kent; Edward Whitley, Conservative MP for the Everton division of Liverpool; James Campbell, Conservative MP for Glasgow and Aberdeen Universities; James Picton, Gladstonian Liberal MP for Leicester, and Harry Lawson, Liberal Unionist MP for London's West St Pancras constituency. They heard evidence over three days from both viewpoints concerning the provisions of the Belfast Constabulary bill then before parliament.[2] Those speaking in favour of the *status quo* included a number of magistrates and the former West Belfast MP Sir James Haslett.

Bowman, who was initially examined by Sexton, contended that Nationalists did not accept the 'decisions of the local justices as tending to promote the administration of justice.' He claimed to be aware of instances where the relatives of [loyalist] people facing charges of a party [political] nature had approached the magistrates beforehand with a view to seeking favourable treatment. He also alleged that magistrates were in the habit of asking where a defendant lived and where he was employed as that would give a clue to his religion and his perceived political sympathies.

'One man will receive a month's imprisonment or a £1 fine, and the next day for the same offence another man will be sentenced to three months without the option of a fine,' said Bowman. 'A large number of the town council are magistrates and they are, therefore, interested in the fines levied as they go into the borough rates,' he continued, claiming that the authority's coffers had been boosted by some £3,000 arising from prosecutions which had followed the summer 1886 disturbances. That money had, he said, been used by the council for compensation payments 'so that the wealthy would not feel the burden so much as it would seem they did.'

'It is highly necessary to withdraw the local justices in Belfast from the administration of justice, and to have the law administered by paid justices,' said Bowman, who alleged: 'The loss of life during the riots was due directly to the interference of the local magistrates.' He also offered the view that 'supreme control' for the preservation of law and order should rest with a commissioner of police who would have the power to 'proclaim processions and the playing of bands and everything of that kind.'

Bowman faced stern cross-examination, telling the MPs that he was not directly a ratepayer, with a rate element being included in his rent. He claimed he had attended the Belfast courts around 150 times during the previous year – never as a plaintiff or as a defendant – thereby giving an indication as to how he spent a large part of his time as secretary of the IPHRA. Bowman told Sir James Corry that the Association had 800 members in Belfast with 'many more Protestants favourable to its views.' Returning to familiar territory he also voiced his distrust of resident magistrates, saying it would be better to appoint paid magistrates who were practising barristers.

He concluded his evidence by claiming that his own home had been 'on the agenda for looting' during the riots. 'I was told so by a workman in Combe's factory [at North Howard Street] who advised me to remove my wife and family,' he told the MPs. He also said he did not know of a single city or town in Ireland where the house of a Protestant had been looted or destroyed by Catholics on account of his faith.

Bowman was one of six witnesses, two Protestant and four Catholic, called to put forward the nationalist viewpoint. The others were solicitor Thomas McClelland, a founder member of the IPHRA; Dr John Tohill, principal of St Malachy's College and joint hon. secretary of the Belfast Catholic Committee; Dr Alexander Dempsey, a leading medical practitioner; businessman Edward Hughes, and trader and general dealer William O'Hare. McClelland, Dempsey and Hughes were all justices of the peace, which allowed them to serve on the bench in the Belfast courts.[3]

That same month brought a significant by-election success for the Liberals which contributed to a feeling that the country was swinging back behind Gladstone and that a sizeable majority in favour of Home Rule would be achieved if there was an early general election.[4]

However, any hopes that the Conservative government would adopt a more conciliatory attitude towards the National League were dashed following a meeting of the Privy Council in Dublin on 19 August when it was decided to introduce a proclamation order under the terms of the Crimes Act on the grounds that the 1,200-branch National League was a 'dangerous association' and that it 'promotes and incites acts of violence and interference with the administration of the law.'[5] The immediate reaction of the IPHRA was to lend the League its support, with Bowman attending a meeting of the Belfast branch three days after the ban was imposed.[6]

Coinciding with the apparent Gladstonian Liberal revival in Britain, a deputation from the British Home Rule Union travelled to Ireland the following month. The Young Ireland Society co-ordinated the visit and Alexander Bowman was assigned the role of accompanying the section of the group undertaking a programme of northern engagements – including meetings planned for Omagh, Strabane, Dungiven, Coleraine, Londonderry, Maghera, Toomebridge, Kilrea, Ballymoney, Ballycastle, Cookstown, Newry and Belfast.[7]

Among the distinguished delegation was political economist Professor Thorold Rogers, Richard Eve, who had fought three unsuccessful elections for the Gladstonian Liberals, English Catholic Wilfred Blunt, and barrister Thomas Hobson.[8] Police notetakers were present at all the venues and the planned meeting and reception for Coleraine, organised by the North Derry Gladstonian Liberal Association, had to be abandoned after the town commissioners refused them access to the town hall.[9] The Omagh meeting came under particularly close scrutiny from the police, with a detective travelling in the same train carriage as the visitors as they travelled to the town.[10]

So many people turned up at St Mary's Hall in Belfast on 21 September for the Home Rule Union delegation that three simultaneous meetings had to be staged – in the major hall, in the minor hall and on the street outside – with a further meeting being arranged at the same hall the following evening.[11] The visitors were joined by two of their number who had spent the earlier days of the trip in the southern half of the country: Charles Conybeare, MP for the Camborne division of Cornwall, and Thomas Lough, Irish-born secretary and founder of the British Home Rule Union. They, too, had faced a heavy police presence on arrival at York Street railway station, with at least a dozen detectives waiting on the platform in case there were any breaches of the Crimes Act.

Three Irish Nationalist MPs attended the meeting – Michael McCartan (South Down), William Reynolds (East Tyrone) and John Pinkerton (Galway City) – as well as 31 priests, eight justices of the peace, a large number of barristers and solicitors, and a wide representation of nationalist organisations, including the Belfast National League and the Belfast Young Ireland Society. The IPHRA was represented by president Thomas Shillington, secretary Alexander Bowman and executive committee members David Briggs and Hugh Hyndman.

Bowman's first speaking role of note during the tour came at a meeting in Ballymoney, Co. Antrim.[12] Eleven days later, on 3 October, as the visit by the English delegation drew to a close, Monaghan town square was the venue for a final demonstration attended by Nationalists from South Tyrone and North Monaghan. Two of the visitors, Edward Pickersgill, MP for Bethnel Green, and barrister Hugh Boyd, defeated candidate for South-East Durham at the 1886 election, were welcomed by Bowman on their arrival by train from Enniskillen.[13] A contingent of police officers remained in the adjacent courthouse during the meeting.

Bowman said there had never been any quarrel with the people of England, indeed until 1885 the ordinary people of England had had no political power and were as helpless as the Irish to protect themselves. He continued:

> We do not want separation from England, but we do want a union of community, of sentiment, of mutual affection, but not the parchment they call union... I do not believe Protestants would be persecuted by Catholics... I would urge upon the Protestants of Ulster to join with their fellow countrymen in their fight for Home Rule. Let all Protestants and Catholics never forget that they are first Irishmen and then Ulstermen and that next to their God they owe their love to Ireland.

Continuing disquiet over government efforts to put down the National League led to an even keener interest among members of the IPHRA in the activities of the Young Ireland Society. David Briggs, who had joined the society that March,[14] occasionally chaired its meetings while another regular attender was association vice-president John Stewart Wallace, who had spoken at a number of the anti-Crimes Bill rallies that May and would play an important part in Bowman's future life. Bowman himself rarely missed a meeting and on 13 October 1887, he took the stage at St Mary's Hall to deliver a lecture entitled 'Watchman, what of the night?' Although the title was taken from the Bible (Isaiah 21:11), the content was strongly political and devoted almost entirely to the previous night's visit to Belfast by Joseph Chamberlain.[15]

Bearing in mind that Bowman's election manifesto two years earlier had been based largely on Chamberlain's *Unauthorised Programme*, he was bitter at the politician's subsequent change of heart as far as Ireland was concerned:

> He was a politician of whom I had the highest hope. A few years ago Mr Chamberlain was wont to speak of Ireland in terms more sympathetic than any other British statesman. At that time he was the recognised leader of the English democracy; but the glory has departed – the mighty has fallen.

Chamberlain, he continued, had asked at the Ulster Hall the previous night why Ulster and Belfast prospered, yet Cork and Waterford were in decline. 'Is Ulster prosperous?' replied Bowman. 'Does Belfast continue to prosper?' He continued:

> Members of the agricultural community in Ulster are unable to pay their rents except out of past savings. As to Belfast, there are thousands of men anxious to have work in order that they may have bread for their wives and families, but they cannot obtain it. Our poorhouses are filled, the utmost resources of private charities are taxed. Can this state of affairs be coincident with prosperity?

Bowman claimed the population of Ulster had fallen by 5.38 per cent in the period 1871 to 1881 – more than had been recorded for any of the other three Irish provinces – and that any prosperity the north enjoyed was due to the linen industry, 'a trade which has been nursed and fostered by government bounties while the woollen, cotton and shipbuilding industries in the south and west are being throttled by hostile tariffs.'

The lecturer turned to a claim by Chamberlain that the rights of Ireland's minority Protestant population should be protected by giving them the power of veto on any legislation which affected their interests. Bowman responded by quoting Chamberlain's own words of four years earlier:

> What we have to deal with, the evil against which we are protesting, is the inordinate influence and power which minorities have obtained in our system; and really it is time for someone to stand up and say a word for downtrodden majorities. Minorities are everywhere; they meet us at every turn; they rule us at every corner. Our object should be to reduce their power and influence.

Bowman went on to mock Chamberlain over an anachronism in his Ulster Hall speech about how the Relief of Derry had 'saved the Union.' He retorted: 'Saving the Union in 1689 and 1690! Why the Union was not in existence till 110 years later. It is sad to find a man, who a few years ago had the brilliant prospects of Mr Chamberlain, proving his utter ignorance of the initial facts of history.'

Praise for Bowman's lecture was led by Briggs, who also referred to his colleague's 'sacrifices in the Home Rule cause.' The meeting closed with a proposal by IPHRA honorary secretary James Johnston that the members of the Home Rule Union deputation who had visited Belfast should all be enrolled as honorary members of the Young Ireland Society.

As for the IPHRA itself, the organisation's first annual meeting followed in November and, despite the failure of the Crimes Bill campaign and the hostile opposition it had encountered, the mood among members remained buoyant, even arrogant, thanks to the visit by the English delegation.[16] The meeting was held in Belfast's Lombard Hall behind closed doors with Shillington in the chair and representatives from both the Belfast and Dublin sections in attendance. An assessment presented to the meeting argued that events over the previous 18 months had in fact defined their aims more clearly and offered renewed faith and confidence in their principles. By laying before parliament his Bill for the Better Government of Ireland, Gladstone, the organisation felt, had transformed a matter of uncertainty into something which was inevitable, the only real question being the timescale.

While disappointed at the outcome of the 1886 general election, the IPHRA drew considerable comfort from the subsequent by-election successes which suggested a swing back to Gladstone. 'That [1886] result was undoubtedly caused by the hesitation of a large number of Liberal voters to support Mr Gladstone's proposals. This hesitation no longer exists,' the report declared.

The association also scoffed at Joseph Chamberlain's proposal for a separate parliament for Ulster. 'As a further indication of the progressive movement amongst Irish Protestants today,' stated the report, 'we rejoice to refer to the manner in which the monstrous proposal to separate the Protestant population of Ulster from the rest of Ireland in the settlement of the Irish Question, has been received by the leaders of opinion in Ulster.'

* * *

The most notorious effect of the proclamation of the National League was the jailing of two dozen Nationalist MPs, as well as newspaper editors and even priests, over speeches delivered at meetings under the auspices of the League or alleged conspiracies to promote the Plan of Campaign. Those sent to prison for periods of up to six months, often with hard labour, numbered some 1,600 over a three-year period to late 1890. They became known as 'Balfour's Criminals' and included John Dillon (East Mayo), William O'Brien (North East Cork), William Redmond (North Fermanagh) and Alex Blane (South Armagh).[17]

Bowman himself sailed close to the wind when he travelled to the village of Dromore in Co. Tyrone on the evening of 5 January 1888, after a National League meeting planned for the following night was proclaimed on the grounds that it would 'occasion terror and alarm.' Immediately after the notices banning the meeting appeared in Dromore, Nationalists began to gather in the streets and a torchlight procession made its way to the railway station to await Bowman's arrival with West Clare Nationalist MP Jeremiah Jordan.[18]

Carrying placards bearing messages such as 'Remember Dillon and O'Brien,' 'Home Rule,' 'Down With Tyranny' and 'God Save Ireland,' the crowd then paraded around the streets of the village before arriving at McCann's Hotel in Church Street, where an effigy of 'Bloody Balfour' was set alight amid cheers. Jordan, an Enniskillen Methodist and former Liberal, and Bowman then spoke – before the banning order took effect. Bowman expressed his 'extreme pleasure' at being there and accused the authorities in Dublin Castle of again 'daring to interfere with the liberties of the rule of Ireland.' The purpose of the following night's meeting, he said, was not to intimidate but to 'express the right of Irish people to manage their own affairs.'

Bowman once again urged his audience to avoid taking any actions that would cause offence to their friends across the water.

> Our fight is now assured of victory because of their sympathy and it is our duty to conduct ourselves as men and show we are prepared to risk all despite what Arthur Balfour and his satellites might do, but also to show at the same time that we respect human life, human liberty and human rights.

The police, limited at that stage to a sergeant and four constables, did not interfere with the proceedings at McCann's Hotel but word quickly spread around the village that a detachment of soldiers stationed in Belfast had already set off by train for Enniskillen. A further contingent of RIC officers as well as 50 soldiers of the Dragoon Guards arrived in Dromore after midnight and took up positions in the unlit streets. Taking advantage of the darkness, National League supporters spirited Bowman out of the hotel to a farmhouse some two miles away in the townland of Lettergash, close to the main Enniskillen to Dromore road.

It was on a hillside there shortly after noon that the first of six meetings took place in defiance of the ban – without a policeman or a soldier in sight, but attended by hundreds of Nationalists and accompanying bands who had arrived from adjacent areas of Counties Fermanagh and Tyrone. With Kilskeery Parish Priest Fr John Bartley chairing the proceedings, the attendance included Fr Peter Connolly, CC, Dromore; Fr James Smyth, CC, Trillick; Fr Maurice Brew, CC, Irvinestown; William McCaughey, secretary of the Kilskeery branch of the National League, and Patrick Muldoon, secretary of the League's Dromore branch. Bowman and Jordan – who described himself as a man who had always been 'law-abiding, constitutional and moral' in his actions – were the main speakers. Jordan said their intention that day was not to evade the police but to encourage the people to continue the 'good work already begun.' He declared: 'We are here to sustain your courage, to animate you to persevere in the good fight, and to steel your hearts against the oppressors. By patience, and if necessary suffering, we will keep steadily marching onward, shoulder to shoulder and foot to foot, and God will give us the victory in due course.'

Bowman, surveying the large and enthusiastic crowd, said he believed they were ready for the 'bloodless' fight. 'There is little to fear for the struggle for Irish Nationality so long as men are actuated by a spirit such as that which has been exhibited by the men of Tyrone,' he stated, continuing:

> You have come here at great disadvantage, but you are here to renew your pledges at the shrine of our country's altar. Ireland in the past struggled on, in spite of coercion, against foreign domination and it is perhaps today the only country that has been occupied for seven centuries by a stronger power and yet remains unconquered. And if you are prepared to continue the struggle, you must be prepared to make any sacrifice the future may require at your hands.

As well as the rally at Lettergash, further meetings in defiance of the Dromore ban were held at Crozier's Hill, about a mile and a half from the village, in Dromore rectory with Fr Bartley presiding, at nearby Fintona, at Drumquin and at Omagh. Jordan and Bowman arrived in time to address the latter two meetings, along with Mid Tyrone Nationalist MP Matthew Kenny. There was just one arrest during the 24-hour period of the drama – a man in Dromore who found himself facing a month in prison for the crime of loudly singing about Home Rule and the proclamation order.

Five days later Bowman was back in Belfast for a meeting of the Young Ireland Society, where the guest speaker was James Dempsey, who had unsuccessfully fought the North Belfast seat against William Ewart 18 months earlier. Dempsey, as the sole Catholic candidate, had also failed to secure a seat for the Nationalists on the town council the previous November. Drawing from his experiences, he spoke of religious and political influences on local government in Belfast and how they weighed heavily against the minority.[19]

Having described how Nationalists could gain their due representation on the council through a different system of dividing Belfast into wards, and an extension of the franchise along the lines of 'one man, one vote,' Bowman said he hoped they would never agree to anything but legitimate representation on the authority.[20] 'Any good men who have obtained admission to the council are utterly powerless in face of the great majority which opposes them,' said Bowman, adding, with considerable foresight:

> I hope this meeting is only the first of a series which will impress
> upon the local authorities and upon the [Irish] Parliamentary Party
> the necessity of making such a change in the municipal government
> of Belfast as will give the minority that representation to which they
> are entitled.

By then Bowman's standing among Belfast's minority
community was considerable and when a discreet meeting was
called on 22 January to honour East Clare Nationalist MP Joseph
Cox – who had four arrest warrants hanging over him since the
previous November – prior to his departure by boat for England,
Bowman was there.[21] Cox, who had spent almost a week touring
Belfast in the company of South Down MP Michael McCartan,
yet seemingly immune from detection, voiced his 'pride and
gratification at meeting such a trusty band of northern
Nationalists.' In a reference to the Protestant Home Rulers, he
declared:

> Boycotting has been carried out to such extremes that many of those
> gentlemen who believe in the righteousness of our cause, and who
> sympathise with us in a practical, though to the public unobservant
> way, are kept back from taking their places publicly on our platforms
> through the dread of the consequences which would follow to their
> professions, their businesses, and their trades, by reason of the illib-
> eral action of the intolerant few who, for the present, exercise such
> sway over the unthinking artisans of this city.

The following night an 11-strong delegation of working men
from London's East End Liberal and Radical Association, headed
by the Rev. C. Fleming Williams, attended the fortnightly meeting
of the Belfast National League in St Mary's Hall, having met
Bowman and other prominent Nationalists for talks that
afternoon.[22] The guest speaker, on the subject of 'Home Rule from
an Englishman's point of view,' was Ernest Tipping, vice-president
of Southport's John Mitchel branch of the National League.
According to Belfast branch president Fr Convery the members
of the delegation, from Tower Hamlets and Hackney, had witnessed
scenes of eviction on the lands of Lord Massereene at Collon near
Drogheda.

Bowman rounded off a busy month with a return to familiar

territory at Annaclone, where he was feted as guest speaker by the local Gladstone branch of the IPHRA in the district's newly-erected hall,[23] and with a visit to Cookstown, Co. Tyrone, where he delivered a lecture on 'The Present Position of the Irish Question' to the local National League branch.[24]

At Annaclone Bowman described how those countries with their own domestic government, including Ireland immediately prior to the Act of Union, had thrived compared to those 'governed by a foreign legislation.' Statistics, Bowman said, showed that since the Act of Union Ireland's prosperity had not increased and within the previous 40 years the population of England had risen by 70 per cent, compared to a 50 per cent drop in Ireland. Having described the benefits an Irish parliament would bring in terms of the development of industries, the encouragement of agriculture, the building of harbours and places of refuge for fishermen, and by the opening up of the country's mineral wealth, Bowman asked: 'Is it not criminal that the gifts of God to this country are allowed to go to waste?' He expanded by saying:

> We have a garrison in Ireland, between military and police, of almost 40,000 men. The people of Ireland, under the most severe provocation, are maintaining a calm and dignified demeanour. They are abstaining from crime and are thus vindicating their right to self-government. In England there is one policeman to every ten thousand people, in Ireland there is one to every two thousand, and yet the crimelessness is shown by the fact that, though in England they have eight criminals for one policeman, in Ireland there are only two for every one.

Bowman closed by declaring: 'If the people stand by their principles and struggle on for their liberties, the bitter past will soon be buried and we will be able to begin the new and better work of building up a grand and a noble history of the future of the Irish race.' After the cheering had died down McClinchy told the meeting he was holding a letter inviting Bowman to lecture in the United States of America. 'I do not yet know, however, whether or not Mr Bowman intends to accept the invitation,' he added. Future events suggest that, while undoubtedly flattered by the request, Bowman was unwilling to go so far because of his fears for the safety of his young family during an extended absence.

The invitation confirmed Bowman's high standing in the eyes

of the nationalist people. It was hardly surprising then that his name was included in a 3,500-strong roll-call of Ireland's leading Home Rulers who formed the reception committee for a visit to Dublin at the beginning of February by John Morley, Gladstone's confidante and former minister, and the Marquess of Ripon, First Lord of the Admiralty in Gladstone's government of 1886.[25]

Morley and Lord Ripon both received the Freedom of Dublin from Timothy (T. D.) Sullivan, another recently released Nationalist MP, who, as a former Lord Mayor of the city and one of its Members of Parliament, was standing in for incapacitated Lord Mayor Thomas Sexton.[26] After addressing a rally at Leinster Hall, the English visitors travelled to the Mansion House where they were presented with illuminated addresses by representatives of 60 different corporate and municipal bodies throughout Ireland. Because of the limited time available it was impossible for the hundreds of individual branches of the National League to deliver similar presentations, but an exception was made for the Belfast branch, as well as for the IPHRA and the North Derry Gladstonian Liberal Association which claimed to represent 3,000 Protestant voters.

Two days before the Dublin demonstration Bowman had travelled to Dromara, Co. Down, the area of his birth some 34 years earlier. The meeting, on the rent question, was intended to be non-party political and succeeded in attracting Catholic and Protestant tenant-farmers in large numbers.[27] However, the only Member of Parliament present was South Down MP Michael McCartan, who was from nearby Leitrim, Castlewellan, while the county's three Conservative representatives made their excuses.

Also noteworthy, for an altogether different reason, was the presence of three local farmers by the name of Rodgers – Robert and William from Derry townland and Thomas from nearby Crossgare townland – who were almost certainly relatives of Alexander Bowman on his mother's side. Robert Rodgers was the Poor Law Guardian for Derry.[28]

Politics were back on the agenda when a delegation from the IPHRA, including Bowman and Hugh Hyndman, travelled to Ballee outside Downpatrick, Co. Down, for a meeting of

Nationalists in late February.[29] Their arrival at the Downpatrick train station was somewhat hampered by the overzealousness of several Belfast and County Down Railway officials who tried to prevent members of the reception committee from setting foot on the platform.

Four resolutions were passed by acclaim: protesting against the administration of the Crimes Act as 'an unwarranted violation of civil liberties,' supporting Gladstone and the Home Rule movement, condemning the 1887 Land Act as 'inadequate to meet the grave necessities of the farming community,' and declaring that no solution to the Irish problem was possible 'except the conferring upon the people of this country the right of self-government in all affairs which are purely Irish.'

Four weeks later the IPHRA organised a meeting in the Lombard Hall with Irish Land Restoration Society chairman the Rev. John Bruce Wallace as guest speaker.[30] He too had become a committed supporter of Home Rule. Also on the platform was James Workman, Bowman's election agent from November 1885, who yet had an important part to play in Bowman's life. Wallace, like Hyndman at Downpatrick and Bowman before, was anxious to dispel any notion that Home Rulers were intent on total independence for Ireland:

> Any desire for separation is fast dying out. It was born of the intense irritation produced by constant misunderstanding, and the contemptuous treatment of the most reasonable Irish demands. It is being killed off by the altered gracious disposition and policy of the Liberal Party. The opponents of Home Rule style themselves 'Unionists' and stigmatise its advocates as 'Separatists,' but the fact is that the chief of the real Unionists is the Grand Old Man himself.

St Patrick's Day 1888 saw Co. Antrim farmers and farm labourers gathering at Deerpark, Glenavy, for a demonstration which drew together speakers from the National League and the IPHRA.[31] Contingents carrying banners and accompanied by bands arrived from Aughagallon, Milltown, Aldergrove, Killead and Ballinderry, as well as Glenavy itself. Shillington and Bowman represented the IPHRA, while Patrick McGarrell and James Brankin, secretaries of the Glenavy and Aughagallon National League branches respectively, joined them on the platform.

Bowman told the demonstration that while the Act of Union had united the legislatures of Great Britain and Ireland its effect had been to separate the peoples.

The meeting closed with Lisburn man John Sinton calling for 'three hearty and ringing cheers for Her Majesty Queen Victoria and the hope that she may be spared in health to visit Dublin to open the Irish parliament after Mr Gladstone's Home Rule bill has become the law of the land.'

Such professions of loyalty did not, however, prevent Bowman from using altogether sharper language when, for the first time, he addressed the Sexton Debating Society at its rooms in Mill Street, Belfast.[32] He was introduced by the chairman, 16-year-old Joseph Devlin,[33] as secretary of the IPHRA and spoke on the subject 'Rays of Hope.'

Reflecting a deepening frustration at the government's anti-nationalist activities, Bowman referred to their shared hope that Ireland would be 'liberated from the thraldom of foreign domination' and that their country might 'by the exertions of her sons, show herself worthy of holding the position of a free nation.' He believed that memories of the men involved in the Fenian movement 'should serve as a stimulus and an incentive to the young men of Ireland of the present day to devote their best energies to the liberation and emancipation of their native land.'

'The work achieved by the men of those days gives good grounds for hoping that a continuation of the struggle will result in success,' said Bowman. After tracing the history of the Home Rule movement from its foundation by Isaac Butt, Bowman contended that 'splendid results have followed the agitation conducted by the leaders of the Irish Party in amending many of the grievances from which the Irish people have suffered.'

He still held out the hope that another general election might not be too far off and that the Home Rule question might again be raised at the polls:

There was never a great struggle fought out at the English polls which was not in the first instant defeated. However, the obtaining of Home Rule is only the first battle in the campaign won. Our next great fight for the improvement of the position of the Irish people must be on the burning question of the land laws for at present the labouring population of Ireland is paying between £25 million and £30 million to an idle and misgoverning aristocracy.

Bowman and fellow Belfast Nationalists again ran the risk of prosecution under the Crimes Act when, in April 1888, they organised a welcoming reception and public meeting for Fr James McFadden, from Gweedore, and Fr Daniel Stephens, from Falcarragh, both in Co. Donegal, who had been released on bail pending appeals against three-month prison sentences imposed for promoting the Plan of Campaign among local tenants.[34]

The two 'criminal' priests, their every move watched by RIC detectives, arrived at the Great Northern Railway terminal from Letterkenny and then travelled on by landau to Patrick Dempsey's Linen Hall Hotel at Donegall Square East, a popular meeting place for Nationalists.[35] Addresses were presented to them by deputations from the Young Ireland Society, the IPHRA, the Belfast National League, the Sexton Debating Society, and the Belfast National Foresters.

Responding, Fr McFadden declared: 'It is the object of our enemies to show to the world there is disunion among the people and that sectarianism poisons our organisation. I am exceedingly pleased, therefore, that the addresses include one from the Protestant community, or from that portion of it at least which cannot be led away by passion.'

Before the party left for St Mary's Hall, one of the organisers, Jeremiah MacVeagh, was approached by District Inspector William Davis of the Royal Irish Constabulary and asked if the promoters of the public meeting would object to the presence of two of its notetakers. Davis was told that the men would be permitted into the hall if they paid the admission charge like everyone else and did not sit at the press table. They duly took seats in the body of the hall, under a banner displaying the message 'Balfour's Criminals, Welcome To Belfast,' and took copious notes.

Within days of their Belfast visit the two priests were back in court where their appeals failed. There was outrage in the nationalist community when Fr McFadden's sentence was increased from three months to six, while Fr Stephens' term was unchanged.[36]

During the same period, and in the face of such unrelenting criticism, Bowman sought to keep the IPHRA in the public eye through letters to the Belfast press. One stood out because the *Northern Whig*, once the willing vehicle for Bowman's views, refused to publish it. The by-then Liberal Unionist paper had previously printed a letter from the Rev. Dr Hugh Hanna on the subject of 'Ulster, Scotland and Home Rule,' but Bowman's lengthy response was rejected by editor Thomas Macknight. Undaunted, he submitted it to the *Morning News* which published his contribution verbatim.[37]

It stressed Bowman's continuing involvement with the IPHRA and how he remained a hated figure in loyalist circles. He referred not only to a 'prejudice-laden atmosphere,' but also to the 'reign of terror under which the advocates of Home Rule are compelled to live in the midst of a community which professes to believe in the fullest civil and religious liberty and right of private judgment.' Bowman challenged Hanna to explain how he could 'give credit for good intentions to those who support the Home Rule policy of the Liberal Party if they happen to live on the other side of the Channel, while we who are in favour of the self-same policy, but happen to live in Ireland, have the vilest motives and designs imputed to us?'

Accusing Hanna of threatening a civil war over the Home Rule issue, Bowman declared:

> Do the gentlemen who indulge in these threats ever think of what civil war involves of man, created in the image of God, being butchered by his fellow; his brother of human energy being devoted to the task of converting this fair world of ours into a charnel house; and of wives made widows and children fatherless? Surely they who talk of civil war cannot have contemplated what consequences it involves?

And on the subject of national identity, Bowman rebuked Hanna for denying Irishmen the 'right to be Irishmen in the same sense and way that Scotchmen are Scotchmen.'

The hostility Bowman referred to in his response to the Hanna letter manifested itself on 11 June, when he travelled to Omagh to deliver a lecture entitled 'The Past and Present of the Irish Question – a Contrast' to the local branch of the National League.[38] As he spoke stone-throwers attacked the venue, the Royal Assembly Hall to the rear of the Royal Arms Hotel in High Street. One missile shattered the window close to the platform, scattering glass over branch officials and grazing Bowman's head. After a few calming words from the lecturer, indicating the justification of their cause and the difficulties they would encounter along the way, the meeting continued uninterrupted. Three days later he delivered the same lecture, without incident, to members of the National League's Derry branch.[39]

Later that same month Loyalists decided to revive the counter-demonstration tactic when a purportedly non-party meeting in sympathy with three local men jailed under the Crimes Act and with the purpose of forming a local tenants' property defence association was announced for Jerrettspass in Co. Armagh.[40] Placards were erected calling for a counter-meeting. However, the protest meeting did not materialise, with local Orangemen disclaiming any knowledge of, or responsibility for, the posters. Nevertheless, the mere threat of a counter-demonstration ensured a heavy police presence.[41]

The meeting had been called over the unwillingness of landowner Captain George Douglas to reduce Poyntzpass tenants' rents by any more than the 10 per cent agreed to the previous year. Furthermore, his tenants were furious that three of their number, Peter Byrne, William John Hanna and Laurence McCourt, had been jailed for sympathising with an evicted tenant and for speaking out on the issue in breach of the Crimes Act. The time had arrived, the farmers felt, to form a mutual defence association, to be named the South Down and Armagh Tenants' Property Defence Association. Bowman's speech denied that the three local men serving sentences in Armagh prison were criminals, saying: 'No man is a criminal unless he has violated the moral code of the community.'

Bowman's last major involvement with the Nationalist movement in Ireland came at a demonstration in Loughguile, Co. Antrim, on 15 August 1888.[42] With the Mitchelstown killings and the jailing of leading nationalist figures still fresh in people's minds, the resolutions reflected a growing bitterness against Lord Salisbury's administration and, in particular, Chief Secretary Balfour. There was particular anger at the death the previous month of John Mandeville, a National League leader and agrarian agitator from Mitchelstown.[43]

Bowman, having referred to Mandeville being 'done to death at Tullamore,' concentrated on the imprisonment of 'the pure-souled and chivalrous Dillon and the patriotic priest of Gweedore.' In closing he again risked his own liberty by urging tenant-farmers to:

Clothe and educate yourselves, your wives and children, fairly remunerate your labourers and if anything remains I would not object to you bestowing it upon your landlords. Society is only capable of being divided into three parts, namely workers, beggars and thieves. The farmer and his labourer belong to the first class. Would anyone venture to assert that the landlord also belongs to this class? No, they are thieves and the worst feature of the whole matter is that they can command the practically unlimited resources of the British government in Ireland to assist them in carrying out their nefarious designs. When men of all creeds and classes become united for the overthrow of misgovernment and unjust privilege, the death knell of class rule will indeed have sounded and a National parliament will have the guidance of our people's destiny.

The end of that same month would witness the first serious challenge at Westminster to the Crimes Act with John Morley proposing an amendment which indicted the government's coercion policy.[44] In a speech lasting one hour and forty minutes William Gladstone declared that in Ireland 'the law has been on one side and justice on the other.' With electoral defeats beginning to gnaw away at the Conservatives' strength, opponents of the government had hope of an alternative future.

THE BIRD OF PASSAGE'S
TRANSITION FROM NATIONALISM
TO SOCIALISM

W<small>ITH HIS OLDER</small> children earning extra pennies by selling newspapers on the streets, the financial strains were taking their toll and Bowman was forced to move away from Belfast and abandon the Home Rule struggle.[1] He would write some years later in a letter to a London newspaper:

> For several years I was the secretary and one of the most active spirits in connection with the Irish Protestant Home Rule Association, until having made it impossible to earn a livelihood in Belfast by reason of the unpopularity of the views I advocated, I had to seek an outlet for my energies in the more tolerant atmosphere of Britain and thus became a bird of passage.[2]

The move, to Glasgow in the first instance, came in the winter of 1888, two months after Bowman had represented the IPHRA at a farewell banquet in the Railway Hotel, Banbridge.[3] It was held for Uriah McClinchy, president of the Gladstone branch at Annaclone, who himself was emigrating to America, having fought in the Civil War there more than 20 years earlier.[4]

At the outset a letter from William Gladstone was read out in which the former Prime Minister praised the services rendered to Ireland by McClinchy and the IPHRA.[5] 'Were the sentiments of the present generation of Irish Protestants unitedly such as those of their forefathers 100 years back,' he wrote, 'all opposition in England to Home Rule would melt away like a morning vapour in the sun.' Claiming that opposition or neutrality from a 'large but diminishing proportion' in England was only serving to delay settlement of the Home Rule issue but could never defeat it, Gladstone concluded: 'There is no more useful service done on the whole wide field of the question than to bring Irish Protestants more and more into the views and convictions of their ancestors, instead of their present new-fangled notions.'

Bowman's decision to move to Glasgow came suddenly. At the farewell dinner for McClinchy in Banbridge, he had fallen into conversation with John Stewart Wallace, by then Liberal candidate for the Limehouse division of London. Wallace was well-known as the inventor of various devices, including fire extinguishers and typewriters, as well as the automatic weighing machines and 'electric shock' machines which were proving popular at places like railway stations and public baths, and held no fewer than 13 patents for his assorted inventions.[6] Within a short time Wallace had offered Bowman the opportunity to work as Glasgow-based agent for the Universal Automatic Machines Co.[7]

At a specially-convened meeting of the executive committee of the IPHRA, held on 30 October in its new office in the Crown Chambers at Royal Avenue, the news was confirmed to members that their long-serving secretary had tendered his resignation.[8] Robert McCalmont, fertiliser manufacturer and defeated Gladstonian Liberal candidate for East Belfast in 1886,[9] presented Bowman with a purse containing 42 gold sovereigns as a token of their esteem.[10] McCalmont regretted that not all the association members had had an opportunity to subscribe because of the short notice. Bowman, moved by his colleagues' generosity, both verbal and financial, said he was conscious that it 'depicts what I ought to have been, rather than what I was.'

Thus ended Alexander Bowman's link with the IPHRA in Belfast. Within months of his departure the room in the Crown Chambers had been taken over by a new National Club headed by solicitor James Johnston, a founding officer of the Home Rule organisation and by then a leading figure in the National League.[11]

Bowman's move to Glasgow came at a time when, with the Conservatives still securely in power despite by-election successes for the Gladstonian Liberals, support in Belfast for Home Rule was tending to rest solely with the National League. Many Protestant Home Rulers had already allied themselves to the League, particularly after the ban was imposed in August 1887, while the association itself would be split irrevocably during the Parnell/O'Shea divorce crisis of 1890, with northern members supporting the anti-Parnellites and the Dublin executive remaining loyal to Parnell.[12] Others felt the future lay with the socialist movement, supporting, for example, the newly-formed Belfast Radical Association.[13]

In crossing to Britain, Bowman was following a well-trodden path. There was a steady flow of Irish immigrants in the nineteenth century to the English midlands, as well as to ports such as Liverpool and Glasgow, with many playing an active role in trade union affairs. Some, like Bowman, would, in time, re-direct their anger over government policies by swapping their Irish Nationalist leanings for left-wing politics. Nor would Bowman have felt out of place, for he had made numerous Scottish contacts, not only through his own earlier trade union activities but also through the Irish Land Restoration Society's sister organisation in Scotland. The latter had been represented by its secretary, James Simpson, at Henry George's meeting in Belfast in January 1885, and by Glaswegian John Shaw Maxwell at a lecture on land nationalisation given by the Rev. Bruce Wallace two months later. By late 1888 Simpson had become a prominent member of the Northern (Britain) branch of the Irish National League.[14] Bowman was also acquainted with Scottish radical journalist James Morrison Davidson, who had stood there as a land restoration candidate in the 1885 general election.[15] And William Gladstone, the statesman Bowman so greatly admired, was MP for the Scottish Midlothian constituency.

Thanks to the amazing generosity of the IPHRA members, Bowman was able to rent a comfortable cottage, 25 South Street, in the relatively rural Whiteinch area, between Glasgow and Clydebank, and, having brought over his family by the end of the year, enrolled his two eldest children at the local Whiteinch

Primary School.[16] William's date of enrolment was 7 January 1889, with Robert following him on 13 May of that same year. Minnie joined her older brothers on 19 March 1890. After a short time the family moved to Gordon Street, which comprised a terrace of new three-storey houses. They lived in one of six apartments in number 25.[17] It was to the rear of the primary school and within yards of an area of magnificent parkland complete with a lake. Bowman ran the automatic machines business from a rented office at 10 Stockwell Place in the city centre.[18]

The Glasgow of the late 1880s was fast becoming a centre for radical thinking and land reformer Henry George and his theories still enjoyed considerable support, particularly from the city's large number of Highland migrants, many of them crofters who had lost their homes, as well as the Irish population.[19] In April 1889 George was entertained to dinner by the Glasgow Eastern branch of the Scottish Land Restoration League.[20] Echoing George's line of thought, the Scottish League advocated that all taxation should be shifted onto the value of land 'irrespective of its use or improvement,' as well as the 'taking of all ground rent for public purposes.' George also delivered a Sunday sermon entitled 'Thy Kingdom Come' in Glasgow's City Hall before a crowd estimated by his sympathisers at some 5,000 with many more turned away.[21]

It was from August of that same year that Bowman raised his own profile, not only in Glasgow but also back home in Belfast. He placed prominent advertisements for his business – offering a 'liberal percentage of the gross receipts paid as rent for the space occupied by each machine' – in *Brotherhood*, which circulated among trade unionists on both sides of the Irish Sea. Given Bowman's long-standing links with its Belfast-based editor Bruce Wallace, the newspaper would prove an ideal vehicle by which he could re-enter the political arena.

In September Bowman gave a lecture on Home Rule to the Bridgeton branch of the Scottish Land Restoration League.[22] Describing Bowman as the former secretary of the IPHRA, *Brotherhood* recorded his 'racy historical account of the reign of coercion, starting from the Irish invasion seven centuries ago, and travelling through such coercion epochs as the reign of Queen Elizabeth and the Cromwellian period, to the present day – seven centuries of suffering and oppression for a large proportion of the Irish people.'

Bowman was subsequently listed among the speakers for the winter session of Sunday evening talks held under the auspices of Glasgow's Henry George Institute in the Waterloo Rooms at Waterloo Street. By then three years old, the Institute sought 'the discussion of social and kindred subjects, both from the moral and the economic point of view.' The 1889-1890 season commenced with a talk on 'Christ and Social Problems' by Bruce Wallace, while 'God's Gift to Man' was the title of Bowman's talk, delivered in November.[23] Demonstrating his ability to combine spiritual and earthly matters, he described nature as God's material gift to man:

> ... the Earth that God created for the children of men; the gift is universal and man's need for it as universal as the gift. Yet in spite of the evident intention of their infinite Father, millions of His children are deprived of any share in His bounty and are condemned to lives of ceaseless toil and misery. The title to the private ownership of land – to the privilege of exacting tribute from the users and improvers of it – is based, not upon right, but on force and fraud; and no transmission of such title by inheritance, or sale, or otherwise, can change its original immoral character. Restitution is thus a duty incumbent on every one of the heirs and successors of those ancient violent or cunning usurpers; and, failing the performance of this duty, taking back the land emerges as a right on the part of the people.

On 1 February 1890, *Brotherhood* reported that Bowman had been elected president of the HGI, while Irish Nationalist MP Michael Davitt, a frequent speaker in Glasgow, had consented to be honorary president of the Scottish Land Restoration League.[24] Bowman was starting to move once again in important circles – a point emphasised by the presence of Keir Hardie, then secretary of the Ayrshire Miners' Union, as guest lecturer at a meeting of the HGI later that same month.[25] The topic for Hardie's talk was 'The eight-hour labour day and its relation to the land question.'[26]

On 19 July 1890, the *Belfast Weekly Star* – which had since incorporated *Brotherhood* – reported that the various strands of the land restoration movement in Glasgow, namely the Bridgeton branch of the Scottish Land Restoration League, the HGI and the South Side Single Tax Association, at a meeting held in Neilson's

Temperance Hotel a fortnight earlier, had decided to form an umbrella organisation – the Scottish Land Restoration Federation – with Bowman elected as president of its 15-strong representative council.

The federation, with an address at Montrose Street in the city, had as its declared object the 'restoration of the land to the people by the imposition of a single tax on the value of land, irrespective of improvements, thereby relieving industry of all taxation.' Methods to achieve its aim included public meetings and organising associations, the affiliation of clubs and other societies, the circulation of literature, and 'other such methods as may be deemed necessary to create a public sentiment against private property in land, and to arouse the people to assert their right to, and recover possession of, the same.'[27]

Six weeks after the launch Henry George was back in Glasgow to address another packed meeting in the city hall. It was held under the auspices of the new federation and Bowman chaired the proceedings. Members of the platform party included Glasgow MP Andrew Provand, several councillors and other 'prominent friends of reform.'[28]

Bowman's activities in Scotland were still being followed back in Ireland. The *Belfast Weekly Star* congratulated him on his election as president of the Scottish Land Restoration Federation.[29] 'Having known him here as a faithful and hardworking colleague in championing the rights of labour, and of the people,' the paper stated, 'we anticipate that a career of great usefulness and progress is before the new federation in the coming year.'

The three organisations which formed the federation continued to exist as separate entities, with Bowman's name joining the list of speakers for the HGI's fifth season of talks in 1890/91. In October his subject was 'Mutual Help' – a duty, he said, which was incumbent on men individually and collectively:

A state which has the bulk of its industrial products monopolised by the few, and denied to the many, is not a wealthy state, but a state where wealthy people dwell. Tested by this rule, Great Britain is, at once, the richest and poorest country in the world. Secure the commonage of nature, which its Creator intended for all, and the root of poverty is destroyed. Free access to natural opportunities will, by uprooting the resources of monopoly, create in its place the necessity for mutual help, and lead to the ultimate Brotherhood of Man.[30]

The following month saw Bowman's re-election as president of the Scottish Land Restoration Federation. His role, as well as conducting meetings, involved visiting neighbouring parts of Scotland to assist with the establishment of new branches. However, funding problems were blamed for the body's inability to circulate 'desirable literature around the country.' Members were advised at the annual meeting that while income had amounted to £43. 14s. 9d., expenditure was £43. 1s. 0d.[31]

During his time in Glasgow and despite his move towards socialism, Bowman clearly retained his personal regard for William Gladstone, for one of his most prized possessions was a souvenir book published by the Scottish Liberal Association following the former Prime Minister's week-long visit to Midlothian and other parts of Scotland in late October 1890.[32] It carried messages of good wishes and tributes to Gladstone from every party association in Scotland and verbatim reports of the five major speeches he had delivered. Many of the contributions stressed continuing support for their leader's Home Rule aspirations and, in a number of instances, similar hopes for Scotland.

At the same time Bowman made sure he kept in touch with matters back home, writing in early 1891 to the *Belfast Weekly Star* to welcome the establishment in Belfast of a 'union for the discussion of social questions.'[33] There was more to the letter than immediately met the eye for Bowman's days in Glasgow were nearing an end and the possibility of moving on or perhaps returning to Belfast would have been on his mind. At the time he was still an agent for the Universal Automatic Machines Co. and had been joined by James Workman, his former flaxdressing colleague and North Belfast election agent, as his assistant.[34] Workman was a former president of the Flaxdressers' Trade and Benevolent Union.[35]

By the late summer of 1891 Rose was expecting her fifth child and the family had been hit by financial difficulties. With Bowman's involvement in a variety of political distractions Workman had all but taken over the agency, to the detriment of the Bowman family's income.[36] The days were also numbered for the *Belfast Weekly Star*, with one of its last reports from Glasgow being an account of a public debate between Bowman and Scotsman John Bruce Glasier, a one-time member of Davitt's Land League and former secretary of the Socialist League's Glasgow branch.[37] The topic was 'the best means of solving the labour problem.' As with Keir Hardie the significance was considerable – Glasier too would become a founding figure of the Labour Party.

In the absence of the *Belfast Weekly Star* and its reports on activities involving Alexander Bowman, one must conclude that he made his decision to leave Glasgow for London having finally lost the battle to make ends meet. His three school-age children were withdrawn from Whiteinch Primary School on 25 March 1892,[38] and in April they were back in Belfast, enrolled at Argyle Place National School, where Bowman's friend James Mitchell Lee was headmaster.[39] The family, without Bowman, moved into the Agnes Street home of his elderly in-laws, the Ritchies,[40] with son William staying at the school until 24 June 1893, and Robert until 5 August of the same year.

With little indication of a financial farewell gift from the Scottish Land Restoration Federation, Bowman's trips home to Belfast over the next three years were few and far between.[41] He had secured employment as the London representative of the Ulster Bacon Curing Co., which had its base in May Street, Belfast. The business advertised each week in *Brotherhood*, giving rise to the conclusion that Bowman had gained the position thanks to the backing of a political ally associated with the company. He was already in London when fourth son Thomas was born in May 1892, with illiterate mother-in-law Isabella Ritchie signing an 'X' on the register in his place.[42]

In the knowledge that Bowman was by then living in the capital city, an invitation was extended to him the following month to attend a dinner in the Holborn Restaurant, hosted by Co. Down-born Queen's Counsel Sir Charles Russell MP, who had represented Parnell successfully at the Parliamentary Commission held into the false allegations in *The Times*.[43] The dinner was for Home Ruler sympathisers, particularly those who had carried on the fight in Ulster. Among the invited guests were Thomas Shillington, still described as president of the IPHRA, Justin McCarthy MP, Thomas Sexton MP, Thomas Dickson MP, Jeremiah Jordan MP, Thomas Lough, John Stewart Wallace, both prospective Liberal parliamentary candidates, the Rev. Bruce Wallace, and the renowned Dublin-born writer Bram Stoker.[44]

Despite the presence of so many former friends and acquaintances, Bowman declined the invitation, pleading a 'pressing business engagement.' The wording of the letter hints that Bowman had lost touch with the Home Rulers and that the invitation to attend the dinner had caught him somewhat by surprise. Given his past devotion to the Home Rule cause, it is hard to imagine he would not have made alternative arrangements for his business appointment had he really wished to attend. It is possible that he was disillusioned with Home Rule politics after the Parnell split. What is certain, however, is that despite his wistful reference to the Home Rule fight, Bowman was being increasingly drawn to socialism and away from the Liberal Party and Irish nationalism as a result of his political work in Scotland. All his future public utterances in relation to Ireland would be devoted to the cause of uniting Irish people under the broad banner of socialist principles.

Following the July 1892 election Gladstone was returned for a fourth and final term as Prime Minister with a 40-seat majority. Unionist candidates won 19 of the 33 Ulster seats. Throughout Ireland Nationalists won 80 seats, against 23 for the Conservatives and Liberal Unionists.

The 82-year-old Prime Minister put Home Rule for Ireland at the top of his government's agenda, knowing he needed Irish Nationalist votes to stay in office. He succeeded in steering a second Home Rule bill – which included provision for 80 Irish representatives to have rights of participation in most Westminster business – through 82 sittings of the House of Commons during 1893, and saw it passed by a 34-vote majority at the third and final reading on 1 September that year. However, few were surprised when, exactly one week later, the Conservative-dominated House of Lords rejected the bill by a then unprecedented 419 votes to 41.[45] His greatest ambition thwarted, by the following February Gladstone had handed over the reigns of office to Lord

Rosebery, his Liberal sucessor as Prime Minister.

As for Bowman, seeking to expand upon those political interests he had cultivated during his years in Glasgow, he rapidly established himself as a speaker at Sunday rallies organised by the Marxist Social Democratic Federation. The Federation had been founded 10 years earlier by Londoner Henry Mayers Hyndman, an Eton-educated former stockbroker who had served on the central executive of the Land League of Great Britain in the early 1880s, and read *Das Kapital* on board a Cunard liner during a business trip to the United States.[46]

Bowman's earliest advertised involvement with the SDF dated from the summer of 1893 onwards, when he was listed in the SDF paper *Justice* as the guest speaker at a number of venues to the north-east of London, including Tottenham, Finsbury Park, Wanstead, Hackney, Bethnel Green, Canning Town, Rotherhithe and Deptford. Although they were never billed as sharing the same platform, Bowman was joined on the SDF lecture rota by George Bernard Shaw, a member of the Fabian Society and one of the period's most effective speakers on socialist issues.[47]

Bowman was living in the Clerkenwell area with eldest half-brother William and had joined the local branch of the SDF.[48] He worked for the Ulster Curing Co. during the week and reserved his Sundays for the lecture circuit. The nature of his employment was important to the fledgling socialist movement, since company representatives travelled from place to place for their work and could be counted upon to spread the political message as well.

However, thoughts of his family back in Belfast were never far from his mind and by early 1894 they had joined Bowman in London. He had saved enough to secure comfortable rented accommodation in the rapidly expanding but still relatively rural suburb of Walthamstow, also in the north-east of the city. Their new home, at 29 Maude Terrace, was a newly-built terraced house in a tree-lined avenue. Sons William and Robert, who, despite the numerous disruptions to their young lives, had both attained a commendable standard of education, were enrolled in the boys' department of the nearby Markhouse Road School from 15 February 1894, with Minnie attending the girls' department.[49]

Within a few months Bowman had joined the SDF's

Walthamstow branch and maintained his role as a Sunday speaker, undertaking engagements in many parts of London. That June he travelled to Brixton where a new branch had been established and debated temperance with a representative from the Norwood Temperance Organisation. According to *Justice*: 'Despite the rain there was a good attendance and a vote taken at the end of the meeting showed that those present were in favour of the Socialist position in the proportion of three to one.'[50]

Given such a high local profile within the organisation and in light of his previous electoral experience in Belfast, Bowman allowed his name to be put forward by the Walthamstow branch as an SDF candidate for the local district council in December 1894, and again, under the more general 'Working Men's candidate' banner, for Essex County Council the following March. In doing so, he found himself caught in the centre of the bitter rivalry between the two local newspapers – the *Walthamstow Guardian* and the newly-launched *Walthamstow Reporter*.

By the time of the first election the family had moved a short distance to a cramped upstairs flat at 57 Warner Road which they shared with half-brother William, and Bowman was working as an insurance agent.[51] Eldest son William had left school on 14 November 1894 and was working in a local cheese and provisions store, while Robert had a part-time job in another Walthamstow shop. It was a clear sign that once again the family's finances were under strain. The ready availability of cheap imported bacon from America had brought his employment with the Belfast firm to an end.[52]

Bowman's new-found position proved sufficient to provoke the wrath of the *Walthamstow Reporter*, which sided with the local controlling Radical Liberal councillors. Describing Bowman as the leader of the 'local Socialistic wreckers,' the paper declared:

This person was utterly unknown in Walthamstow until a few weeks back. He has never performed one act for the benefit of the working men of the town. Yet he desires to be regarded by his 30 followers as the grand elector of Walthamstow. He describes himself by the very indefinite and elastic title of 'Insurance Agent.' But, whatever he may be, he is not the kind of man to be taken on trust, more especially when he and his few henchmen are the pets of Sammy Herbert's organ.[53]

Portrait of Alexander Bowman from 1902, the year after he served as president of the Irish Trade Union Congress.

William Ewart, Bowman's Conservative opponent for the North Belfast seat in the 1885 General Election.
COURTESY OF THE LATE SIR IVAN EWART

Belfast's Central Library largely owes its existence to a strong public lobby in the 1880s, led on behalf of the working class by Belfast Trades Council.
CENTENARY POSTCARD PUBLISHED IN 1988 BY THE LIBRARY

The six labour councillors elected to Belfast Corporation in November 1897.

BACK, FROM LEFT: Murray Davis, Pottinger ward; William Liddell, St George's; Edward McInnes, Victoria.

FRONT, FROM LEFT: Alexander Bowman, Duncairn; Robert Gageby, Shankill, and Alex Taylor, Court.

Hugh Bowman's butcher's shop at Agnes Street, Belfast.
Included are two of Hugh's eight children, Johnston
and Elizabeth Rogers Bowman.

The Falls swimming
baths at the turn of
the century.

Alexander Bowman's children

Charles Edward Bowman
(1895–1923)

Minnie Grimmett Bowman
(1885–1968)
on her engagement day

Thomas Rodgers Bowman
(1892–1964)

Robert Ritchie Bowman CBE (1883–1970) and William James Bowman (1881–1958)

Hugh Bowman MBE (1887–1965) and his mother Rose (1852–1947) at the former's home in Bangor.

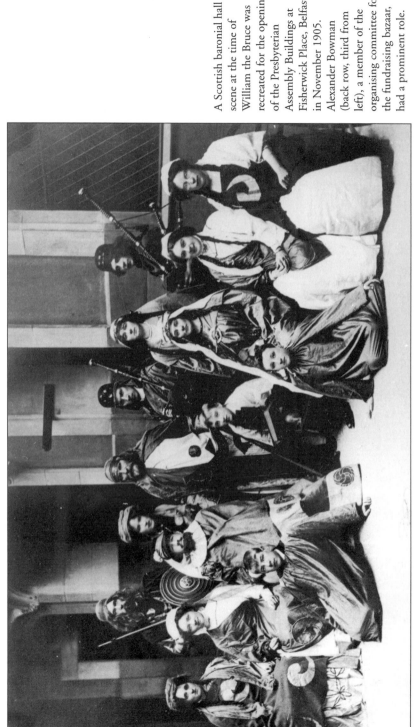

A Scottish baronial hall scene at the time of William the Bruce was recreated for the opening of the Presbyterian Assembly Buildings at Fisherwick Place, Belfast, in November 1905. Alexander Bowman (back row, third from left), a member of the organising committee for the fundraising bazaar, had a prominent role.

For good measure the *Walthamstow Reporter* also accused the SDF of forming an alliance with local Conservatives in a bid to bring down the Radical Liberals.[54]

Bowman was one of 15 SDF candidates – they were also known as the Social Democrats and Labour Party and the Labour and Progressive group – seeking a share of the 18 seats in Walthamstow's four electoral wards. He stood with five other SDF members in the James' Street six-seat ward and all attended a rally in the local Workmen's Hall on 12 December 1894, three days before the poll. Only the *Walthamstow Guardian* covered the meeting,[55] with one of the candidates, newspaper compositor Herbert Arnold, being reported as stating that it was the first time the 'Labour Party' had taken any action to secure a voice in the affairs of the parish. 'One of the Radical candidates has said they must kick the working men into common sense,' he declared, 'but the working men will not stand being kicked or hit. They will act as they consider right and to their interest.'

Bowman added that it was the Radicals who were splitting the vote in Walthamstow. 'Not one of them is a *bona fide* working man,' he claimed. 'The time has come when the working class must be heard. The battle has begun and we must fight it to the bitter end.' The battle, however, was not to be won in Walthamstow for none of the 15 SDF candidates standing for the council even came close to securing a seat. In a low poll, with 1,716 voting out of 3,624 on the register, all six seats in the St James' ward went to Radical candidates, with the SDF hopefuls recording six of the seven lowest votes.[56] There was some consolation for Bowman whose 209-vote total was the highest achieved by any SDF candidate in Walthamstow. In a sympathetic editorial, the *Walthamstow Guardian* said the Radicals had subjected the SDF candidates to the 'most bitter and unfair personal attacks.'[57]

Within days of his election defeat Bowman had the consolation of welcoming an old acquaintance to Walthamstow, with the Rev. Bruce Wallace being the guest speaker for a meeting of the SDF branch.[58] By then minister of the Brotherhood Church at London's Letchworth Road,[59] his topic was 'Christianity and Socialism.'

Nor did the district council setback spell an end to the electoral activities of the SDF in Walthamstow, for two months later it was agreed to put Bowman's name forward for the High Street ward seat in the triennial elections to Essex County Council.[60] His opponent was Courtenay Warner, who was also Liberal MP for Somerset's Northern division.[61] Having described candidate Warner as a 'splendid Radical MP' and a 'most generous friend to every good cause,' the *Walthamstow Reporter* declared that he would be opposed by 'an untried and, comparatively, an unknown man, who, if elected, would be incapable of performing the duties of the position.'[62]

Warner, who had been a county councillor in another local ward for six years, was the nominee of the Radical and Progressive Association, while Bowman stood as the Independent Working Men's candidate.[63] The latter's election advertisement in the *Walthamstow Guardian* declared: 'We are opposed to the dictatorial and tyrannical conduct of the ultra Radicals which has so disguised Walthamstow in the past. Justice and fair play to all parties is required.'[64]

Bowman's election address indicated that he had been requested to seek election to the county council by a 'large and representative meeting of delegates from the United Workers' Organisation, the Christian Socialist League and the Social Democratic Federation.' Bowman wrote:

> The electors of Walthamstow have the chance to elect men who, in respect to betterment, taxation of land values, acquisition of sources of public convenience, and supply of everything which is in the nature of a monopoly, the strict enforcement of the Weights and Measures Act, and all other laws – such as the Allotments Act – which tend to the improvement of the condition of the people, are in sympathy with that policy which has made the London County Council in some degree worthy of the greatest and most wealthy city of the age.
>
> The question of the unemployed is also one which must be faced and dealt with. I am therefore in favour of the county council using all the powers it possesses, and, in so far as they are inadequate, I should advocate the security of further powers. Entrust me with your suffrages and I shall do my best to justify the wisdom of your choice.[65]

Despite such noble intentions, the *Walthamstow Reporter* was not too far off the mark, for Bowman polled just 94 votes against

Warner's 449, giving the latter a 355-vote majority. Once again it was a low poll, with 558 out of 1,649 on the register for the 2 March election choosing to vote.[66]

Back-to-back electoral defeats ultimately had little to do with Bowman's decision to return to Belfast. In a speech prior to the December 1894 election he admitted he 'could only be in Walthamstow for another five months.'[67] Job insecurity and dwindling finances meant that at times during his stay in the London suburb Bowman had been forced to shuttle his family back and forth to his in-laws in Belfast.[68] By the time of the district council election Rose was expecting her sixth child. Bowman, aware of this, had decided it was time to make a permanent move back to Belfast.

The county council election, which Bowman must have realised he had little or no chance of winning, was a temporary distraction and the family was back in Ireland by the summer time – but not before son Robert had completed his schooling by 21 June 1895,[69] and Bowman had witnessed, one can assume with a certain degree of satisfaction, the defeat of Courtenay Warner in July's general election.

Lord Rosebery had gone to the country after his government was defeated by seven votes in a division connected to the administration of the army. The election saw the return of the Conservatives and their Liberal Unionist allies with a 152-seat majority over the Gladstonian Liberals and Irish Nationalists. It was the most crushing victory since the Liberals took office with a 370-seat majority in 1832. With Lord Salisbury once again at the helm, it meant that, at least for the foreseeable future, Belfast loyalists would have nothing to fear from a socialist-minded 'bird of passage' with fast-receding if not already abandoned Home Rule sympathies.[70]

And, perhaps mindful of his own unsettled upbringing, Bowman had decided, once and for all, that his six children would have a better chance back in Belfast in a settled family environment. One can only wonder what would have happened had he actually won a seat on Walthamstow District Council or the more influential Essex County Council. Given his new-found socialist contacts and an unquestionable ability to get his message across to the right audience, it is not beyond the bounds of possibility that he too, along with Hardie, Glasier and MacDonald, might have had a significant role to play in the birth of the British Labour Party.[71]

BACK IN THE BELFAST FOLD
AND ELECTION SUCCESS

T HE RETURN OF the Bowman family to Belfast can be dated by the enrolment of third son Hugh and daughter Minnie at the Agnes Street National Schools from 5 August 1895.[1] With resources limited, initially they lodged with Rose's sister Minnie, her husband William McHenry, and twins Arthur and Ella at 205 Tennent Street.[2] Soon Bowman was back in the trade union fold, acting as organiser in his spare time for the Belfast Municipal Employees' and Other Workers' Association.[3] Equally importantly, certainly from a financial point of view, he resumed work as a flaxdresser after an absence of more than 10 years from the job.[4] The family also moved into their own rented home at 29 Upper Meenan Street, close to the Shankill Road.[5]

It was not unusual for a general union comprising, in the main, unskilled workers to seek the services of an outsider, particularly one with acknowledged organisational skills. While the position was unpaid apart from expenses, it did represent a chance for Bowman to regain his trade union credentials in the city – although he did not rejoin the trades council until the beginning of 1897 through nomination by the flaxdressers' union.[6]

Despite the political differences and bitterness of a decade earlier,

Bowman's forthright and non-party approach as the leader of workers' delegations to meetings of Belfast Corporation made an impression on fellow trade unionists, including members of the Belfast United Trades and Labour Council – renamed to reflect a change to the representation of skilled and unskilled workers.[7] Bowman's return to trade union circles can also be linked to his continuing role as a public speaker, along with figures like John Bruce Glasier and future Prime Minister Ramsay MacDonald, at meetings of the relatively short-lived local branch of the Independent Labour Party. The ILP had been established in the city in 1892 and was boosted the following year by the decision of the British TUC to hold its annual Congress in Belfast.[8]

Although the ILP suffered as a result of the sectarian nature of Ulster politics,[9] to Bowman, who served briefly as its lecture secretary, it was a means by which he could continue to promote the socialist principles he had learned in Glasgow and London. It also indicated that Bowman's political sympathies were beginning to move from Marxism back towards the centre.

The party newspaper, *Labour Leader*, edited by Keir Hardie, included a report from the Belfast ILP in October 1896 which indicated that after a lapse of some months the branch 'once more asserts itself with that unslaughtered vitality characteristic of the party.' The same edition referred to 'the energetic efforts of our lecture secretary Comrade Alexander Bowman, who has been a powerful acquisition to the branch.' He also addressed the branch about atrocities in Armenia, his 'usual forcible and trenchant style eliciting the applause of a large audience,' while in November the newspaper stated that he was 'on the warpath on behalf of dockers, scavengers and other free and happy Britons.'[10]

An early sign of his renewed involvement with the trade union movement came in November 1896, when he led a deputation to a meeting of Belfast Corporation to seek a wage increase for the city's street sweepers and to appeal for changes to the rules applying to their employment.[11] He pointed out that if a man arrived for work even a few minutes late he lost half a day's pay, and he complained that workmen completing 30 years of service with the corporation had their wages cut from 16s. 6d. a week to just 7s. a week. He was accompanied by William Walker, a member of the trades council and a key local figure in the ILP.[12]

Responding, Lord Mayor William Pirrie told the delegation it was the first time he had heard any request for extra money for their employees and he was sure the appropriate committees would 'give every attention to the remarks put before the corporation.' He added that he was 'very glad to know that punctuality is being insisted upon by the department as otherwise it would be impossible for work to be done.'

The *Labour Leader* exaggerated what had been a reasonably civil encounter between councillors and deputation, but included a perceptive comment: 'There was a regular combat, bloodless of course. Bowman fairly pulverised the council with his sharp sarcasms, Walker followed suit with characteristic audacity – should these two invincibles stand for council honours any time, they should go in flying.'[13]

Bowman and Walker returned to the corporation for its quarterly meeting in May 1897, to represent pipelayers employed by the gas committee.[14] They argued that the men often had to travel long distances from their homes to arrive at work by 6.15am, but they did not receive any extra pay or allowances. Bowman suggested that the men should be allowed to meet at a central point at 6am and then take as long as was necessary to reach the place where their services were required. The same policy, he claimed, had been followed for many years by the corporation's police committee and he urged the members to instruct their gas committee to adopt a similar plan.

It was an argument the pair did not win. While chairman Sir William McCammond, presiding in Lord Mayor Pirrie's absence, assured the delegation that the corporation would not wish to see any of its employees suffering 'either a grievance or an injustice,' another member, Sir Daniel Dixon, pointed out that each case was treated on its merits but an allowance was certainly paid where work was carried out beyond the municipal boundaries. His view that the members of the delegation were 'in error' was supported by gas service manager James Stelfox, who told councillors that the maximum distance to be walked without the allowance applying was one-and-a-half miles in any direction from the centre of the White Linen Hall and that had been agreed following consultations with the trade unions.[15]

At the beginning of November Bowman paid a further visit to the town hall as secretary of the Municipal Employees' Association, to seek a wage increase for labourers employed by the corporation.[16] Bowman urged the councillors to standardise the wages paid to labourers at £1 a week, pointing out that workers in Britain's major cities were already earning that amount. Lord Mayor Pirrie promised the matter would be given 'careful consideration.'

The elections, which arrived before those deliberations could take place, were the first to be held since an extension of the city boundaries the year before to create 15 wards, each with an alderman and three councillors, giving a total of 60 members. Previously there had been 10 aldermen and 30 councillors.[17] Belfast Trades Council was clearly aware that the already-widened franchise, linked with the extended boundaries, offered working-class candidates considerable hope of success. It would not be their first bid for town hall honours. Two labour candidates, Samuel Monro and Murray Davis, had stood unsuccessfully in 1891 and 1893 in the old Cromac and Dock wards respectively.[18] Also in 1891 Belfast barrister Thomas Harrison had won a seat as an independent in the St Anne's ward, having run with the approval of the trades council.[19]

For the November 1897 elections the trades council selected candidates in seven wards where they felt they stood the best hope of victory. Bowman, who had chaired several meetings of the council when president Richard Wortley was unable to attend, was the choice for Duncairn. The other labour candidates were Murray Davis – Pottinger, secretary of the Belfast Operative Bakers' Society; William Liddell – St. George's and Dock, secretary of the Operative House and Ship Painters' and Decorators' Union; Edward McInnes – Victoria, district delegate of the National Amalgamated Union of Labourers; Robert Gageby – Shankill, secretary of the Flaxdressers' Union; and Alex Taylor – Court, Irish Linenlappers' Union and secretary to Belfast Trades Council.

Trades council members also pledged their continuing support for Thomas Harrison in Woodvale, although the seat had been left open to him by the local Conservative Association,[20] and offered their backing to Conservative candidate William McClure in Ormeau, on the grounds that he had always been recognised as a fair employer by the Amalgamated Society of Tailors.[21] Bowman would surely have allowed himself a wry smile at such a blatantly political gesture, given the council's stand against him 11 years earlier.

The six labour candidates stood on a manifesto which included demands for corporation direct labour, fair wages for municipal workers and a fair wage clause for public contracts. Crucially, the trades council had also been boosted in the eyes of the electorate through its positive role in a public health inquiry, which, in exposing inefficiency and corruption, had pointed the finger at a number of corporation members and officials. Outbreaks of typhoid in the city that year had caused no fewer than 354 deaths.[22] In addition, the trades council was actively involved in a lengthy lockout which had hit the British engineering industry, including a number of Belfast firms.

For many members of the public the first opportunity to see the election candidates in action came at a massive demonstration in support of the engineers, organised by the trades council.[23] Following a procession of affiliated trade unionists and accompanying bands, from Agnes Street through the streets of the city, speakers addressed a large crowd from three platforms erected at Ormeau Park. The same resolution, proposed from each platform, condemned the Employers' Federation for 'making a small strike in London the pretext for a national lockout' and accused the federation of a 'vicious attack' on their movement. Bowman spoke on the lockout and the eight-hour working day the strikers were seeking.

Buoyed by the success of the demonstration, the trades council was ready to do battle at the polls. Bowman handed in his election papers on 16 November 1897.[24] Given the short time left to the 24 November polling day, he launched into a series of public meetings – not in halls but literally on street corners. It might have been early winter but Bowman had little trouble attracting crowds of 1,500 to 2,000 each night. It was no mean feat considering the electoral area, which had been created by splitting the old Dock ward into separate Dock and Duncairn wards, had a population of 20,863 and an electorate of 3,527.[25]

At a meeting held at the junction of Upper Canning Street and Glenrosa Street within hours of handing in his nomination papers, Bowman referred to the absence of labour representation on the corporation in the past:

> If I am elected I will take good care that the working man's interests are maintained in the future. I am not the owner of any jerry-built houses and therefore I have no axe to grind. I will do all I can to remedy the present state of the public health; to increase the remuneration received by the scavengers who do very necessary work for the corporation; to prevent the giving of contracts to unfair shops; to municipalise the tramway system of the city; to increase the open spaces and breathing places for the people; and to prevail upon the corporation, with its favourable borrowing powers, to borrow money at the low rate of two-and-a-half per cent, as it can do, and lend it to the ratepayers so they can become the owners of the houses they inhabit.[26]

The crowd, having greeted his promises with loud applause, dispersed to the strains of 'The Cock of the North,' played by a band of pipers.

The following night's rally, on a vacant site at the junction of Ivan Street and York Road, heard Bowman deriding the other candidates as 'this family party.' In addition to Sir William McCammond, Conservative, who was standing against independent Samuel Lawther in the separate election for the aldermanship of Duncairn, the four remaining candidates seeking the three corporation seats included Sir William's son James and his brother-in-law John Thompson, both Conservatives, also Robert Wilson, Independent, and Dr Timothy White, Conservative. Bowman said while he 'yielded to no man' in his admiration for Sir William McCammond, he wondered if it was right that he and his family should seek to prevent the 3,700 working families in the ward from having labour representation.[27] Bowman promised that, if elected, he would ensure 'the foundations of houses are concreted and that every house will have a nine-foot rear, so that the contents of the ashpits and other refuse will not require to be conveyed through the living apartments.' Houses, he continued, were being built without passages and when complaints were raised the reply was that the plans had been passed 'so long ago.' And with the exhortation 'Plump for Bowman,' he added: 'Send me to the town hall and I will do all that in me lies to remedy this glaring error. I want nothing more than justice and will be satisfied with nothing less.'[28]

The next meeting attracted 1,000 to 1,500 people to an assembly point at Whitla Street, where chairman David Carlisle asserted: 'It is time the horny-handed sons of toil had someone to look after their interests. Reforms are urgently needed in this city – there is more disease in it at present than before the dying corporation put the pigs out of the poor man's yard.'

Bowman trusted that on election day the 'family' opposed to him would be 'so ill municipally that the family physician [Conservative candidate Dr White] will have an opportunity to display his skills in ministering to the injured.' When challenged to state if he held atheistic views, Bowman said he did not think the electors had the right to inquire into any man's particular theological views. However, he was quite happy to say he believed 'most firmly in the power outside ourselves, beyond our comprehension, that makes for righteousness and I call that power God.' And he added: 'If the questioner does not believe me, then I would refer him to my minister, the Rev. George Magill, of Cliftonville Presbyterian Church, for confirmation.'[29]

Tuesday night, 22 November, saw the Bowman bandwagon leaving the Painters' Hall at Great George's Street bound for Greencastle – thus becoming the first candidate to canvass at the north end of the Duncairn ward.[30] The party travelled in a brake, hired by Belfast Trades Council, which was illuminated by torchlight. According to the *Belfast Evening Telegraph* they were accompanied by a piper in Highland costume 'whose pipes, by their warlike tone, lent vigour to the scene which presaged the triumphant entry of this candidate into Greencastle.' Some 2,000 people gathered outside the Railway Hotel to hear the speakers who were introduced by carpenter William McAlister, treasurer of Belfast Trades Council. The loudest cheers were reserved for Bowman who promised that he would endeavour to provide 'healthy homes, perfect sanitation, municipal swimming baths, branch libraries and higher wages for labour done,' and declared that in his capacity as organiser of the local Municipal Employees' Association, he had been campaigning for a one shilling a week increase in labourers' wages. 'Every working man, in order to keep a wife and family, should be paid one pound per week,' he added.

* * *

All six trades council-backed candidates were triumphant, with all but one heading the polls. In Duncairn, with electors entitled to vote for a maximum of three candidates, the result was: Bowman 1,249; White 1,196; Wilson 1,010; Thompson 839, and McCammond 767. In the election for the aldermanship, shipbuilder Samuel Lawther defeated Sir William McCammond by 1,797 votes to 704, thus completing the rout of the 'family party.'[31]

Liddell, the only labour candidate who did not top the poll, captured the third and final seat in the St. George's ward but finished last in Dock. Electoral success was also achieved by the two trades council-endorsed candidates, Thomas Harrison in Woodvale and William McClure in Ormeau, as well as by coachbuilder Frank Johnston in Shankill. Although Johnston, like McClure, ran as a Conservative Association candidate, he was a former secretary of the trades council.[32]

The *Belfast News-Letter*, at one time a bulwark of anti-trade union opinion,[33] had encouraged its readers to support Gageby in the Shankill ward.[34] After the results were announced it declared that the trades council nominees had no special following, 'rather they were standing on principles which were not political' – although there was a clear reference to Bowman's activities of 1886 and beyond:

> One of them is said to be what is sometimes called a Protestant Home Ruler, and all of them stood on a platform which has more to do with the interests of trade unionism than with the interests of any political party. Some of the labour candidates will, we believe, prove useful in the deliberations of the corporation.[35]

The same paper, in brief profiles of the successful candidates, claimed inaccurately that Bowman had stood as a 'Separatist' in the 1885 North Belfast election. The fact that Bowman chose not to correct the mistake, as he would most surely have done a decade earlier, suggests he did not feel any need to answer for his past actions and had entered a new phase in his life.

The elections returned 33 Conservatives, the six labour members, five Liberal Unionists and eight independents,[36] plus two aldermen and six councillors nominated by the city's Catholic Association.[37] While Catholics were encouraged to vote for labour candidates elsewhere, the Catholic Association's strength lay in the Falls and Smithfield wards where it achieved an electoral clean sweep.[38]

The success of the six labour candidates had an impact far beyond Belfast. E. L. Richardson, former president of Dublin Trades Council,[39] who would himself win a seat on Dublin Corporation in January 1898, wrote:

> Your victories have sent a thrill of pride and satisfaction throughout the whole of Ireland's labour forces and fittingly demonstrate what should, and would, no doubt, be accomplished in Dublin, Cork, Limerick and other centres had the workers therein a similar franchise to that enjoyed by the sturdy Belfastmen.[40]

A similar message of good wishes was conveyed from Waterford Trades Council to their Belfast counterparts.

There was also unanimous agreement among members of the trades council at the same meeting that the six labour councillors should have 'a common programme in harmony with trade unionism, and that they should not be holding separate views and be running antagonistic to each other to the defeat of a true labour policy.'

Bowman would prove a faithful attender at meetings of Belfast Corporation and its sub-committees, rarely missing a session despite their noon start and the requirement to take time off from work to attend. His maiden speech was on a motion to set aside money towards a proposed swimming pool for the north end of the city. Little realising that one day he would work for the corporation as a pool superintendent, Bowman, along with four of his labour colleagues, voted in favour of the motion which was narrowly defeated by 22 to 20.[41]

At the January 1898 monthly meeting trade union matters came to the fore, with members receiving a deputation from the trades council.[42] The visitors, familiar faces to the labour members, repeated the earlier call for an increase in labourers' wages. Councillors again agreed to give the views expressed by the delegation 'careful consideration' but, in reality, the labour members were very much in a minority and it would take time to win over many of the old guard. The vast majority of councillors were well-to-do Conservative businessmen who had little affinity with the working classes.

At the same meeting efforts were made to put the sub-committee structure into place, with each of the 60 councillors and aldermen being nominated to serve on a total of three committees, with those committees being graded in importance. The idea was that to ensure equal ward representation each councillor should serve on a major committee, a middle-ranking one and a minor one. In Bowman's case he was given places on the police, markets and cemeteries sub-committees, which meant the number of meetings he had to attend rose significantly. Bowman supported the plan, declaring that with the heavy volume of work facing the corporation and the 'comparatively untrained condition of many of the members, this requires our loyal acceptance.'[43]

The first major difference of opinion between that old guard and the labour representatives emerged at the January meeting. Trade in Belfast was still being hit by the dispute involving the city's engineers. The labour members, in consequence, put forward a motion that 'an instruction go out to all labour-employing committees of the corporation to give preference of employment to all labourers rendered idle as a consequence of the stagnation of trade caused by the lockout of the Belfast engineers.' Bowman, seconding the proposal, said there was a 'large quantity of necessary work to be done' and he could not see why it could not be undertaken with so many men in pressing need of employment. However, the main objection to the motion from other members was that the labour leaders were the very people responsible for the industrial action. Instead, a tamer version was adopted, calling on the committees to 'push forward such authorised public works as are necessary in order that as much useful and remunerative work as possible may be done during the present regrettable circumstances.'

On a somewhat lighter note the meeting closed with a proposal to invite tenders for the purchase of 19 robes and 19 cocked hats for the new members failing to attract a seconder. Lord Mayor

James Henderson pointed out that 'the late John G. McGee supplied the present gowns and cocked hats to the corporation when the Queen visited Belfast [in 1849] and I am afraid the members will have to wait some time before they get new ones.'

The corporation's February meeting saw a further debate on workers' wages, fuelled by the decision of the authority to increase the salaries of several of its already well-paid senior staff.[44] Bowman described it as 'a decision which offends my sense of justice.' However, the labour members, who a week earlier had organised a public protest meeting on the issue,[45] recorded a noteworthy victory, securing backing for a resolution, albeit watered down, to spend an extra half-penny on the rates to increase the wages of around 1,100 workers who were paid less than £1 a week.

Bowman also proposed that the Press be admitted to all corporation meetings but the proposal, backed by the other labour members, was defeated by 19 votes to 14.[46]

He was finding himself able to represent the working people of Belfast on two fronts – as an elected representative and as a member of the trades council. With corporation meetings very much rubber-stamping mundane issues, at times he would have found trades council membership altogether more rewarding. In January 1898, and emphasising the importance he still placed in the trades council, Bowman had allowed his name to go forward for the presidency but he was defeated 46 votes to 22 by Richard Wortley. He was, however, returned as vice-president that year.[47]

At a trades council meeting in March Bowman proposed a resolution which criticised certain elements of the new Local Government (Ireland) bill, one he cited being a requirement that all property occupiers should pay rates. He said such a measure would 'press harshly and unfairly on the wage-earning classes.' The resolution, passed without dissent, called for a deputation to seek the corporation's support in opposing the offending clause.[48]

The Local Government bill was still troubling trades council members at their meeting in May,[49] with Bowman condemning Sir James Haslett, who was also MP for North Belfast, over an amendment he believed Haslett would propose at Westminster – that local authorities should pay pensions only to those retiring members of staff who were paid salaries. Bowman, speaking for the corporation workers he still represented, claimed they would be excluded from pension schemes and urged trades council secretary Alex Taylor to write to all MPs who would be 'favourable to the interests of the workers' to oppose such an amendment. Fellow labour representative William Liddell offered a contrary view, suggesting that in fact Haslett was seeking, through his amendment, to extend the scope of superannuation payments to include the ordinary workers. Liddell won the trades council's support for a call to 'labour and local Members of Parliament to see that the amendment applies to all workers as well as officials in the employment of local bodies.'

Two weeks later Bowman spoke at length about the 'marvellous penchant for employing an extraordinary number of apprentices' by Messrs. Herdman in their flaxdressing department at Sion Mills.[50] Noting that one shop in the factory employed 36 apprentices, he said: 'The Flaxdressers' Union has to grapple with this difficulty all over the trade, and we have been fairly successful, except in the case of this particular firm.' Warning that a flaxdressers' strike would be called if other measures failed, Bowman hoped for the sympathy and support of the council 'if war should come.'

The meeting was also noteworthy since it took place two days after the death, on 19 May 1898, of William Gladstone. Gladstone was still a national institution and his death was an event of major importance. Bowman chose, however, not to reflect publicly on the man he had idolised for so many years.

Bowman was also involved in a lighter though ultimately quite far-reaching matter when the trades council, pursuing an issue which had been on its books for several years, agreed to write to Sir Charles Dilke, Liberal MP for Chelsea, requesting him to move an amendment to the Local Government (Ireland) bill, 'conferring upon local bodies in Ireland the power already possessed by similar bodies in England and Scotland to strike such a rate as may be required to provide music in the public parks.' Seconding the call, Bowman expressed the opinion that 'if music were introduced into the city parks it would considerably brighten them up and add very much to the people's enjoyment.' The council's approach to Dilke helped to bring about the provision of bandstands in public parks the length and breadth of the country.

At a trades council meeting in July Bowman claimed that 'suffering and death' resulted from the use of poisonous phosphorus in the manufacture of matches by British companies. He won the backing of the trades council for a call to go out to the Home Secretary to have the chemical banned.[51] During a corporation meeting that same day Bowman won support for a call, against the recommendation of the gas sub-committee, to award a week's holidays to the authority's lamplighters, stokers and other employees who were required to work seven days a week. Victory was achieved despite sarcastic comments from several Conservative members to the effect that being a lamplighter was 'recreation and not work,' and that the men were already paid the wages of trained men for 'comparatively easy work.'

July also afforded the trades council an early opportunity to re-test its electoral strength following the resignation of Sir Daniel Dixon as alderman for Dock ward. The council put forward one of its number, Robert Fleming, believing that as it already had six councillors on the corporation it had every right to a labour alderman. Fleming faced opposition from Conservative Henry Hutton, who had topped the councillors' poll in Dock the previous November, and independent James McClelland. Two public meetings were held in the Painters' Hall prior to the election on 22 July, with speakers, including Bowman, claiming the absence of a trades council-nominated alderman denied them a place on the corporation's important general purposes committee.[52]

Fleming's campaign came unstuck when it was gleefully reported in the Conservative press that in an effort to bolster his flagging support he had sought and gained the backing of the city's Catholic Association which had decided against fielding its own candidate.[53] The labour nominee vehemently denied that he was a Nationalist or that he had ever donated money to any nationalist causes, but, with two trades union secretaries working for Hutton's return, the damage was done. In a low poll timber merchant Hutton received 1,091 votes compared to the 446 cast for Fleming and 226 for McClelland.[54] Having had their fingers burnt, the trades council decided not to field a candidate in the resulting by-election for Hutton's existing seat.

The highlight of a busy first year for the newly-elected councillors came on 18 October with the laying of the foundation stone for the new City Hall in Donegall Square.[55]

The corporation's December meeting saw a disagreement between Bowman and labour colleague Davis over the quality of the gas supplied to the city's houses and street lamps. Bowman's call for an investigation was supported by Thomas Harrison who described the gas as 'simply disgraceful.' Davis, a member of the gas committee, was stung by the criticism and retorted that the gas was supplied in accordance with an Act of Parliament. 'I would venture to say there are no towns in Ireland, and very few in England and Scotland, as well-lighted as Belfast,' he added.

Town clerk Sir Samuel Black told members that tests were regularly conducted at the gasworks and members were free to watch them being carried out. He refuted any suggestion that there were 'two qualities of gas' in Belfast and said problems invariably arose where the gas burners were in a poor condition. 'If the gentlemen who consume gas in their houses would see that their burners were properly attended to, they would have no complaint to make about the quality,' the town clerk added. Harrison challenged him to explain why it was that sometimes they had good gas, yet the following week, with the same burners, it had become 'wretched.' Refusing to be beaten, Black replied: 'I suppose in the meantime the burners have got out of order.'

Bowman, who had first raised the issue, gained the welcome support of former Lord Mayor Pirrie who said they all knew the gas was 'as bad as can be' and the labour member had been right to draw it to their attention. 'At the same time we should thank the company for supplying gas of this quality,' Pirrie declared. 'By so doing, we now have more applications for electric light than our works can supply.'[56]

Several days later Bowman might have felt he had travelled back a decade or more to the days of protesting against the manner in which Ireland was governed from Westminster. Under the auspices of the Irish Financial Reform League, a public meeting was held in the annexe of the Ulster Hall to promote Ireland's claim for a reconsideration of its financial relations with Great

Britain.[57] The distinguished platform party included Dublin's Lord Mayor, Alderman Daniel Tallon.

They were seeking Belfast's support for a campaign backed by a Royal Commission which had concluded that, when one contrasted the relative resources of the two islands, Ireland contributed too much to the British Exchequer. Cross-party support was very much in evidence. Pottinger Conservative councillor John McCormick proposed the main resolution which sought immediate action from the government:

> That in the opinion of this meeting it is imperative on Irishmen of all political parties to join in the effort now being made by the Irish Financial Reform League to redress the burden of Imperial taxation, which, after investigation by a Royal Commission, has been found to press unduly on the resources of Ireland and to be in contravention of Article Seven of the Act of Union.

* * *

The beginning of 1899 brought mixed fortunes for the trades council representatives on the corporation. On 1 January Robert Gageby's term of office came to an abrupt end after it was discovered that his name had been mistakenly struck off the electoral register. The error only came to light when Gageby decided to stand for the vacant aldermanship in Shankill.[58] Not only was he unable to stand for that election but the law required his enforced retirement as a councillor. Nevertheless, the January elections afforded the trades council another test of its staying power. The newly-introduced Local Government (Ireland) Act not only shifted the date of the polls from November to January, but it also required that one-third of the councillors should seek re-election each year, commencing with those who had secured the least number of votes in November 1897.[59]

Since five of the six trades council representatives had topped the poll, just one needed to seek re-election. William Liddell retained his seat, defeating a Conservative by 1,190 votes to 938. In Duncairn independent member Robert Wilson had decided to stand down and, given Bowman's earlier success, it was decided to pit trades council president John Murphy against previously-defeated Conservative candidate John Thompson. However, Thompson easily defeated Murphy by 1,534 votes to 399.[60]

It would take several months to resolve the situation in Shankill. Ultimately, Gageby's seat went, without recourse to an election, to Conservative Association nominee James Pearson, who was also a member of the trades council.[61]

At the first corporation meeting after the elections, Bowman failed in a bid to have the traditional starting time shifted from noon to 3pm.[62] And he was equally unsuccessful during a debate about the city's public library when he suggested that betting information should be 'blotted out from the papers kept in the newsroom as the library is crowded with those people anxious to read this news.'[63]

Despite such minor disappointments, the broader picture was looking bright as far as the trades council was concerned. Another provision of the Local Government (Ireland) Act was the requirement to hold elections for two poor law guardians for each of the 15 Belfast electoral wards. It was agreed to nominate William Walker for Duncairn and he broke further new ground for the trades council by topping the poll of three candidates. One result of his election was the provision by the trades council of Christmas treats and summer excursions for children and the elderly in Belfast's workhouses.[64]

Proving that, while limited to just five representatives, the labour members were making an impact in the city, the pro-Conservative *Belfast Evening Telegraph* willingly conceded:

> The labour party, as they are sometimes called, have every right to claim they have comported themselves with credit to themselves and benefit to the artisans of the community. The health of the city has been placed in the forefront of the labour programme and many of the suggestions made on this score have been adopted.[65]

* * *

The May meeting of the corporation heralded disappointing news for the labour members, with the formal announcement that Thomas Harrison was resigning his Woodvale seat after eight years because of increasing demands on his law practice.[66] While Harrison's vacant seat was filled by a Liberal Unionist without recourse to an election,[67] the labour members still had an opportunity to flex their electoral muscles following the death that same month of Pottinger alderman William McCormick. Three candidates, including McCormick's son John, presented themselves to the electorate. The others were Conservative nominee Dr. Alfred (A.V.) Browne, already a councillor for Pottinger, and a second independent, builder William Hill.[68]

Four of the five labour councillors, along with former member Robert Gageby, spoke in McCormick's favour at a series of public meetings,[69] pointing to his sympathetic approach in the past to working-class issues. The election saw victory for McCormick who received 1,911 votes to the 1,805 cast for Browne, with just nine going to Hill.[70]

Arising from McCormick's success, his own corporation seat in Victoria fell vacant, with two candidates stepping forward: Conservative nominee Dr James King-Kerr and, once again, William Hill. Emphasising that they judged a candidate not on his political affiliations but on a perception of his actions, the labour grouping lent their support to the Conservative.[71]

Thanks in no small part to the labour backing, King-Kerr was elected with a 270-vote majority.[72] By way of returning the compliment, he lent his support to a call by Bowman in July for the provision of more drinking fountains around the city.[73] Indicating that his temperance views were as sincere as ever, Bowman told colleagues how he often heard complaints from men 'with conscientious objections to entering public houses' that there were too few drinking fountains in the city. 'How,' he asked, 'can the many temperance people in Belfast expect people to be teetotal if no provision has been made for their needs?' Another member retorted: 'A man who is ashamed to go into a public house when he is thirsty deserves to die of thirst.'

OLD WOUNDS REOPENED
FOR THE APOSTLE OF SOCIALISM

IN JULY 1899 THE five trades council members managed to sail
the corporation into uncharted waters – by coaxing it to seek a
sworn inquiry into the manner in which a controversial case had
been handled by two of the city's magistrates. Quay labourer
Alexander Hopkins, from Sandy Row, had accused two police
constables of assaulting him as he made his way home from a
meeting in Clifton Street Orange Hall. The policemen counter-
charged Hopkins, an Orangeman, Salvation Army member and
teetotaller, with indecent behaviour for 'following' prostitutes.[1]

The three magistrates hearing the case dismissed Hopkins'
allegations against the officers but two held that Hopkins had
been guilty of indecent behaviour. Chief magistrate John Burke's
decision to limit the fine to £1 meant that the defendant had no
right of appeal. The case became a *cause célèbre* – with Unionists,
trade unionists, Orangemen, temperance supporters, and church
ministers taking Hopkins' side on the grounds that his previous
good character had been sullied, while others felt the integrity of
the two magistrates who had found him guilty, both Catholics,
was being called into question.[2]

The labour councillors called for a special meeting of Belfast

Corporation but Lord Mayor Otto Jaffe refused on the grounds that it was 'not within the province of the corporation to interfere with the magistrates in the execution of their duty.' However, the law permitted councillors to requisition their own meeting. It was held on 19 July and there was unanimous support for a resolution seeking a sworn inquiry into the case. The resolution was forwarded to Chief Secretary Gerald Balfour at Dublin Castle.[3]

Within days the Hopkins case was being raised at Westminster for differing reasons by the rather unlikely trio of William Johnston, John Dillon and Michael Davitt.[4] The matter was brought to a speedy end in a subsequent letter from Balfour to the corporation rejecting the call for an inquiry.[5]

Two months later Sir Samuel Black took centre stage for a debate which echoed events back in January 1886 when Bowman had joined the public outcry over a proposed £75 a year increase for the town clerk, lifting his salary then to £2,000. At that time Bowman condemned the increase outright but in 1899 he and his labour colleagues chose a more conciliatory, although equally fruitless tack when the corporation's finance committee recommended a £400 a year pay rise to lift Black's salary to £4,000. The committee argued that under the new Local Government (Ireland) Act he would be entitled to various fees in his capacity as town clerk and the £400 increase would represent an all-inclusive payment.[6] The labour members, who during the same meeting had been unsuccessful in their efforts to win a shilling a week increase for the corporation's scavengers, stuck to their guns and put forward an amendment calling for the issue to be referred to the Local Government Board. It was defeated by 26 votes to 14 and Black, indicating that he had no plans for retirement, received his increase.[7]

The tactic of requisitioning a meeting was used again in November 1899 when Bowman and his fellow labour councillors put forward a radical plan to impose a tax on land values.[8] The twin aims of the proposal were to reduce the financial burden already facing Belfast's ratepayers and to discourage speculators from buying city centre sites and leaving them vacant, with no rates due, until they could be sold on to developers for a healthy profit. Bowman explained to the small number of councillors who attended the special meeting how two months earlier 114 rating authorities had sent delegates to a conference in Glasgow 'where they affirmed the principle of taxing land values for the relief of local burdens, and 30 others not represented sent sympathetic messages.'

Bowman also pointed out that Glasgow Corporation had prepared a bill for consideration at the next session of parliament, seeking authority for the Scottish city to levy a tax on land values. 'Every public improvement augments land values at the ratepayers' expense,' he said. His resolution urged the corporation's law committee to follow Glasgow's lead and to seek the appropriate powers. Enjoying across-the-board support, the resolution was passed with a sizeable majority.

* * *

As the labour representatives were not required to seek re-election in January 1900, and there was little likelihood of success in any of the other wards, there was no official trades council involvement in the campaigning. One contest did, however, attract the interest of individual members. In the Ormeau ward Cllr James Dawson was nominated for re-election by the Belfast Conservative Association. He faced Dr James Williamson, a former Conservative Association member who was running as an independent.

A campaign meeting for Williamson was chaired by trades council treasurer William Nicholl.[9] The corporation, he said, had been failing to operate the fair wages clause, which involved the payment of the agreed trade union rate of pay on building contracts, and Dawson was one of the chief culprits.

The following night Dawson enjoyed the support of four corporation colleagues, all with trade union links, including Bowman. Introducing a strongly political note, Murray Davis praised the Conservative Association for helping to place Unionist working men on the electoral register:

> ... and for that reason, if for no other, the Association deserves some consideration from us. If some of you attended the corporation and saw the actions of the nationalist members you would very soon put your hands in your pockets and assist the Association in the registration work it performs from year to year.[10]

Bowman steered clear of politics, preferring to praise Dawson for his efforts in the corporation chamber to improve the city's sanitation and to provide better conditions for working men.

At a subsequent meeting of the trades council, standing orders were suspended to allow Nicholl to 'call attention to the contest in Ormeau ward and to review the conduct of some of the representatives of labour in connection therewith.'[11] Claiming that trade unionism had been 'dragged through the mire,' Nicholl asked the trades council to 'defend in the future the true interests of trade unionism by repudiating the actions of men who are at complete variance with the labour question.' He singled out Bowman for a particularly vitriolic attack. To a shout from the floor of 'Wipe the councillor off,' he claimed that Bowman's role as 'the Apostle of Socialism' was totally at odds with some of his remarks at the Dawson meeting. The trades council, added Nicholl, had been made a laughing stock.

Davis defended his right as an elector in Ormeau ward to choose between the two candidates, adding: 'I have always endeavoured to support the trades council, but it strikes me that the council has shirked its own responsibilities very materially. How much has it paid Mr Bowman and Mr Taylor during the past six or seven months?'

Bowman insisted that at a meeting of their own executive committee Dawson was preferred to Williamson. 'If there is diversity of opinion in the executive,' he said, 'then my allegiance to the trades council is not called upon to determine the course of action I decide to take. And I would challenge anyone to say if I have ever done anything contrary to the interests of the working men.' He also took up Davis' point about payments to councillors and what he perceived was a threat from Nicholl to withhold that support:

> If you take nothing from nothing, what remains? I have not been paid overtime for last July and not a single farthing for the intervening months. And when a man threatens starvation to me until my will becomes the will of someone else, then I think it is only right I should tell him I have been undergoing a process of starvation for the past six months.

The resolution censuring the councillors for backing Dawson was defeated by 20 votes to 17. Nor did the matter end there as far as William Walker was concerned. Angered by trades council links with Conservatism, he indicated that at their next meeting he would move a motion calling on the body to:

> ... repudiate the action of Cllr Bowman in the contest in Ormeau ward and, believing him to have flagrantly violated his pledges not only to the trades council but to his constituents, hereby calls upon him to resign his seat as councillor for Duncairn ward.

In the intervening period the election in Ormeau saw the defeat of Dawson by Williamson – by 1,689 votes to 1,183.[12]

When the trades council held its annual general meeting at the end of January,[13] any pride Bowman might have derived from being returned for a third consecutive term as vice-president, with John Murphy as president, would have been tempered by the knowledge that the new secretary was Walker, with Nicholl again taking on the duties of treasurer. After the completion of the normal business, which included changing the body's full name to the United Trades and Labour Council of Belfast and District, and raising the annual dues from 2d. per union member to 3d., Murphy called on Walker to propose his censure motion.

Before Walker could say anything, William Liddell rose to his feet and said it would be wrong for the trades council to try Bowman twice for the same alleged offence. Murphy ruled that the part of the motion which referred to 'violating pledges to the trades council' was out of order, but he indicated that they could debate the portion relating to Bowman's Duncairn constituents.

Neither Bowman nor Walker found that acceptable. Bowman said he was ready to defend his actions 'in the most public way,' while Walker told Murphy he was unwilling to confine himself to such restrictions, adding: 'I have had the opportunity to hear a good number of Mr Bowman's speeches and will take the matter to his constituents in Duncairn ward.' Bowman, paraphrasing from Shakespeare's *Julius Caesar*, retorted: 'That is the better course. We shall meet at Philippi!'[14]

* * *

Bowman's loyalty to Queen Victoria remained beyond question. When it was announced in March 1900 that the monarch planned to visit Dublin the following month, Bowman joined his corporation colleagues at a special meeting when it was agreed to request that she consider adding Belfast to her itinerary.[15] The city fathers were clearly disappointed that the Queen had been unable or unwilling to travel north. However, regret turned to joy when it was announced on 26 April, the day of Queen Victoria's departure from Ireland, that a baronetcy was being conferred on Lord Mayor Sir Robert McConnell.[16] The corporation's first meeting after the Queen's visit was dominated by the honour. Speaking on behalf of the labour group, Bowman said he and his colleagues:

> ... look with pleasure upon the very distinguished honour conferred upon the Lord Mayor by her Majesty, because we recognise the fact that he is of the people, that he has risen with the rise of Belfast, that he has grown with its growth, and that, in honouring Sir Robert McConnell, Her Majesty is really honouring one of the most living and progressive cities in Europe.[17]

One of Bowman's pet subjects, the provision of public libraries, was raised at Belfast Corporation's meeting in August, when members were told that several suitable sites were under consideration for a branch library at Ballymacarrett.[18] They also heard that a room had been inspected at the Falls Road public baths which, it was felt, would be suitable for a reading room. Bowman told colleagues he wanted to see a library provided in Duncairn but former Lord Mayor Sir James Henderson pleaded for patience and 'breathing space' for the library committee.

The Duncairn councillor began to seek his own breathing space over the next few months with a fall-off in attendances at corporation meetings being recorded. He was by then chairman of the parliamentary committee of the Irish Trade Union Congress. However, there would be time for one more important election campaign – and in his own North Belfast parliamentary constituency.

In the wake of the national celebrations which had followed Boer War successes, Lord Salisbury decided that late September would be an appropriate time to go to the country to seek a new mandate. Three of Belfast's four constituencies saw the return without opposition of their sitting members – Conservatives William Johnston and Gustav Wolff in South and East Belfast respectively, and Liberal Unionist Hugh Arnold-Forster in West Belfast. In North Belfast, however, barrister and former councillor

Thomas Harrison decided to challenge sitting MP Sir James Haslett. Harrison claimed he was standing 'at the request of a large and influential deputation of working men' – mirroring almost exactly the words used when Bowman was persuaded to stand for election 15 years earlier.[19]

Harrison described himself as a Liberal Unionist but the Belfast Liberal Unionist Association quickly disowned him, saying he had not been one of their members since March 1892.[20] It was reacting to a particularly virulent editorial in the *Belfast News-Letter* which described Harrison's candidature as 'a flagrant violation of the first condition of the Unionist alliance, in that North Belfast is a Conservative seat and Mr Harrison is a Liberal Unionist.'[21]

Harrison's manifesto included a number of demands which he felt clearly would appeal to the working-class electorate of North Belfast.[22] To emphasise his continuing support for labour issues, Harrison was one of the principal speakers when a large demonstration was mounted in Belfast on 29 September under the auspices of the trades council and the Amalgamated Society of Carpenters and Joiners, whose members had been on strike for 22 weeks.[23] Accompanied by a number of bands, thousands marched from Carlisle Circus to Ormeau Park, where three platforms had been set up. Presiding over the three were Bowman, Murphy and strikers' representative James Baxter.

Two days later, in a reciprocal gesture, Bowman joined Harrison at Ligoniel for an open-air election meeting outside McClelland's Mill, which – in a further echo of events in 1885 – was constantly interrupted by barracking.[24] Bowman, who was soon forced to abandon his speech because of hooting and shouting, said the drop in Belfast's death rate from 25 per 1,000 six years earlier to a level of 19 per 1,000 was largely due to Harrison's efforts. And clearly angered by the hatred spilling out at the meeting, Bowman declared tellingly: 'For the past 20 years I have stood up for the cause of the working man. I would have done much better if I had fought for myself rather than the people – but I chose to fight their fight rather than my own.'

Earlier that same day Bowman had attended a meeting of Belfast Corporation.[25] Before the normal proceedings began, members met in private session to discuss a proposal to confer the Freedom of the City on Lord Roberts, who had just received an earldom for his exemplary leadership during the Boer War. Although no record was released of what was said during the 'in committee' meeting, Bowman was identified by the *Belfast News-Letter* as a supporting speaker. All the members, with the exception of James Dempsey, rose to their feet in support of conferring the honour on Lord Roberts, who had served as Commander-in-Chief in Ireland between 1895 and 1899. For Bowman much water had flowed under the bridge since his membership of the Belfast Peace Society and his condemnation of Lord Salisbury's government of Ireland 'by whips and swords and guns.'[26]

The following evening Harrison held another campaign meeting, but the venue had to be changed from the corner of Agnes Street and the Crumlin Road to the Oldpark Road because of the likelihood of a violent confrontation between supporters of the two candidates.[27] Once again the meeting was marred by rowdyism, with rotten eggs being thrown at the speakers. Two further meetings were held on the evening of 3 October, one at Greencastle and the other at York Road, opposite Jennymount Mill.[28] Bowman chaired the Greencastle rally and commended Harrison for his work as legal adviser to the trades council, pointing out he had sought 'neither fee nor reward' for his efforts. Labour councillor William Liddell praised him for supporting the fair wages clause and for his successful efforts to have the pay of corporation labourers raised from 14s. a week to 19/6d.

The result of the election was a further reflection of 1885, with Harrison polling 1,855 votes to Haslett's total of 4,172. Given an increase in the electorate, the result was little different, proportionately, to the Ewart-Bowman encounter. The general election witnessed a resounding victory for Lord Salisbury's government, with the Conservative/ Liberal Unionist alliance winning over 400 seats.[29]

The hostility Bowman had encountered at Ligoniel and William Walker's ill-disguised threat earlier in the year represented all-too-clear reminders of the bitterness he had faced in Belfast in the latter half of the 1880s. They were key elements behind his decision in the winter of 1900 not to seek re-election. Another was the continuing reluctance, or inability, of the trades council to make good lost earnings to representatives who were not full-time trade union officials, specifically Bowman and Taylor.[30] Certainly in Bowman's case his work as a flaxdresser, by then part-time, invariably took second place. He had proved a conscientious attender of the corporation and its sub-committees. During the three years and two months he held office he had attended more than 500 meetings and missed just 70.[31]

Money was an issue which had been raised at trades council meetings with increasing frequency the longer he remained on the municipal authority. As early as February 1898, just two months after the elections, members considered a request that 'until we have sufficient municipal funds to pay Councillor Bowman, we pay him out of the funds of the committee.'[32] A municipal labour representation fund had been set up prior to the elections but was already exhausted. The motion was adopted but only after members had decided to delete the specific reference to Bowman. A fortnight later, following a lengthy debate on the subject of selling penny ballot tickets to raise funds for their councillors, members voted for a motion proposed by Bowman that:

> ... in the opinion of this meeting it is expedient to raise a municipal election fund, and with that object in mind that one penny, three-penny and sixpenny tickets be printed and offered for sale to those who sympathise with the representation of labour at municipal or other local boards.[33]

It was estimated in 1899 that the sum of £100 per year was necessary to pay for the lost time of Cllrs Bowman and Taylor and Poor Law Guardian Walker. The figure represented two-thirds of the council's annual income and in fact the trio received just £50 between them. The following year saw £17 being distributed to the three members.[34] The matter dragged on without adequate resolution. Then, in November 1900 – around the time Bowman would have determined not to seek re-election – the trades council adopted a motion proposed by William Walker that: 'We recommend this council to endorse the candidature of those members who may seek re-election, but undertake no financial obligation therewith.'[35]

It is likely that Walker, having bided his time from earlier in the year and upon seeing further signs in the corporation chamber that his former ILP colleague was losing his radical edge, put forward the proposal in the knowledge that it would push Bowman to stand down. It was an action which helped to set in motion the train of events which would ultimately lead to the severing of Bowman's ties with the trade union movement.

Bowman's final meeting as a member of Belfast Corporation took place on 1 January 1901. It was a six-hour session and included lunch, compliments of Lord Mayor Sir Robert McConnell.[36] But the story had not quite ended, for when nominations opened on January 7 for candidates to fill a number of vacant seats, Bowman's name was put forward – but for the Windsor ward in the south of the city.[37] His proposers, both old friends, were Thomas Adair, of Wellesley Avenue, and Joseph Cairns, of Dublin Road.[38] The two were doubtless well-intentioned, but they were acting without Bowman's approval, for he withdrew his name before the nominations closed two days later.

The other four councillors who had to seek re-election were initially joined by four more Belfast Trades Council-endorsed candidates: joiner William Walker (for Duncairn), compositor John Murphy (St. Anne's), iron turner Thomas Hughes (Smithfield) and tailor Daniel McDevitt (Falls). All were nominated in anticipation that agreement could be reached with the other parties. However, no agreement was achieved and, consequently, all six withdrew.[39] Alex Taylor also pulled out of the election following a row over his close ties with a contractor to the corporation.[40] In the knowledge that Robert Gageby was being returned unopposed in Shankill,[41] votes of confidence were passed for the remaining two contesting candidates, Murray Davis and Edward McInnes. There was success in low polls for both candidates.[42] However, the six seats it had gained in 1897 proved to be the trades council's best showing at any one time until 1920.[43]

THE IRISH TRADE UNION
CONGRESS YEARS

D ESPITE THE RENEWED hostility he was experiencing in Belfast trade union circles, Bowman's activities on the wider labour stage were leading him towards his career highpoint – serving as president at the 1901 Irish Trade Union Congress in Sligo. The Irish TUC, which first met in 1894, was born largely out of delegates' dissatisfaction with their impact when attending its British counterpart, a dissatisfaction heightened in 1895 by a bar imposed on trades council representatives.

Bowman had his earliest involvement with the Irish TUC in 1898 when the fifth annual meeting of delegates was held in the Exhibition Hall at Belfast's Botanic Gardens Park.[1] He would attend a total of four Congresses, representing both the Belfast Municipal Employees' and Other Workers' Association and the Flaxdressers' Union.[2]

Listed as a member of the reception committee for the Belfast Congress, Bowman's role was limited, although he was elected to serve on both the standing orders committee and, more importantly, the parliamentary committee. His tally of 52 votes was just 12 fewer than the 64 cast for the latter body's chairman, Derry tailor James McCarron. The eight successful candidates included Belfast Corporation colleagues Alex Taylor and Murray Davis.[3]

During a debate at Congress on labour in the flax industry, Bowman seconded a motion proposed by Belfast flax roughers' delegate John McParland that boys under the age of 18 should not be permitted to engage in flax roughing. Painting a grim picture of working conditions facing the flax-spinning industry, the same resolution called for the Factories and Workshops Acts to be amended 'so as to make it compulsory on all employers to heat by artificial means during the winter months all workshops or machine rooms where men or boys are engaged in the roughing, machining or sorting of flax.' The motion was passed after the delegates had considered the advisability of having steam pipes in the workshops lest the flax was in some way damaged.[4]

On the social side, Bowman helped to organise an excursion to Larne for a two-hour trip on board the mail steamer *Princess May* as far as Garron Point. On returning to the harbour the delegates travelled by brake to the King's Arms Hotel for dinner.[5] Following the close of the Congress some 100 delegates paid a visit to the fire station at Chichester Street where they were given a guided tour by superintendent George Parker.[6]

* * *

The following May Congress stayed north, with Derry's Guildhall serving as the venue. James McCarron was the unanimous choice for president, while Bowman was credited as being the main organiser.[7] Bowman played an active role in the Congress debates, winning support for a motion on the need for 'more-effective propaganda in the best interests of trade unionism in Ireland.' He urged Congress to pay more attention to the work of trades and promote organisation in each town where it met.[8]

The Guildhall was the venue on the second evening for a workers' rally, chaired by McCarron. One of the main addresses was given by Bowman who again called for better organisation among workers and the promotion of 'everything that makes for justice and righteousness.'

Not in Derry – Derry is but a provincial city; not in Ireland – Ireland is but a speck in the Western sea; not in Britain – Britain is but a combination of inconsiderable isles in which the sun of civilisation has been late in rising. Rather, we ask you to join with your fellows, whether black, white or yellow in colour, for the sake of humanity, whether they are pagans, Hindus, or Moslems, recognising the fact that political and religious distinctions are devices of your enemies.[9]

Despite Bowman's impassioned plea, the Derry Congress ended on a sour note, with Dublin Councillor William Leahy having to apologise with some reluctance for expressing anti-British sentiments at the closing banquet in the Guildhall.[10] Instead of the customary toast to the Queen's health, McCarron proposed the 'Prosperity of Ireland,' with the hope that 'all classes of our fellow countrymen will combine to work together for the welfare of our land.' While Bowman, in responding, confined his remarks to stating that the principal aim of Congress was to remove those obstacles which kept working men divided, Leahy declared – using words he could have borrowed from Bowman a dozen years earlier – that the union between Britain and Ireland had been secured by 'fraud and perjury.'

With several delegates protesting at the introduction of such a divisive issue, particularly at a celebratory banquet, the Congress president ruled Leahy out of order, noting that at trades council meetings in Derry they never allowed politics to be discussed. 'Cllr Leahy must remember that he is not speaking in Dublin, but in a different atmosphere,' said McCarron, 'and so he must cut his coat according to his cloth, so to speak.' Barely repentant, Leahy said he regretted 'having offended the sensibilities of any gentleman present, but I drink to the prosperity of Ireland and I wish her to be a nation.'

At the next meeting of Belfast Trades Council William Walker complained that delegates had given priority to the 'Irish Question' and no effort had been made to pursue 'anything practical to help trades unionism.'[11] He contended that unless Congress personnel were different the following year, the trades council's affiliation should be ended.

Bowman's trade union star rose still higher in 1900, when Lord Mayor Sir Thomas Pile welcomed delegates to Dublin's City Hall for their three-day gathering from 4 to 6 June.[12] Bowman was re-elected to serve a third consecutive term on the parliamentary committee.[13]

Consideration of the parliamentary committee's annual report led to a heated confrontation between Bowman and Walker and confirmed that the tensions were barely beneath the surface.[14] Walker branded the report as 'remarkable for its omissions.' There was no reference, he said, to his resolution – passed unanimously at the Derry Congress – to appoint a special committee to consider funding for an appeal to the House of Lords. The case, Quinn v. Leathem, had also been the subject of much discussion at meetings of Belfast Trades Council in the intervening period.[15]

The dispute, between the North of Ireland Operative Butchers' Society and Belfast flesher Henry Leathem, was raised at the Dublin Congress at the point when adequate subscriptions had already been raised, but not at the behest of the parliamentary committee. Walker proposed a new motion to the effect that its members were guilty of a 'grave dereliction of duty' in that they had failed to carry through the resolution apart from sending out a circular to which there had been no response. He went on to accuse the delegates of 'only coming together for a holiday and not to do business.'

Bowman, who had seconded Walker's Derry resolution, stepped into the fray and admitted that the parliamentary committee could not have pursued the matter without committing itself to considerable expenditure in terms of both time and money. When the costs towards the appeal were eventually lodged six weeks previously, he added, it had been only through the 'goodwill and friendship of a professional gentleman in Belfast.' Walker accused him of lying, which prompted Bowman to retort: 'I insist now, as a man who has a reputation in the trades union and labour world, that Mr Walker should say what statement I made is absolutely untrue.'

The row intensified with Walker making allegations about lodgment and withdrawal dates and calling on the parliamentary committee to produce bank-books to support his claims. Congress president George Leahy warned that the adoption of Walker's motion would be disastrous, amounting to a direct vote of censure on the parliamentary committee. In the resulting poll it was defeated by 61 votes to six.

Elsewhere during the Congress Bowman supported resolutions

calling for better safety measures for railwaymen, and, returning to a familiar theme, deploring rural depopulation.[16] The Dublin Congress closed with Bowman's re-election to the parliamentary committee.[17]

When the Quinn v. Leathem appeal was subsequently raised at a meeting that June of Belfast Trades Council, members faced complaints from butchers' representatives that 'criticisms of a very unfriendly kind had been passed upon their case.'[18] Accepting the point, a resolution was agreed unanimously by the trades council urging the butchers to 'prosecute their appeal.' The trades council also advised the butchers to affiliate with the British TUC and it was decided to print circulars for distribution to delegates attending the annual Congress, scheduled for Huddersfield in the first week of September. In July, to lend further support to the fight, Bowman and Walker were delegated to accompany butchers' representatives to the British Congress, Bowman on behalf of the Flaxdressers' Union and Walker on behalf of the trades council.[19] TUC records show that the 120-strong butchers' union joined by way of a £1 affiliation payment to the parliamentary committee. The newly-affiliated union was represented at the Huddersfield Congress by Belfast butcher John Sykes, of Ratcliffe Street.[20] At the trades council's next meeting Walker, Bowman and Sykes reported on the visit to Huddersfield and it was agreed that their canvass of delegates before the conference commenced had been fully justified and suitably productive, since the body had agreed to seek the support of general trades throughout the United Kingdom for the butchers' case.[21]

* * *

On 23 January 1901 Bowman led a delegation from the parliamentary committee to meet Chief Secretary George Wyndham at Dublin Castle.[22] The delegation covered a number of topics – outworking in the tailoring trade, a proposed Factories and Workshops bill, the Merchandise Marks Act, the Workmen's Compensation Act, the Plumbers' Registration bill, Housing of the Working Classes Acts, the establishment of a receiving depot for War Office contracts in Ireland, dangerous trades and sanitation, the appointment of female factory inspectors, the Workmen's Compensation Act as it affected railway workers, night work in bakehouses, and the operation of the fair wages clause in public contracts in Ireland.

Bowman, delegated to speak about dangerous trades and sanitation, claimed that as the law existed it was impossible to adequately supervise factories and workshops in Ireland. He referred from personal experience to trades which were 'not dangerous by reason of dangerous or unfenced machinery being employed, but because of the vegetable, textile or mineral dust generated.' Returning to familiar territory, he continued:

> Consumption, which is one of the most terrible scourges under which people groan, is largely occasioned by bad ventilation and the prevalence of dust where large bodies of men and women are compelled to work from morning till night. I do not want anything done to injure a trade already sufficiently handicapped, but where imperfect ventilation exists the inspector should be asked to exercise greater diligence in having it improved. We want additional zeal put forth, not by the inspectors, because they are doing all they can, but by the Administration in increasing the numbers of those officers. There is also a crying necessity for female inspectors, having regard to the fact that when bad sanitary conditions prevail, women are loath to complain except to members of their own sex. There is not one female inspector in Ireland, yet there are in Belfast alone between 50,000 and 60,000 women employed every day.

Wyndham, who, at the conclusion of the submissions complimented the delegates on the clear presentation of their case, assured them that while Ireland did not have its own Minister of Trade, his door as Chief Secretary was always open to them. Referring to Bowman's point about the dangers created by dust and other substances, Wyndham spoke of his own personal regret that it was difficult, even impossible, not to draw a distinction between accidents and injuries to health. He hoped that the success to date of the Workmen's Compensation Act would 'encourage statesmen in future to advance and apply the principles of that Act wherever they can be properly applied.'

The Chief Secretary also supported Bowman's call for female factory inspectors, saying he was aware of women being employed in that capacity in England. 'If there are none in Ireland, then the industries which employ a great number of women justify that concession,' added Wyndham.

When 75 Irish TUC delegates representing 52,000 workers next gathered for their three-day Congress – in Sligo Town Hall from Whit Monday, 27 May 1901 – Alexander Bowman was sole nominee for the presidency.[23] Sligo Trades Council president Patrick J. Farrell made the formal proposal, with local secretary Francis Gallagher seconding. The election of the representative from the Belfast Municipal Employees' and Other Workers' Association was unanimous.[24]

Bowman's presidential address has stood the test of time and if it contained a message drawn from his activities of 15 years earlier, it was that first and foremost they were Irishmen and that their country was one of which they could be justly proud.[25] He commenced by justifying the existence of Congress.

While their cross-channel counterparts had progressed to the point where they were campaigning for higher wage levels and the improvement of working conditions, the position in Ireland was very different. Bowman pointed out that the island's main industries were of an agricultural nature and that work was carried out under the 'most hampering and depressing' conditions. Textile, metal-working, shipbuilding and brewing trades, with their linked industries, he said, only furnished employment for an 'inconsiderable proportion of our people.'

However, he saw hope that a golden age lay before Ireland in the 'not too distant future' through the establishment of the new Department of Agriculture and Technical Instruction. The duty of Irish trade and labour unions, he declared, was to assist by every means in their power to create and establish Irish industries. Bowman continued:

> We, as workers, can do much to create, foster and stimulate in the minds of the young men and women of this country a desire for a complete technical training. When Young Ireland, thus trained, enters upon its life work it will do so with muscles more susceptible and faculties imbued, in some degree at least, with affection for its work. A people possessing the innate artistic and imaginative qualities of the Irish race, fitted by proper training, is quite certain to be able to render a good account of itself as artisans or as manufacturers. Thus shall Ireland cease to be the Cinderella of the nations and adopt the role of Mercury.

> We must ever bear in mind that no one of the all too many sections

into which the population of this country is divided has a monopoly on patriotism. Our people are so sharply divided by race, by religion, and by politics, that they have never been able, under present conditions, to make a really effective, hearty, and unanimous effort for the well-being of our common country. In trades unionism we have a platform broad enough and an ideal lofty enough for every Irishman.

He also issued an earnest plea to those many Irish people who chose to invest their wealth outside the island. 'Let us join hands,' Bowman declared: 'You have the capital, we the muscles and the skill, and by the judicious blending of the forces of Capital and Labour this land of ours, so long a reproach to Western civilisation, may – nay, shall – be made to blossom as the rose.'

Bowman pointed to the importation of millions of pounds worth of raw flax each year and claimed that with the proper training their own farmers and village workers could 'so treat the native flax that in fibre it would compare most favourably with the best we get from Belgium or Holland.'

He drew his presidential address to a close by urging the 'promotion of the health and vitality of our people' if they were to stand a fair chance in the markets of the world. If people were to enjoy good health, he said, they needed proper food, suitable clothing and sanitary dwellings.

Bowman concluded with four lines of verse written by the British poet Philip James Bailey:

We live in deeds, not years; in thoughts, not breaths;
In feelings, not in figures on a dial.
We should count time by heart-throbs. He most lives
Who thinks most, feels the noblest, acts the best.[26]

The second day of Congress saw delegates and local trade unionists, accompanied by the Mayor of Sligo, enjoying an excursion to Lissadell, home of Sir Josselyn Gore-Booth.[27]

Given his role as president of Congress, Bowman's participation in the normal cut and thrust of debate was restricted largely to ensuring that business ran smoothly. Nevertheless, he topped the poll for the eight-member parliamentary committee with 37 votes, while Walker narrowly failed to be elected with 19 votes.[28]

The Sligo Congress drew to a close with delegates backing a

vote of thanks proposed by Dublin delegate William Leahy, who referred to the 'brilliant' manner in which Bowman had discharged his duties. To mark the occasion Bowman was presented with the silver-plated order bell inscribed with his name. In the last important speech he would ever give, Bowman replied:

> I have some little experience of public affairs and I strove earnestly to prevent friction or the introduction of anything tending to defeat, but welcomed everything calculated to unite the workers of Ireland. If I succeeded, as your resolution induces me to believe I did, then I am satisfied.[29]

During the early summer months of 1901 Bowman fulfilled his usual work in connection with Belfast Trades Council. When it came, the ending of his 20-year association with the trade union movement was sudden. He chaired the council's meeting on 8 August – but never returned. His life as a trade unionist and socialist politician was over.[30]

A NEW LIFE ON THE FALLS ROAD

FOLLOWING HIS retirement from the corporation, and sorely in need of money, Bowman had resumed flaxdressing on a full-time basis with a move to the Edenderry Mill on the Crumlin Road.[1] He was then encouraged by friends, seemingly against his will, to submit an application for the vacant position of superintendent of the five-year-old Falls Road baths.[2]

Mounting disillusionment with local politics, particularly the ever-present hostility displayed by colleagues like William Walker, is one explanation for Bowman's decision to take such a drastic change of direction. An additional factor was the progress his own brother Hugh had been making – for by the turn of the century he was a master butcher with two shops to his name, one at Shankill Road and the other at Duncairn Street. A third would follow at Agnes Street and a fourth at Antrim Road.[3]

At the time of his marriage in 1885, and as recently as 1892, Hugh had been earning a living as a breadserver. By 1894 he was a bakery manager and by the end of the decade he was on his way to creating his own business empire as a butcher. While they worshipped at the same Cliftonville Presbyterian Church and their children attended the same school at Agnes Street, the brothers had little else in common. The younger man, who had few memories of his rural Co. Down background, was a Conservative and Unionist, and a freemason.

Hugh would father eight children. However, having a large family was not a source of any financial embarrassment to Alexander's brother. Rather, he enjoyed a measure of good fortune thanks to his wife's side of the family. There was always plenty of support for Hugh and Lizzie and when father-in-law George Blackwood died on 4 March 1901, Lizzie was a main beneficiary.

It is not hard to imagine the strong-willed Rose Bowman telling her husband that while she had always backed his endeavours, his friends were right – the time had now come to put his own family first. He had devoted more than 25 years to championing the rights of working people but had little to show for it but his pride. With Bowman already approaching his late forties it was time to lay down some permanent roots, especially as the Falls Road position offered a house for the superintendent and his family. Bowman applied for the job with some reluctance, little realising it would afford him another opportunity, albeit in a totally different way, to work for the good of the people.

The Falls Road post had fallen vacant following the death on 10 June 1901, of its first superintendent, Joseph Mitchell – president of the trades council at the time of the Home Rule controversy. At a meeting of the council's executive committee three days later, chaired by Bowman, a message of sympathy was expressed to Mitchell's family.[4] Bowman would have been aware that to seek the salaried managerial position would mean an end to his trade union membership, and, in light of the corporation's ruling against Edward de Cobain some 16 years earlier, a ban on any further active involvement in politics.

The chairman of the corporation's newly-created baths and lodging house committee was Robert Gageby, Bowman's long-time political and trade union colleague. One can only speculate on the role Gageby played in the appointment of the new pool superintendent but it could not have done Bowman any harm. It is also likely that because of Bowman's earlier and well-publicised views on Home Rule, his appointment would have gone down well with people living in the largely-Catholic Falls area.

The corporation's baths committee decided to fill vacancies at both the Falls Road and Ormeau Avenue baths with residential superintendents.[5] The previously-agreed salary for a superintendent was £100 per annum but, following the intervention of the full corporation, it was agreed that the starting salary for the two posts would be £80, rising in £5 increments over four years to £100.[6] Advertisements were placed in the daily papers inviting candidates to attend for interview on 22 August 1901.[7]

No fewer than 115 applications were received for the two positions. The Falls Road appointment was dealt with first and after the candidates had been reduced to six the final result saw Bowman securing 'the majority of votes.' The same procedure was followed for the Ormeau Avenue appointment, with the successful applicant being Bowman's old adversary Thomas Johnston, the former trades council vice-president who had branded him 'a Republican and one of the deepest dye' at a meeting in support of William Ewart in the run-up to the 1885 election.[8] It is not recorded in the baths and lodging house committee minutes if there were any strong objections to the appointment of the former labour councillor as Falls Road superintendent. The only hint came at the committee's next meeting when Gageby indicated that a notice of motion, submitted by committee member John McDonnell, had been withdrawn and would not be discussed.[9]

Belfast Trades Council minutes for the period following Bowman's sudden departure indicated no expressions of regret or otherwise. A meeting-by-meeting roll call for 1901 showed his attendances ceased from 8 August and the final mention of his name was in the minutes of the 1902 annual general meeting when it was reported that Bowman had been replaced by William Brown as a delegate of the Flaxdressers' Union. At the same meeting William Walker was elected president of the trades council.[10]

Bowman remained a member of the Irish Trade Union Congress's parliamentary committee for the year 1901-1902, his name appearing in the annual report for the 1902 Congress in Cork. The parliamentary committee described Bowman's absence as 'unavoidable' when members met John Redmond, leader of the reunited Nationalists, and other MPs from the Irish

Parliamentary Party at Dublin's Mansion House on 10 January 1902.[11]

If anyone gained from Bowman's departure it was William Walker, by then district secretary of the Amalgamated Society of Carpenters and Joiners. In 1904 he won Bowman's former Duncairn seat on the corporation. The following year he became the first candidate officially affiliated to the Labour Representation Committee – renamed the Labour Party from 1906 – to stand for parliament in Ireland. It was in Bowman's old North Belfast hunting ground and Ramsay MacDonald, secretary of the LRC, was his election agent. Walker lost out to Sir Daniel Dixon, then Lord Mayor, by 474 votes – polling 3,966 to the Conservative victor's 4,440.[12]

* * *

Relucant or not, Bowman accepted the job at the Falls Road baths and moved his family into the spacious accommodation at adjacent North Howard Street.[13] It was to become the family's ninth address at least inside six years – after a short spell with the McHenrys at 205 Tennent Street they had lived at nos. 24, 26 and 29 Upper Meenan Street. Then, on resuming full-time flaxdressing at the Edenderry Mill, the family lived at no fewer than three addresses in almost as many months: 25 Heather Street, 19 Fingal Street and 62 Bray Street, all within easy reach of the Crumlin Road.[14] At the baths his first monthly salary was £6. 13s. 4d., while the entire fortnightly wage bill rarely exceeded £15. 5s. 6d. It covered a fireman to heat the baths, the senior pool attendant, male and female attendants, and other ancillary staff.[15]

The new pool superintendent never gave anything but 100 per cent commitment to the post, which involved the baths being open seven days a week, including early morning opening on a Sunday.[16] He set about the task with the same zeal he had put into his earlier endeavours, introducing various well-received innovations at the pool. An early example was the conversion of one of the lesser-used pools at a cost of just £35 into a gymnasium and recreation room. He first put the idea to the baths and lodging house committee in September 1902.[17] Within a week the members had backed the proposal and it was agreed to purchase two sets of parallel bars, a vaulting horse, two dozen Indian clubs and two dozen dumb bells.[18]

The facility was officially opened at an impressive ceremony two months later. According to the *Belfast News-Letter* the gymnasium was the first of its kind in Belfast 'under municipal auspices and if the effort succeeds the other baths in the city might be similarly fitted up.'[19] The report continued: 'One penny will be charged for admission, entitling the visitor to the use of all the appliances, and Mr George McCreedy, who is a well-known gymnast, has kindly consented to attend on a number of evenings during the week in order to give instruction.'

As well as making use of an otherwise disused pool in the winter months, committee chairman Gageby declared that the corporation was providing 'healthy, useful, profitable and pleasing recreation' in the form of a reading room.

In October 1904 the *Ireland's Saturday Night* newspaper reported on the display which had formally inaugurated the new gymnastics season at Falls Road. The report again highlighted Bowman's role, saying he had introduced:

> ... some important and valued innovations, which have extended the benefits to be derived from the institution. Until a few years ago the swimming pools were practically deserted during the winter months – a regrettable fact, having regard to the circumstance that the building and site cost a sum of nearly £16,000. Now they are in constant use by all sorts of swimming and athletic clubs, the members of which number over 1,000 regular and enthusiastic patrons. Any amount from 1,000 to 1,500 persons use the baths and gymnasium weekly; and the gymnasium area was used by about 8,000 last winter. The first class swimming bath, which is open throughout the winter, has a spacious pond and is kept in splendid condition, the water being perfectly pure and crystal clear.[20]

During the course of the evening the Woodvale gymnastics team, assisted by Sgt Major Leggett, instructor at the Victoria Barracks, gave an exhibition of work on the parallel bars, rings and horizontal bars. Two clown gymnasts, alias Jack Coulter and Sgt McMullen of the Royal Irish Rifles, provided more of the evening's entertainment and 'evoked considerable merriment.' In addition there was a musical programme.

Hearty thanks to the Lord Mayor and the many contributors to the programme were accorded on the proposal of superintendent Bowman – a far cry from the resolutions he had once put before the trades council and corporation, yet the pool was without doubt a source of immense pride to him. By May 1906 he was able to report that annual receipts had risen from £348 to £529 since 1902 and that numbers using the pool and its facilities each year had risen from 38,750 to 74,946.[21] Among the reasons given for the increase in usage was Bowman's contact with local schools, including Clifton Park National School, which led to children attending the pool for swimming lessons.[22] In addition, he was able to draw on his old contacts in the flax trade to encourage employers to send their young half-time workers to the pool to enjoy the baths at schoolboy rates. Those taking advantage of the scheme included Messrs Greeves and Co., the New Northern Spinning Company and the Falls Flax Spinning Company, with Greeves and Co. sending along 300 children every fortnight.[23] So great were the numbers – since for many it was the only proper access they had to a bath – that Bowman was forced to scrap a plan to convert one of the pools into a skating rink.[24]

It was not all plain sailing for the superintendent and in September 1907 he had to report to the baths committee that the gymnastics instructor, ex-Sgt Gregg of the Royal Irish Rifles, had been suspended for being under the influence of alcohol on several occasions.[25] The instructor resigned from the position in December and was replaced by John French.[26]

In February 1908 Bowman put forward a plan for the reading room which had fallen into disuse following the opening of a new Carnegie Library on the Falls Road. An earlier suggestion put to the committee was to allow workers from Greeves to use the room as a creche but Bowman had a better idea. He proposed the installation of new Lassar-type individual baths, describing them as 'the last word in regards to baths at this moment.'[27] He told councillors they were cheaper to fit, more economical to use, requiring less than half the normal quantity of water, and 'beyond comparison more sanitary.' Committee members liked the idea and agreed to set aside £250 for the scheme which included two small dressing rooms for each of the five Lassar baths. Bowman also suggested that representatives from the local mills should be invited along to the opening to see the advantages for themselves. So impressed were the committee members with the whole idea that they instructed their superintendent to visit Manchester and Liverpool to see the working of Lassar and other baths in newly-opened pool complexes there.[28] The new facility was opened in September and proved an immediate success.[29]

During the summer of 1908 Bowman's style of management came under close scrutiny after partiality charges were levelled against him by some of his staff. He requested that a sub-committee be appointed to enquire into the matter and three members, Cllrs John Shaw and Michael McKeown, along with Alderman George Doran, met to consider the claims.[30] Bowman's accusers were questioned and admitted their allegations were groundless. After apologising to the committee members and the superintendent the staff members were told they 'must be loyal and respectful to the superintendent and acknowledge his authority and position in the establishment in the future.'

The following Spring Bowman, with an eye to matters of hygiene, drew councillors' attention to the 'necessity for some provision for children cleansing their bodies before entering the swimming ponds.' However, they baulked at the expense involved in providing footbaths and, instead, instructed Bowman to arrange for bathers to use the Lassar baths before entering the pools. He did not give up on the idea and the committee agreed to spend £5. 15s. on the installation of five copper footsprays.[31]

In that same year, 1909, Bowman's efforts on behalf of the amateur swimming fraternity in Ulster were acknowledged when he was elected president of the Irish Amateur Swimming Association, having held the same position with the Ulster Swimming Council.[32] The post was rotated around the four provinces and that year the honour fell to Ulster. He undertook his presidential duties with typical dedication. His Falls Road responsibilities were not ignored and in an effort to make better use of the complex in the winter months it was agreed that the larger of the two pools should be covered over for use as a gymnasium.[33] Not only did it save the corporation money on the heating bill but it also created more space for new equipment.

The effect was immediate for between January and March of 1910 Bowman was able to report the continuing successes of the Falls Baths team over squads from the YMCA, McQuiston

Memorial Church and City of Belfast – the latter victory by the slimmest margin, just one-third of a point, securing the coveted Junior Shield in the annual competition run by the Ulster Gymnastics Association.[34] Members of the baths committee expressed delight at the Falls Road team's success and commended the efforts of gymnastics instructor John Conway and the superintendent. They also agreed during February to increase Bowman's annual salary to £110, rising in two £5 stages.[35]

In August 1910, in an echo back to Bowman's days in Glasgow, Messrs W. & J. Avery Ltd. complained to the corporation that when their representative called at the Falls Road baths to empty the penny-in-the-slot machine, he found the door was open and there were just seven pennies in the money bag. The committee instructed Bowman to see in future that a careful watch was kept over the apparatus.[36]

Bowman faced his first major crisis in 1912 when councillors, having had their attention drawn to the pool's by then declining income, decided that the chairman, vice-chairman and three members should meet in special session and report back as to the probable cause and on the future running of the baths.[37] Their concern was over figures which showed that income for the year ending on 10 August stood at £229. 12s. 8d. compared to £341. 7s. 5d. for the same period the previous year. Bowman showed the councillors a usage table for the previous 12 years and they went away satisfied that there was 'no special cause for the present circumstances.' The matter quickly passed and Bowman, enjoying a new salary of £120,[38] was able to report the following year that takings had steadily improved – income for the year ending November 1913 stood at £449. 0s. 5d.[39]

The advent of the First World War heralded few opportunities for change at the baths. An order from the corporation to halt all expenditure for the remainder of the 1915/16 financial year 'which it is possible to stop without injuriously affecting public health or otherwise seriously prejudicing public interests,' linked with the payment of war bonuses to all employees earning under 30/- a week, saw to that. There were no more warm baths for a penny on Thursdays, while a decision by the committee to increase some charges angered local clubs as well as the Ulster Council of the

Irish Amateur Swimming Association.[40]

Early in 1915 it was agreed that provision would be made for soldiers to use the pools and an instruction went out from Belfast Corporation that all its facilities would close between 1.30pm and 5pm on 8 May during the march-past of the 36th (Ulster) Division. Fourteen months later thousands of those volunteers would die at the Somme.[41] Staffing problems were created by corporation workers joining the forces but, in general, life at the pool carried on much as normal. In October 1917 the St Peter's Swimming Club was granted free use of the pool to hold a gala the following month to raise funds for the city's Mater Infirmorum Hospital – but the decision was 'not to be taken as a precedent for similar applications.'[42]

The end of the war, rather than bringing with it continued austerity, saw Bowman earning a quite substantial salary – his annual income was £130 by 1919, rising the following year to £150 and being supplemented by a bonus of £88. 12s. 0d.[43] Takings at the pool were also climbing – but not for long. In 1919 they reached £1,143. 18s. 2d., but fell back the following year to £913. 15s. 10d. The drop in income was linked to the turbulent state of the city in the months leading up to the creation of Northern Ireland. In December 1920 the baths committee decided that in view of the great reduction in the number of users they would have to dispense with the services of four members of staff (out of nine), although every effort was promised to find them alternative employment with the corporation.[44]

The following June acting superintendent Richard Ferguson – Bowman was taking his annual fortnight's leave – reported that he had found it necessary to close the baths early for three days running 'owing to disturbances in the neighbourhood.'[45] Dozens of people lost their lives in the sectarian violence which flared up that summer and beyond.[46] Committee chairman David Thompson, also mindful of the continuing drop in takings, reacted by ordering that the baths should be shut and the staff were given one week's notice. Horrified local residents successfully petitioned the committee to reconsider its decision and the employees were immediately reinstated.[47] Things began to look a little brighter for the pool and early in 1922 Bowman was able to report that

3,093 swimmers' tickets had been issued for the three months ending on 28 January compared to just 650 for the corresponding period the previous year.[48]

It was the lull before the storm for during 1922 hundreds more died as a result of 'The Troubles.' In March matters hit home when Bowman reported that three armed men had entered the ticket office and robbed staff of 10/- from the cash drawer.[49] Later that same month the committee again had to order the closure of the pool 'in view of the disturbed state of the district and the intimidation of members of staff.'[50] Although the move was backed by the full corporation when it met on 3 April, it remained open until 22 June when the complex was commandeered by the Royal Ulster Constabulary under the Civil Authorities (Special Powers) Act of 1922.[51]

It was agreed that the staff – fireman, two male pool attendants, gym instructor, baths attendant, ticket clerk, female attendant and two laundresses – would be placed on one week's notice and that the committee would 'endeavour to utilise their services elsewhere for holiday relief.' The corporation did not regain possession of the baths until 7 November 1922, and they did not reopen the facility until 12 days later. By then Bowman had already retired with Richard Ferguson replacing him as temporary supervisor.[52]

THE CHURCH CONNECTION

DURING HIS YEARS as an employee of the corporation Bowman proved a faithful and very active member of Donegall Road Presbyterian Church. He and Rose had previously worshipped at Argyle Place (up to 1883), Donegall Street (up to 1885), Cliftonville (1885-88), Whiteinch and Walthamstow (1888 to 1895), and Cliftonville again (up to 1903).

Bowman's minister at Cliftonville, the Rev. George Magill, tendered his resignation in 1902 and the church had no minister until the installation of the Rev. George Thompson in May 1903.[1] In the intervening period and subsequently the Bowmans worshipped at Donegall Road. Not only was it considerably nearer, but members of Rose's family also attended the church, as did Alex Boyd, Bowman's successor as organiser for the municipal employees and a future member of Belfast Corporation.[2] Bowman's name appeared on the communicants' roll from November 1903, with Rose following in February 1904.[3]

Bowman immersed himself in church work from the outset. Within months of joining the congregation he was asked to attend a committee meeting to outline a scheme he had devised to help liquidate the church's debt. It involved dividing the congregation into five districts with one elder and three or four members of the committee being delegated to each area to undertake a systematic collection. The idea was eventually adopted and Bowman himself was allocated the area from the 'New Bridge along Roden Street, including the streets off same, as far as the river; right hand side of the street to Excise Street, along same and Distillery Street, and back to Donegall Road.' He was assisted by elder Archibald Irwin and Messrs James Coulter, Robert McBride and William Weir.[4]

Bowman, who by then had joined the committee, also played a major part in the negotiations in 1904 to acquire the nearby Elmwood Church mission hall.[5] He also actively involved himself in a number of fundraising efforts for the church. They included a four-day 'grand united church extension bazaar,' held from 15 to 18 November 1905, at the then newly-opened Assembly Buildings in Fisherwick Place.[6] The idea behind the bazaar, originally planned for 1904 but delayed because the building work had not been completed, was to assist those Belfast congregations which needed help to build new churches or to clear existing debts.

The Presbyterian Church's extension committee approved a proposal to hold the bazaar which was declared open by the Countess of Aberdeen.[7] The participating congregations included Donegall Road, Broadway, Castleton, Woodvale, Bloomfield, Oldpark, Ulsterville and Cregagh,[8] all of which were described by the *Belfast News-Letter* as 'young and vigorous but still labouring under the burden of debt amounting in the aggregate to about £10,000.' With wife Rose helping at the Donegall Road stall, Bowman was keen to see every family in the congregation contributing towards the bazaar. A special souvenir booklet was published, with Bowman serving on the organising committee.[9]

According to the booklet, the main hall of the Assembly Buildings was ringed by stalls representing the eight congregations, while those of the assisting congregations occupied the centre of the hall and the front of the platform. The corridor on the Fisherwick Place side was set aside for archery, and the opposite corridor featured a rifle range. An air gun range was to be found in the corridor behind the Moderator's chair, while the refreshment stall was in the dispatch office and part of the main lobby. The waiting room was used for missionary exhibits and limelight views, as well as a missionary peepshow.

On the second floor the minor hall was used for national exhibitions. On the first day it represented Irish peasant life with an Irish cottage and features usually associated with an Irish fair, together with songs and dances. The next day it was a Scottish showpiece, the room being decorated to represent an old baronial hall in the time of Robert the Bruce, with pipers and knights and ladies with pipes and reels. The following day the theme was 'National Sports of the Three Kingdoms' – England, Ireland and Scotland – while on the final day the Anglo-Japanese Alliance was depicted with 'living pictures of the English colonies and a tug-o-war between Japan and England,' the emphasis being placed on the 'naval excellence of both nations.'

The bazaar was so successful that the admission charge had to be increased to curb numbers, thereby raising a substantial sum for the various participating congregations.

Although Bowman was no longer involved actively in politics, he spoke on the subject of socialism in Bethany Presbyterian Church at Agnes Street in 1906.[10] It was at a time when a number of clergymen were taking a keen interest in social issues as they affected their parishioners. The minister at Bethany, the Rev. Samuel Simms, was renowned as a fearless advocate of temperance and Christian standards in daily life.[11] There is nothing to suggest that Bowman was doing anything other than that which he had always done well – debating a subject he understood before an audience. He might well have missed the cut and thrust of the debating chamber at city hall or the trades council, but the evidence points to a man quite content with his new life at the Falls Road baths and an ever-deepening involvement with church work.

While the Assembly Buildings bazaar had proved a great success, Bowman's call for a repeat at the same venue in 1909 failed to win the support of his church.[12] Nevertheless, efforts to wipe out the Donegall Road debt continued apace, with a two-day sale of work being staged on 8/9 December 1911.

Bowman was one of nine ordained as elders on 27 March 1912, at a service in the Shankill Road Mission Hall conducted by the Rev. Dr William McKean, minister of 1st Ballymacarrett.[13] That same year he represented the 500 families of the Donegall Road congregation at the Presbyterian General Assembly.[14]

At a Donegall Road committee meeting in May 1913, it was agreed without dissent that a memorial against Home Rule – to be presented at that year's Assembly – would be referred to the congregation from the pulpit on the following two Sundays and that all members of the church aged over 16 would be invited to sign a copy if they so wished.[15] If Bowman still had views on Home Rule, he kept them to himself.[16]

As he grew older Bowman's health deteriorated but he still served the church in a number of ways, helping with the choir, of which fourth son Thomas was a member, and the Sunday School, assisting with fundraising through the collection of stipends and as a member of the pew committee, as well as overseeing repairs to the church buildings. He often took the chair for committee meetings in the absence of his minister, the Rev. John McIlrath, and in the early months of 1920 he helped to bring about the union of Donegall Road with Fountainville after the latter had been destroyed in a fire.[17] He was also briefly on the committee of the newly-named Richview Presbyterian Church.[18]

Alexander and Rose Bowman, by then 67 and 68 respectively, were admitted by certificate to once again receive communion at Argyle Place in April 1921.[19] Not only did it represent the completing of the circle for the couple, who were returning to their earliest roots in the city, it was much nearer the swimming pool and the move reflected Bowman's increasing infirmity.

FINAL DAYS AND THE
NEXT GENERATION

BOWMAN HAD held the Falls Baths position for 21 years when he decided it was time to retire. He was 68 and his health had deteriorated. In early June 1922 he forwarded a medical certificate to the baths and lodging house committee which indicated he was suffering from the nervous condition neurasthenia. Committee members were sympathetic and granted him leave of absence on full salary.[1] It was while he was off sick that the RUC commandeered the baths and enforced its closure. At the end of July he formally resigned with effect from 31 August.[2]

Two weeks later it was agreed that Bowman should be accorded a retirement pension of £191. 17s. 5d. a year (£15. 19s. 9d. a month), representing two-thirds of his salary including allowances which by then stood at £287. 16s. 2d.[3]

He and Rose resided for a short time with son Hugh and his family at 65 Rushfield Avenue, off the Ormeau Road, but then moved to Black Hill, outside Carrickfergus, to help youngest son Charles run a chicken farm.[4] Like his father, however, the young man was in failing health and died on 8 March 1923. It was a terrible blow for Alexander and Rose who returned to Rushfield Avenue, Hugh and his family having moved to

Dufferin Avenue in Bangor, Co. Down. It was in that small terraced-house in the city that Alexander Bowman succumbed to bronchitis and heart disease on Monday, 3 November 1924. Members of his family were present, including son William who added his signature to the death certificate.[5] He gave his father's age as 68 while the *Northern Whig* reported he was 72.[6] In fact, Bowman was 70.

Two days later Bowman was buried in Victoria cemetery, Carrickfergus, following a service conducted by the Revs. John McIlrath and Robert Anderson at Cooke Centenary Presbyterian Church on Belfast's Ormeau Road. During the final 18 months of his life Bowman had found it more convenient to attend Cooke church. He had become a communicant in 1923 and attended his final communion service in October 1924.[7] The funeral was private but a number of his friends from public and private life were there to pay their final respects. In the newspaper obituary,[8] he was described as 'a one-time well-known trade unionist and a former member of the Belfast City Council in the Labour interest.' The report recalled his presidency of Congress, municipal employment, and church connections and, almost as an afterthought, proffered an eight-word sentence: 'In later life Mr Bowman was a Unionist.' It was probably inserted by his family to avoid any potentially embarrassing references to his past sympathies for the nationalist cause, particularly at a time when community tensions were still high in Northern Ireland. While he might not have termed himself an Ulster Unionist, Bowman had almost certainly abandoned his earlier Liberalism, Nationalism, and radical Socialism.

The *Ireland's Saturday Night* carried a warm tribute in its swimming notes, referring to Alexander Bowman's time 'a good many years ago' when he had served as president of the Irish Amateur Swimming Association.[9]

The same edition reported that at a meeting of the Ulster Swimming Council, held on the day Bowman died, Samuel Doak, the president, recalled Bowman's services to the body and to swimming in general through his work at the Falls Road baths. His proposal that a message of condolence be sent to the bereaved relatives was passed 'in respectful silence.'

There were tributes also from the Richview (formerly Donegall

Road) Kirk Session, and from Belfast Corporation's baths and lodging house committee.[10] The committee sanctioned the payment of £1. 12s. 0d. to his estate – the final pension sum for the first few days of November.[11] Alexander Bowman's total estate amounted to £283. 3s. 5d., a further commentary on his life of service for others. In his will, made on 24 June 1920, he left everything to Rose.[12]

When the British TUC returned to Belfast for its annual Congress in September 1929, tribute was paid to the efforts of the city's early trade unionists, including Bowman. A souvenir booklet, published to mark the gathering in the Grosvenor Hall, recalled the heady days of 1885 thus:

> The late Mr Alex. Bowman was the candidate for North Belfast, his opponent being the late Sir William Ewart. Labour was defeated at the polls, but this contest was the beginning of good propaganda work carried on for many years by a small but enthusiastic band of workers.[13]

As a final political footnote, Bowman had lived long enough to witness the formation, on 22 January 1924, of Britain's first Labour government, with James Ramsay MacDonald as Prime Minister. MacDonald, who led a minority administration, tendered his resignation on 4 November of that same year – the day after Bowman's death.[14]

* * *

Rose and Alexander – known to his grandchildren as 'Fanter' – had five sons and a daughter: William James (born 6 August 1881), Robert Ritchie (10 September 1883), Minnie Grimmett (9 August 1885), Hugh (5 November 1887), Thomas Rodgers (19 May 1892) and Charles Edward (16 January 1895).

William attended school in Belfast (St Paul's), Glasgow (Whiteinch), Belfast again (Argyle Place) and Walthamstow (Markhouse Road). His first employment was with a cheesemonger and provision store in Walthamstow. On returning to Belfast in 1895 there was no question of him going back to school because of the precarious state of the family's finances. After a number of jobs around the city his father helped him to secure a position with the surveyor's department of Belfast Corporation. After almost 42 years of service he retired on 31 October 1941, and died in 1958. He had married Millie (née Roberts) in 1907 and they had five children – Alexander, Frederick Roberts, Robert Ritchie, Millicent and Elizabeth Eleanor.

R. R. Bowman, who attended the same four schools as William, began his working life at the age of 11 with a part-time job in a Walthamstow shop. Back in Belfast, his father helped him to gain an apprenticeship with coachbuilder Frank Johnston, the former secretary of Belfast Trades Council who had served on the corporation at the same time as Alexander Bowman. R. R. later took advantage of an opportunity, available through his trade union membership, to sit for a scholarship to Ruskin College, Oxford. He had attended night classes and spent many hours after work with a retired school principal making up for lost time in the classroom. He secured first place at the second attempt and spent two academic years at Oxford. In 1911, at the end of the second year, R. R. became the first Irishman to sit for the Oxford University Diploma in Economics and Political Science, achieving three A-pluses and two As, said then to be a record.

He gained a position with the Ministry of Labour's divisional office in Dublin. Between 1914 and 1919 he was manager of the Belfast Employment Exchange and in 1920 he was appointed secretary of the Irish Trade Boards. The new Northern Ireland government sought his services as a principal officer under the Minister of Labour. After three years R. R. became assistant secretary in charge of the administration of unemployment assurances, industrial relations, Factory Acts and the instruction of unemployed juveniles. From 1932 he was Northern Ireland representative on the International Labour Committee set up by the imperial government. Following the death in November 1939 of the Permanent Secretary, Major Hamilton Conacher, he was selected to fill the position, and retired in 1949 – three years after receiving the CBE from King George VI during a visit to Belfast.

R.R., who married Margaret (née Page) in 1913 and had no children, was renowned following his retirement for his horticultural expertise. When he died in 1970 he was the last surviving child of Alexander and Rose Bowman.

Daughter Minnie Grimmett received her schooling at Whiteinch Primary, Argyle Place, Markhouse Road and Agnes Street schools.

As a young woman she made full use of the facilities at the Falls Road baths, enjoying swimming and gymnastics.[15] She married John Alexander Howard on Christmas Day 1911 and they had two children, Rosemary Grimmett and John Alexander junior. Howard was in the Merchant Navy and served with it during the First World War. He rose to be chief engineer with the Head Line, operating from Belfast, and then left the sea in April 1918 to work as an aeronautical inspector with the city's fledging aircraft industry.[16] The family lived at Norfolk Drive off the Glen Road until the troubles started in 1919/20. To protect their homes from nationalist efforts to evict them, Protestant men patrolled Norfolk Drive – some with revolvers kept after the war, and John Alexander Howard with Indian clubs borrowed from the Falls Road baths.

In spite of such measures the family, under threat of being burned out, quit their home at 24 hours' notice, and found themselves compelled to change houses with a Catholic family living in a Protestant area. In 1925 they moved to Dunmurry, five miles from Belfast, where Minnie continued to reside until her death in 1968, her husband having predeceased her in 1956.

Third son Hugh, who received his early schooling at Markhouse Road and Agnes Street, sat the civil service entrance examination and was posted to the Ministry of Labour in Dublin, serving there until 1913. He was then sent north to the Shankill Road Labour Exchange where he held the post of assistant manager. When the Ministry of Munitions was formed during the 1914-18 war, a call went out to all labour exchanges, seeking officers with engineering experience. Hugh crossed to London, was put in charge of a section and was later appointed inspector of construction of war factories. For his work in the ministry he was awarded the MBE.

On returning to Ireland he was again posted to the Ministry of Labour. After his brother became assistant secretary of that department it was not considered advisable to have two brothers in the same ministry, so Hugh was transferred to the Ministry of Education and later the Ministry of Agriculture where he was assistant principal officer until his retirement. Outside his working life he was co-opted onto Bangor Borough Council and was a founding director of Bangor Football Club. Hugh, who died in 1965, was married to Annie (née McAreavey) on Boxing Day

1912. They had four sons and two daughters – Eric, Geoffrey, Hugh junior, Edgar, Helen and Rosaleen.[17]

Fourth son Thomas was born in Belfast during the time spent there before the family moved to Walthamstow. After spells with Harland and Wolff in Belfast and Southampton, John Brown at Clydebank and at one of the east coast ports in England, he emigrated to the United States in 1923. Tommy found employment with a shipyard at New London, Connecticut. During the Depression things were at their bleakest financially, but he managed to find work as a labourer to a carpenter repairing the fish holds on a wharf owned by a New England company with a fleet of trawlers.

When the trawlers arrived for overhaul he was put to work on the engines and gave such satisfactory service that he was eventually appointed assistant marine supervisor at the company's headquarters in Boston. He saw out his working career at the Boston Naval Yard. In the late 1920s he had become an American citizen and in July 1935, at the Second Congregational Church of New London, Tommy married Dorothy (née Little), who was part-descended from American Indians. They had no family and Tommy died in May 1964.[18]

Charles was born in London and educated in Belfast. In his late teens he joined the corporation's works department, remaining there until failing health compelled him to quit. After a spell of recuperation he successfully competed for a scholarship at Dublin's Royal Albert College (Agriculture and Botany). Influenza was rife when the first year examinations at the college were in progress. Charles fell victim and its ravages undermined his constitution. Although he attempted to regain his health by running the chicken farm at Black Hill, outside Carrickfergus, he died in 1923, aged just 28. He had never married.

Alexander Bowman's widow Rose lived on at 65 Rushfield Avenue until 1939 when she joined daughter Minnie Howard in Dunmurry. After the war she went to Bangor to stay with son Hugh at Bryansburn Road and was subsequently admitted to hospital. When she passed away on 1 October 1947, Rose was just two days short of her 95th birthday.

Although financial pressures had ultimately brought Alexander

Bowman's political career to a premature end, he merits his place in Irish history as the island's pioneering labour parliamentary candidate, as one of the first wave of non-party political working-class local government representatives, and as the leader of 52,000 workers when he presided over the Irish Trade Union Congress. Patrick McKeown, his true name, sought little if anything for himself, preferring to struggle for the betterment of others, often at great personal cost. His role in the early development of trade union and labour politics in Belfast and elsewhere in the United Kingdom has been somewhat overlooked with the passage of time. The purpose of this book has been to ensure that, unlike so many of his Victorian contemporaries, Alexander Bowman's name will not be forgotten and to testify to his worth as a ...People's Champion.

NOTES

THE McKEOWN BOY FROM DERRY, DROMARA

1 The most detailed profile appeared in the *Belfast Evening Telegraph* (hereafter *BET*) on 20 December 1897, following Bowman's election to Belfast Corporation three weeks earlier. It included a sketch drawing. The paper's name changed to the *Belfast Telegraph* in 1918.

2 General Register Office, Dublin, for complete version of marriage certificate from Eglinton Presbyterian Church, Belfast. The microfilmed copy at the Public Record Office of Northern Ireland (hereafter PRONI), MIC/1P/40, does not include vital additional comments by the minister.

3 National Archives, Dublin, for 1911 census returns for Belfast.

4 See the *Belfast News-Letter* (hereafter *BNL*), 13 March 1954.

5 See *History of Congregations in the Presbyterian Church in Ireland*, no author cited, Presbyterian Historical Society of Ireland (Belfast 1982),

p.125. Argyle Place Presbyterian Church records courtesy of West Kirk Presbyterian Church.

6 *Belfast and Province of Ulster Directory* (hereafter *Belfast Directory*), 1854-55, pp.609-610. See also the section on the Parish of Dromara in Angelique Day and Patrick McWilliams, *O.S. Memoirs* (*Mid Down*) (Belfast 1992), pp.62-69.

7 See PRONI, *Primary Valuation of Ireland* (hereafter Griffith), Lisburn Union, Co. Down (Dublin, 1863), pp.38-39.

8 PRONI, *Census of Ireland for the Year 1861* (Dublin 1863), p.167.

9 Griffith, Lisburn Union, Co. Down, pp.38-39. The rateable valuation of Patrick's property was £9, while William's was £4. 15s.

10 Ordnance Survey map for 1834, PRONI, OS/6/3/29/1, shows a single dwelling on the land later held by William McKeown. It also features on the map used by Griffith, PRONI,

VAL/2A/3/29A. However, the 1931 revision, PRONI, OS/6/3/29/4, shows the house to have been demolished.

11 *Census of Ireland for the Year 1861*, p.176, shows that Burren's population in 1861 stood at 460 in 85 dwellings, a reduction from 509 people a decade earlier.

12 Tithe applotment books for the Derry townland, dated 1 November 1826, PRONI, FIN/5A/112, pp. 13-15, show that Patrick McKeown farmed six acres of land and paid an annual tithe of 8/4d. The records for Burren townland, PRONI, FIN/5A/112, p.5, include James and Bernard McKeown, hence the conclusion that the three were descended from the Patrick McKeown buried in the Dromara parish graveyard.

13 Records for St Michael's Church, Dromara, for the period 1844-1920, are PRONI, MIC/1D/24; also CR/2/3 (baptisms only).

14 General Register Office, Dublin, for copy of civil marriage certificate. The original register is held by Lisburn Borough Council, Co. Antrim.

15 Baptismal records for December 1845, April 1847 and October 1851, PRONI, MIC/1D/24, identify William McKeown as sponsor for three neighbouring children, indicating St. Michael's to have been his church. The absence of earlier records prevents any examination of his church activities prior to 1844.

16 The decision not to baptise Hugh in the Catholic faith could well have followed the death of the senior Patrick McKeown. His death could also have prompted the gradual introduction of the name Alexander for the older boy. See also note 24.

17 Census returns for Glasgow, 1891, at Mitchell Library, Glasgow.

18 Queen's University, Belfast, British Parliamentary Papers (hereafter BPP), Belfast Constabulary Bill (1887) x., pp.693-862.

19 Belfast City Hall, Register of Births, Marriages and Deaths.

20 *Northern Whig* (hereafter *NW*) and *BNL*, 4 November 1924.

21 Bowman's birthday was recorded as 16 March in a diary kept by his daughter, Minnie.

22 General Register Office, Dublin. William McKeown's death certificate reveals that he died from a tuberculated liver, a cancerous condition he had suffered over a number of months, coupled with the onset of jaundice in the final weeks. His death occurred at Derry, Dromara, in the presence of his wife and was registered by her at the Annahilt office of the Lisburn Union six days later.

23 BPP, Belfast Constabulary Bill (1887) x., pp.693-862. Bowman cited 1865 as the year he arrived in Belfast. He stated: 'I have been living there since 1865; twenty-two-and-a-half years.' As the date of his appearance at Westminster was 13 August, one can calculate that the family's departure from Dromara occurred within days or weeks of McKeown's death.

24 McKeown's father Patrick must have predeceased him, there being no record of his death in the post-1864 registers. Burial records for St Michael's Church, PRONI, MIC/1D/24, show that no McKeowns were buried there, leading to the conclusion that the family plot was within the Catholic section of Dromara's parish graveyard. There is a gravestone there for a William McKeown, but inscriptions indicate he was a prominent local Orangeman.

25 Staff at the Banbridge Heritage Development Company have

painstakingly compiled a record on computer of births, marriages and deaths registered by churches within the general Banbridge district, in some cases dating back to the 1700s. In addition to those records, the office also holds details for Loughaghery Presbyterian Church, Co. Down. Loughaghery records are also at PRONI, CR/3/8/1.

26 If John Bowman's middle initial 'A,' which appears in his baptismal record, stood for Alexander, it follows that it was a likely source of the new name given to young Patrick McKeown. Alternatively, one of his mother's cousins, baptised Betty Rogers in 1808, married an Alexander Bothwell and their first-born was also christened Alexander.

27 Elizabeth Rogers' parents, William and Jane (nee Steel), both probably born in the 1780s, were married at Loughaghery Church on 22 December 1805. This is the oldest confirmed date of any family link to Alexander Bowman.

28 Author's conclusion. PRONI, FIN/ 5A/112, pp. 13-15, as well as identifying Patrick McKeown as a Derry farmer, also name a 'Widow Bowman' as having a four-acre holding in 1826. The suggestion that the land was taken over by the McKeowns is based on the increased size of the McKeown farm and the absence of any Bowman tenants in Derry by the time the Griffith valuation was compiled.

29 Various editions of the *Belfast Directory* show Bowmans living in the general Shankill area. See also PRONI, MIC/1P/89, First Dromara Presbyterian Church, and MIC/1P/ 393, Second Dromara Presbyterian Church, which mention several Ro(d)gers with Belfast addresses in burial records.

30 The author believes that William Bowman, variously listed as a storekeeper and a labourer, who lived at Cambrai Street (linking the Shankill and Crumlin Roads) from the late 1860s, was Alexander Bowman's eldest half-brother. After his marriage to Mary Swindle in Clifton Street Presbyterian Church in 1872, William Bowman moved to adjacent Tennent Street, where near neighbours were the Blackwoods – including Hugh's future wife Lizzie. William and Mary Bowman's first child, born on 5 September 1873, was christened Eliza at Argyle Place Presbyterian Church by the Rev. Lamont Hutchinson.

31 There is a lingering mystery over the absence of any baptismal record for Hugh although there is little doubt he was the youngest child of William and Elizabeth McKeown.

32 See PRONI, MIC/1P/394, Cliftonville Presbyterian Church.

33 *Ibid.*, 1892. The misspelling of son Thomas's middle name as 'Rodgers' can be blamed on Bowman's absence due to work commitments in London. A date of death for Alexander and Hugh's mother Elizabeth has proved elusive.

34 Hugh Bowman's wife Lizzie was one of eight children of Belfast grocer George Blackwood and his wife Mary. Both George and Mary, daughter of Thomas Johnston, a Carrickfergus grocer, who died in 1901 and 1908 respectively, were buried in Carrickfergus's North Road cemetery. With Hugh Bowman's own background somewhat obscured, it was hardly surprising the couple opted for Carrickfergus when youngest child Isabel died from diptheria at the age of 11 in 1914. Alexander followed the lead taken by his brother when his [Alexander's] youngest son, Charles, died in 1923. Not only are Alexander and Rose and various members of their family buried at Victoria cemetery, so too are Hugh and Lizzie and a number of their descendants. See George Rutherford, *Old Families of Carrickfergus and Ballynure*

(Belfast 1995), p.174.

35 *MN*, 31 October 1885. W. A. Maguire, *Belfast: Site and City* (Keele 1993), p80, refers to shortcomings of the half-timer system.

36 The location of the farm where General Monro was arrested is discussed in the appendix to the reprint of W. G. Lyttle's *Betsy Gray* (Newcastle, Co. Down 1997), p.164.

37 When Bowman visited the Agnes Street National Schools as a councillor in 1899, he spoke of his own childhood days 'when my face was as fresh and my heart as free from care...' See *BNL*, 25 November 1899.

38 Maguire, p.79. Before 1874 the minimum age was eight, thereafter 10.

39 The *Belfast Directory* for 1863/64, p.39, places the Brookfield power-loom linen weaving factory at 40 Agnes Street, while the 1880 edition, p.90, gives the Agnes Street Factory as occupant of that address.

40 See Betty Messenger, *Picking up the Linen Threads – Life in Ulster's Mills* (Belfast 1978), pp.82-100, and John W. Boyle, *The Irish Labour Movement* (Washington, D.C. 1988), p.124, for a description of the associated health problems.

41 BPP, Belfast Constabulary Bill (1887) x., pp.693-862. Bowman told MPs he had been reading the *Northern Whig* 'practically every day' for nine-tenths of his life.

42 *Ibid.* Bowman said he had worked in 'a very large number of large workshops in Belfast.'

43 Michael Liggett, *A District Called Ardoyne* (Belfast 1994).

44 *Irish Linen – A History of William Ewart and Son Ltd.,* no author cited, company publication (Belfast 1964).

45 Records of William Bowman (eldest son of Alexander Bowman).

46 The couple were married on 5 November 1851, at Dundrod Presbyterian Church, Co. Antrim.

47 Records held at Dundonald Presbyterian Church. Rose Bowman's age was given correctly in the 1891 census as 38. However, she had 'lost' a year by the time her husband completed the 1911 census form, giving her age then as 57. Like many women from the Victorian era, she was modest about revealing her true age and, according to surviving grandchildren, had 'lost' as many as five years by the time of her death on 1 October 1947, two days short of her 95th birthday.

48 The link between Robert Ritchie and Rose Ritchie is the author's conclusion based on available family information. Ritchie died aged 67 in 1912. See linen industry dispute report in *NW*, 13 July 1874.

49 Confirmed by Presbyterian Historical Society of Ireland, Belfast.

50 James M. Lee was appointed principal of Argyle Place School in 1884. He died aged 51 in 1910.

THE EMERGENCE OF A TRADE UNION LEADER

1 David Bleakley, 'Trade Union Beginnings in Belfast and District with special reference to the period 1881-1900, and to the work of the Belfast and District United Trades Council during that period' (MA, QUB 1955), p.44; W. A. Maguire, *Belfast: Site and City* (Keele 1993), pp.69-70. City status was granted by Queen Victoria in 1888.

2 Rev. Robert Milford, *The Shankill Road* (Belfast 1971), p.7; Bleakley, p.44.

3 Kitchen houses were built on the three up, two down principle – a kitchen and a scullery downstairs, with three small bedrooms upstairs. The toilet would have been in an outhouse in the narrow backyard.

Coal ashes and other waste had to be carried through the house and out the front door for disposal. See Paul Hamilton, *Up the Shankill* (Belfast 1979), p.36.

4 *Belfast Evening Telegraph* (hereafter *BET*) profile, 20 December 1897. It was a widely-held view that excessive drinking was the source of many of the social ills of the time, hence the strong support among early trade unionists like Bowman for the temperance movement.

5 The Bible Temperance Association's adherents in hundreds of church congregations in Ireland, including 40 in Belfast, used unfermented wine at the Lord's Table, thereby wholly avoiding alcohol. See the Rev. George Hay Shanks, *An examination of Rev. Dr Murphy's tract on Wine in the Bible* (Belfast 1869), at Linen Hall Library, Belfast.

6 *BET*, 20 December 1897.

7 *Northern Whig* (hereafter *NW*), 5 April 1881. The 1874 Factory Act had limited the working week in factories to 56 hours, with workshops covered by the legislation from 1878. See Maguire, p.78.

8 Arthur Marsh, Victoria Ryan, John B. Smethurst, *Historical Directory of Trades Unions*, vol. 4 (Aldershot 1994), p.281. The Flaxdressers' Union, founded in 1872, provided unemployment, sickness, burial and emigration benefits, the latter at a rate of £5. 10s., refundable if the recipient returned within five years. John W. Boyle, *The Irish Labour Movement* (Washington, D.C. 1988), pp.98-99, notes that trade unions associated with the linen industry 'contributed a number of leaders to Belfast labour politics.'

9 Examples of writers who support this view include Peter Collins, 'The Belfast Trades Council' (Ph. D.,

University of Ulster 1988), p.12: 'Belfast Trades Council was largely established due to the shared experiences...,' and Ann McKee, *Belfast Trades Council: the first 100 years* (Belfast 1983), p.4: '... had its origins in a meeting to support tenters...'

10 *NW*, 27 March 1880.

11 *Ibid.*, 5 April 1881.

12 *Ibid.*, 2 April 1881.

13 *Ibid.*, 5 April 1881.

14 *Ibid.*, 7 April 1881.

15 *Ibid.*, 5 April 1881.

16 *Ibid.*, 7 April 1881.

17 *Ibid.*, 16 April 1881.

18 *Ibid.*

19 *Ibid.*, 21 April 1881.

20 *Ibid.*

21 Advertisement for meeting in *NW*, 10 May 1881.

22 *Ibid.*, 12 May 1881.

23 *Ibid.*, 17 May 1881.

24 This date is cited by Belfast Trades Council on its letter headings, etc. See McKee, p.4.

25 According to the British TUC Library, London, the affiliation took effect from 18 August 1883.

26 Bleakley, p.58.

27 The first report on Belfast Trades Council proceedings appeared in the *Northern Whig* on 10 January 1882.

28 McKee, p.4.

29 Several writers on the subject suggest that little is known of the council's early deliberations since the minute books are missing for the first four years up to 1885. Peter Collins, p.12, claims 'little or nothing is known of the earliest years of the council... nor were accounts of its proceedings given in any of the newspapers of the period.' Likewise, Alan Carr, *The Early Belfast Labour Movement, part 1, 1885-1893* (Belfast 1974), p.6, states '... since the press were not admitted to trades council meetings until 1891, there is no record of the

business of the council.'

30 *NW*, 23 January 1882.

31 *Ibid.*, 6 February 1882.

32 During its first year, seven subjects were debated by 123 speakers at 22 meetings, with attendances averaging 200 per meeting. See *NW*, 6 April 1883, for a review of the first year. Society president James Flinn (d.1898) told members: 'If public speaking were not countenanced, and if men and women were not encouraged to disseminate whatever knowledge they possessed, the paths of knowledge would be blocked up and a barrier put to the expansion of free thought.'

33 *NW*, 15 February 1882.

34 *Ibid.*, 22 May 1882.

35 *Ibid.*, 2 June 1882. The Library Act, passed in 1850 and extended to Ireland in 1854 – with additional legislation in 1855 reducing the population qualification from 10,000 to 5,000 – permitted the establishment of free public libraries and museums, as well as schools of science and art. It also required a council to first obtain the consent of a two-thirds majority of ratepayers and limited the authority to a maximum tax of one penny in the pound. See Gordon Wheeler's 'A History of Belfast Central Library', in *Linen Hall Review*, 5:2 (Belfast 1988).

36 Mayor [Sir] Edward Porter Cowan was a sympathetic Liberal.

37 Wheeler.

38 *Ibid.* Belfast's population was around 230,000 at the time, indicating how few were voting ratepayers.

39 *NW*, 20 February 1882.

40 British TUC Library, London, British Trades Union Congress, *Reports* (hereafter British TUC, *Reports*), 1882, p.2. Extensive coverage of the Congress can also be found in *The Times*, 19-23, 25 September 1882.

41 *Belfast Directory* for 1884, p.410.

42 British TUC, *Reports*, 1882, p.2.

43 *Ibid.*, p.17.

44 *Ibid.*, pp.19-21.

45 *Ibid.*, p.22. Debate surrounded a proposed amendment which sought to limit the power to contract out of the Employers' Liability Act. See *The Times*, 19 September 1882, for an editorial on the subject.

46 British TUC, *Reports*, 1882, pp.26-27.

47 Also see Boyle, p.129.

48 British TUC, *Reports*, 1882, p.37. The £10 voting qualification for municipal elections was established through the Irish Municipal Corporations Act of 1840. See Ian Budge and Cornelius O'Leary, *Belfast; Approach to Crisis: A Study of Belfast Politics* (London 1973), p.51.

49 British TUC, *Reports*, 1882, p.36.

50 *NW*, 7 May 1883.

51 *Ibid.*, 21 May 1883.

52 *Ibid.*, 19 June 1883.

53 *Ibid.*, 25 June 1883. The fund had reached £85 a week before the exhibition.

54 *Ibid.*, 4 July 1883.

55 *Ibid.*, 5 November 1883. There is no trace of the photograph. If it has survived, it would be the earliest known to feature members of Belfast Trades Council.

56 *Ibid.*, 3 December 1883.

57 British TUC, *Reports*, 1883, p.17. For additional Congress coverage see *The Times*, 11-15, 17 September 1883.

58 British TUC, *Reports*, 1883, p.33.

59 *Ibid.*, p.44.

60 *NW*, 17 September 1883. These words by Bowman were not recorded in the official Congress report.

61 West Belfast MP Thomas Sexton (d.1932) would use his party's

influence at Westminster to have a section added into the Municipal Corporation of Belfast Act of 1887 abolishing the £10 rateable valuation requirement in favour of household suffrage. This would have the effect of giving the vote to householders, including women, in Belfast municipal elections 12 years before the rest of Ireland. See Budge and O'Leary, p.117 and p.132, note 55.

62 British TUC, *Reports*, 1883, p.45.

GLADSTONE AND THE LIBERAL CAUSE

1   Records of William Bowman (eldest son of Alexander Bowman).

2   *Northern Whig* (hereafter *NW*), 17 March 1884.

3   *Ibid.*, 7 April 1884. Robert Meharg (1858-1936) was the longest-lived of the founding figures in the Belfast Trades Council.

4   *NW*, 5 May 1884. By this time the Liberal Party had established itself as the party with which many new working-class voters living in urban constituencies identified themselves. See Clive Behagg, *Labour and Reform, Working Class Movements, 1815-1914* (London 1991), p.93. Also W. A. Maguire, *Belfast: Site and City* (Keele 1993), pp.93-94, for details of the Liberal Party's efforts to secure the support of working-class voters in Belfast.

5   For report of Assembly Hall meeting see *NW*, 4 June 1884. The suggestion that these meetings represented the commencement of Bowman's open involvement with the Liberal Party in Belfast is based on the absence of his name from a comprehensive list of those attending the Belfast Liberal Association's first annual meeting at the Lombard Hall two years earlier. See *NW*, 28 January 1882. Likewise, the 1883 annual meeting, *NW*, 26 January 1883. The raising of the

issue by Thomas Johnston more than three years into the life of the trades council suggests that prior to 1884 Bowman had not been involved, at any rate in a position of any influence, in party politics.

6   The Representation of the People (Ireland) Act of 1868 had reduced the previous £8 rateable valuation qualification for voters to the £4 figure Bowman mentioned at the Manchester Congress, and had introduced a lodger franchise. The 1884 Representation of the People Act [known as the Reform Act] would create a uniform householder and lodger franchise for the whole of the United Kingdom. It would extend the right to vote in Ireland to all male householders in both counties and boroughs, and to lodgers in the counties.

7   *NW*, 10 June 1884.

8   There were fears amongst members of the House of Lords, where the Conservatives had an in-built majority, that increased representation of the working classes in the House of Commons could ultimately lead to moves to curtail their powers. Hence the Lords' desire for what amounted to an accompanying readjustment of political power.

9   *NW*, 17 October 1884.

10 This was 7,000 more than the figure Bowman had cited at the Nottingham Congress a year earlier. Curiously, the number of voters in Belfast at the 1880 general election was 21,188, while the total for the four new Belfast constituencies in November 1885, **after** the Representation of the People Act had taken effect, was 30,368. See Brian M. Walker, *Parliamentary Election Results in Ireland, 1801-1922* (Dublin 1978), pp.123,130. To explain the anomaly, it is possible that Bowman was

anticipating the proposed figure but believed it to be still inadequate.

11 *NW*, 6 December 1884.

12 The Corrupt Practices Act of 1883 ensured there would be rigorous control over election expenses, thereby preventing wealthy candidates from literally buying their way to success.

13 The Independent Order of Good Templars, one of the strongest general temperance organisations, reached Belfast in 1870. By the mid-1880s it had 2,000 adult members in 35 lodges, as well as several thousand under-16s in a juvenile branch. Details in *Belfast Directory* for 1884, p.91. Bowman's temperance work went largely unreported. He chaired a gospel temperance meeting in October 1885 at the Working Men's Institute in Queen's Street, Belfast. During the meeting he 'urged upon all interested in the financial, moral and religious progress of the country, the pre-eminent claims of temperance reform.' See *NW*, 7 October 1885.

14 This account of the society's formation appeared in *Brotherhood*, 30 November 1889, which was edited by the organisation's one-time chairman, the Rev. John Bruce Wallace (d.1939). There is no evidence that Bowman was among the founding members. It seems more likely that he joined during his period of political awakening in the early to mid-1880s.

15 *NW*, 20 December 1884.

16 *Ibid.,* 23 January 1885.

17 *Belfast News-Letter* (hereafter *BNL*), 23 January 1885.

18 *Ibid.,* 27 February 1885. Kate Newmann, *Dictionary of Ulster Biography* (Belfast 1993), p.99, reveals that, like Bowman, Hanna was a native of Dromara.

19 *BNL*, 27 January 1885.

20 De Cobain was elected later that year as independent Conservative MP for East Belfast. He was required to resign his position with the town council owing to his active involvement in politics.

21 Debates were reported in the *NW* as follows: assimilating the franchise, 16 January 1883; intoxicating drink, 23 January 1883; new laws, 20 March 1883; Home Rule, 31 October 1883; the franchise bill, 21 and 28 October 1884; the government's Irish policy, 4 November 1884; Oliver Cromwell, 11 November 1884.

22 Few details were carried in the press of the arguments put forward by speakers at meetings of the Belfast Debating Society. This was one of the exceptions and may well have provided valuable ammunition for Bowman's political enemies during the November 1885 election campaign.

23 *NW, BNL*, 30 January 1885.

24 *NW*, 21 March 1885.

25 *Ibid.,* 6 May 1885.

26 *Ibid.,* 25 June 1885.

27 *Ibid.,* 4 August 1885.

28 The articles, summarised here from various *NW* reports, appeared under the heading *The Maiden Tribute of Modern Babylon* and also became known as the *Pall Mall Revelations*.

29 The almost immediate outcome of the *Pall Mall Gazette* reports was the passing of a Criminal Law Amendment Act raising the age of consent to 16 after years of obstruction and opposition in parliament.

30 *NW*, 20 October 1885. At the conclusion of the trial Stead was found guilty of taking the 13-year-old from her father against his will and also of aiding and abetting an indecent assault which arose from an examination of the girl by a female

co-accused. It was the Crown's contention that Stead, through his actions, was tempting poor parents to commit crimes, while the defendant claimed if he had not 'bought' the girl, she would have been sold to someone else with a more evil purpose. It had also been his aim to ensure the Criminal Law Amendment bill was passed by parliament. Stead – who would lose his life when the Titanic sank – was sentenced to three months' imprisonment. There was extensive coverage of the Stead trial in the Belfast daily newspapers during October and November 1885.

31 *NW*, 12 August 1885.

32 *Ibid.*, 25 September 1885.

33 William Woodall introduced women suffrage bills in the House of Commons in 1884, 1889 and 1891, all unsuccessfully.

THE WORKING MEN'S CANDIDATE

1 *Northern Whig* (hereafter *NW*), *Belfast News-Letter* (hereafter *BNL*), *Morning New*s (hereafter *MN*), 10 October 1885.

2 *Lurgan Times*, 31 October 1885.

3 See Arthur Marsh, Victoria Ryan, John B. Smethurst, *Historical Directory of Trades Unions*, vol. 4 (Aldershot 1994), p.277, with additional information by Mats Greiff, School of Education, Lunds University, Malmo, Sweden.

4 For details of legislation, introduced between 1800 and 1875, which aided the progression of trade unions from being illegal organisations, with no rights in law, to legal organisations with a role in the workplace, see Clive Behagg, *Labour and Reform, Working Class Movements, 1815-1914* (London 1991), pp.78-79.

5 Mats Greiff.

6 Advertisement in *BNL*, 25 November 1885.

7 This extended account of the proceedings draws together the coverage from four newspapers, *BNL*, *NW* and *MN*, of 31 October 1885, and the *Weekly Northern Whig* (hereafter *WNW*), of 7 November 1885. Each newspaper published an edited report of the meeting and a more complete picture is gained by combining elements from the four.

8 The age given by Workman would support Bowman's erroneous claim that he was born in 1855.

9 Henry Broadhurst and miner Thomas Burt, who represented Morpeth from 1874. A third labour-minded MP, Alexander Macdonald, was elected for Stafford in 1874 but died in 1881. See Behagg, p.93. All three were elected to Westminster as Liberals.

10 At that September's TUC in Stockport, Broadhurst told delegates: 'The next general election will be to the people as the seed time to the farmer. If you do not bestir yourselves most vigorously in seed-sowing, you cannot reap the harvest of legislation.' See *NW*, 10 September 1885.

11 See *History of Congregations in the Presbyterian Church in Ireland*, no author cited, Presbyterian Historical Society of Ireland (Belfast 1982), p.125. Two weeks after the meeting, on Friday, 13 November 1885, the Rev. George Magill (d.1923) officiated at the marriage of Bowman's brother Hugh to Lizzie Blackwood at Ekenhead Presbyterian Church. See PRONI, MIC/1P/8.

12 Nomination details were published in the Belfast press on 25 November 1885.

13 See Brian M. Walker, *Parliamentary Election Results in Ireland, 1801-*

1922 (Dublin 1978), p.130. East Belfast: Edward de Cobain (Ind. Con.), 3,033; Sir James Corry (Con.), 2,929; Robert W. Murray (Lib.), 870. South Belfast: William Johnston (Ind. Con.), 3,610; John Workman (Lib.), 990; Robert Seeds (Ind. Con.), 871.

14 Several authors have claimed that Bowman was officially adopted as the Liberal Party candidate in North Belfast. John W. Boyle was probably the first to counter the view, in *The Irish Labour Movement* (Washington, D.C. 1978), p.342. Boyle had the distinct advantage of interviewing Bowman's son Robert before his death in 1970. Another who avoids the mistake is Ann McKee, *Belfast Trades Council: the first 100 years* (Belfast 1983), who refers to Bowman 'fighting working-class issues,' p.11. The mistaken view is put forward by J. D. Clarkson, *Labour and Nationalism in Ireland* (New York 1925), p.349; Andrew Boyd, *The Rise of the Irish Trade Unions* (Tralee 1985), pp.74-75; Peter Collins, 'The Belfast Trades Council' (Ph. D., University of Ulster 1988), p.39; Ian Budge and Cornelius O'Leary, *Belfast; Approach to Crisis: A Study of Belfast Politics* (London 1973), p.104; Arthur Mitchell, *Labour in Irish Politics, 1890-1930* (Dublin 1974), p.18, and Emmet O'Connor, *A Labour History of Ireland, 1824-1960* (Dublin 1992), p.39. As Boyle points out, p.346, all appear to have followed Clarkson who was guided, incorrectly, by *The Constitutional Year Book for 1911*, p.213.

15 *NW, BNL*, 25 November 1885.

16 *Belfast Directory*, 1887.

17 *BET*, 31 October 1885.

18 Maguire, p.92.

19 *NW*, 2 November 1885.

20 *MN*, 31 October 1885.

21 *NW*, 14 November 1885; also *WNW*, 21 November 1885.

22 *MN*, 14 November 1885.

23 Robert McClung, 'Recollections of the Belfast Labour Movement' (written in 1929, hereafter Recollections), a manuscript in the author's possession. McClung (d.1945) recalled Bowman's selection as a labour candidate in October 1885, and stated he was in the audience at the meeting in Foyle Street which launched Bowman's election campaign. He attended the second meeting at which Bowman and his supporters were targeted by rival supporters with bags of flour 'supplied by the Tory machine' which left them 'as white as millers.' McClung also recounted the incident in which Bowman's home was attacked.

24 *NW*, 17 November 1885. The term 'bo-man,' as used by Hugh Hanna, was a Scots word meaning bogeyman, goblin or even the Devil. See *Scottish National Dictionary*, vol.2 (Edinburgh 1941), p.192.

25 *NW, MN*, 19 November 1885; *WNW*, 21 November 1885.

26 Boyle, p.344. This tends to bear out the view that the anti-Bowman campaign by Ewart sympathisers was orchestrated and not done on the spur of the moment.

27 Boyle states, p.344, that Benjamin Hobson was on the committee of the Ulster Liberal Association. Hobson (d.1927) was also the father of future leading Irish Republican Bulmer Hobson.

28 Bowman was responding to points made by Ewart on trade issues at his election meetings.

29 Boyle, p.343.

30 Although the *MN* identified Bowman's backer as Joseph Cumming, the *NW* of the same date, 19 November 1885, referred to him

as James Cumming. The speaker may have been Dr James Cuming (sic), a professor of medicine at Queen's College, Belfast.

31 *MN*, 19 November 1885.

32 *NW*, 21 November 1885.

33 *Ibid.*, 26 November 1885.

34 *Ibid.*, 25 November 1885.

35 Thomas Johnston is described by Boyle, p.345, as the 'forerunner of a prolific succession of Unionist workingmen.' His bitter accusation that Bowman was a Republican was groundless. The editorial in *NW*, 2 November 1885, following the launch of Bowman's campaign, indicated that his 'convictions on ordinary party questions... have not been very prominent.' Robert McClung, Recollections (1929), acknowledged that anti-Home Rule fears were rife among the working classes in 1885. With regard to Bowman, he wrote: 'The Pope and Home Rule for Ireland played a big part in the fight which took place. Bowman had no intention of handing North Belfast over to the Pope, although the Tories declared he would.'

36 *NW*, 26 November 1885.

37 *BNL*, 25 November 1885.

38 *MN*, *NW*, 26 November 1885.

39 Brian M. Walker, *Ulster Politics, The Formative Years, 1868-86* (Belfast 1989), p.211, for Parnell's pre-election message to Nationalists. Although Thomas Sexton lost the 1885 West Belfast election, he would win the seat the following year.

40 *BNL*, 27 November 1885. A map showing the electoral boundaries which applied for the 1885 election can be viewed at Belfast Central Library.

41 *BNL*, 28 November 1885; Walker (1978), p.130, states that the electorate in North Belfast was 6,831, while the contemporary *BNL*

gave a figure of 6,810.

42 *BNL*, 28 November 1885. William Ewart died in London in 1889.

43 *NW*, 9 January 1886.

44 James Dempsey had previously served on the executive committee of the Belfast Liberal Association, advocating better representation for minorities. See *NW*, 28 January 1882. Also Maguire, p.93, for reference to the Liberals' failure to retain the support of Catholic voters.

45 Walker (1978), p.137; also Boyle, p.345. The *NW* of 27 November 1885, reported: 'Mr Bowman seemed to have gained the Catholic vote generally, in accordance with a hint dropped at a meeting of Nationalists in town.'

46 *NW*, 28 November 1885.

HOME RULER

1 P. J. O. McCann, 'The Protestant Home Rule Movement, 1885-95' (MA, UCD 1972), pp.1-12.

2 Ramsay Colles, *The History of Ulster*, vol. 4 (London 1920), pp.213-214.

3 *Northern Whig* (hereafter *NW*), 15 January 1886.

4 Bowman cited Gladstone's Land Act of 1870 which had given a measure of legal protection to tenants they had not previously enjoyed, although it failed to control rents. The 1881 Act, also introduced by Gladstone's government, gave tenants security of tenure, fair rents to be settled by arbitration, and the legal right to sell their interest in their holdings. See 'The Land Question in Ulster,' by Frank Thompson, in Eamon Phoenix (ed.), *A Century of Northern Life* (Belfast 1995), pp.122-123.

5 *NW*, 30 January 1886.

6 The figures quoted at the meeting show that, unlike ordinary MPs, government ministers were paid a salary. Belfast's town clerk should

not be confused with Randalstown farmer Samuel Black mentioned in chapter three.

7   *NW*, 13 February 1886.

8   *Ibid.*, 17 February 1886.

9   *Ibid.*, 19 February 1886.

10 *Ibid.*, letter by Bowman.

11 Such a call to the Liberals was issued following a meeting chaired by William Ewart at the Conservatives' Constitutional Club in May Street. See *NW*, 9 January 1886. Support for the move was voiced in a number of letters published by the same paper the following week: 12, 13 January 1886, passim.

12 *Ibid.*, 16 January 1886.

13 Gladstone's appeal took the form of an open letter to Lord De Vesci, dated 12 February 1886, and published in the *NW*, 16 February 1886. Lord De Vesci's reply appeared in the same paper the following day. Reference to the exchange can also be found in *The Ulster Liberal Unionist Association, A Sketch of its History* (Belfast 1913), p.13.

14 This report of the proceedings is drawn from the coverage in *NW*, *Morning News* (hereafter *MN*), and *Belfast News-Letter* (hereafter *BNL*), 20 March 1886. McCann, p.15, calculates the attendance to have been 200.

15 Brian M. Walker, *Ulster Politics, The Formative Years, 1868-86*, (Belfast 1989), pp.193-194, passim.

16 Seconder James Lee was not the schoolteacher of the same name. Lee succeeded Samuel Black as president of the Ulster Land Committee and died in 1897.

17 *NW, MN*, 20 March 1886.

18 *BNL*, 29 March 1886.

19 *NW, MN, BNL*, 9 April 1886.

20 Colles, p.218.

21 *NW*, 9 April 1886.

22 *MN*, 9 April 1886.

23 McCann, pp.15-16, 32-33, 36-37, 143-144.

THE RESIGNATION FROM BELFAST TRADES COUNCIL

1   *Northern Whig* (hereafter *NW*), *Morning News* (hereafter *MN*), *Belfast News-Letter* (hereafter *BNL*), 1 May 1886; *Weekly Northern Whig*, 8 May 1886.

2   *BNL*, 7 May 1886.

3   *NW*, 10 May 1886.

4   The fullest version appears in the *MN* of 13 May 1886. Former bricklayer George Howell was MP for Bethnel Green.

5   *NW*, 17 May 1886.

6   Linen Hall Library, Belfast, Belfast Trades Council minutes (hereafter BTC minutes), 15 May 1886.

7   *NW, BNL*, 18 May 1886.

8   *NW*, 20 May 1886.

9   *Ibid.* It is likely the trades council was unable to find anyone willing to take on the duties of secretary, hence Bowman's retention of the post despite earning a living as a commercial traveller. He had retained his membership of the Flaxdressers' Union.

10 *MN*, 21 May 1886; *NW*, 24 May 1886.

11 The *MN* was the only Belfast daily newspaper to carry a report of the inaugural meeting the next day, 22 May 1886. The size of the attendance was subsequently challenged by other newspapers.

12 James Loughlin, 'The Irish Protestant Home Rule Association and Nationalist Politics,' in *Irish Historical Studies*, xxiv, no. 95 (May 1985), p.343. For more about Thomas Shillington, with whom Bowman was linked for several years, see *BET*, 2 January 1911 (appointment as Irish Privy Councillor); *Portadown News*, 31 January 1925 (obituary).

13 *MN*, 23 April 1886.

14 Thomas McClelland (1813-1897) was a highly respected figure in Belfast legal circles, serving as president of the Northern Law Society.

15 P. J. O. McCann, 'The Protestant Home Rule Movement, 1885-95' (MA, UCD 1972), pp.34-36, in discussing the ideology of the Irish Protestant Home Rule Association, contends that none of its members desired complete separation from Britain. Northern members generally subscribed to the view that had the imperial parliament governed Ireland 'properly and fairly,' the Irish people, or at least the Protestant Home Rulers, would have had no cause or justification for demanding their own parliament.

16 Loughlin, pp.346, 356-358.

17 McCann, p.24, contends that while the association was a small minority group, that should not be allowed to discolour its relative importance at the time.

18 *MN*, 26 May 1886, for additional editorial comments.

19 *NW*, 24, 27 May 1886.

20 See McCann, p.29, for details of branches and the division of Ireland with Belfast as the parent body; also, p.47, for the expansion of branches.

21 *NW*, 1 June 1886.

22 *MN*, 31 May 1886.

23 BTC minutes, 5 June 1886.

24 *Ibid.*, 12 June 1886; *NW*, 14 June 1886.

25 BTC minutes, 18 June 1886.

26 *Ibid.*, 4 February 1887, indicate that Bowman had been delegated to attend a meeting of the town council to discuss the furnishing of the new free library, but was replaced by another member. A slight element of confusion exists when interpreting the hand-written minutes owing to the presence on the council of Henry Bowman, delegate of the Boilermakers' and Iron Shipbuilders' No. 2 Union. He would chair the council's meeting on 3 September 1887.

27 Some authorities cite the voting figures as 341 to 311, omitting the two tellers recorded for each side.

28 *NW*, 15 June 1886. For details of the birth of the Ulster Unionists, see Ian Budge and Cornelius O'Leary, *Belfast; Approach to Crisis: A Study of Belfast Politics* (London 1973), pp.105-106.

29 *NW*, 15 June 1886.

30 *Ibid.*, 29, 31 May 1886.

31 *Ibid.*, 11, 25 June 1886. James Johnston was a practising solicitor in Ireland between 1885 and 1896.

32 *MN*, 25 June 1886.

33 *NW*, 26, 28 June 1886. Queen's County is now known as Co. Laois.

34 Brian M. Walker, *Parliamentary Election Results in Ireland, 1801-1922* (Dublin 1978), pp.130 and 134. Nationalists often put forward their strongest candidates in several constituencies. If successful in more than one, the victor would chose which he wished to represent and a by-election would usually see the return of another Nationalist.

35 *Belfast Directory* for 1887, p.328. The office was no. 6 on the first floor, located between a stockbroker and an insurance agent.

36 *MN*, 1 July 1886.

37 *Ibid.*, *NW*, 3 July 1886.

38 *MN*, 8 July 1886.

39 *NW*, 8 July 1886. For details of the West Belfast election contest, see also McCann, pp.42-43.

40 *Ibid.*, p.44. Calculating votes was a precise art. The *MN* of 17 October 1887, reported that, according to its Derry correspondent: 'The revision of voters' lists for the City of Derry gives the Catholic Nationalists a majority of 74. These added to the votes of 52 Protestant Home Rulers

will give a majority in a contest of 178 to the Nationalist candidate.'

41 Walker (1978), pp.193-194. According to McCann, p.46, six of the Nationalist MPs were members of the Protestant Home Rule movement.

42 Author's conclusion based on newspaper reports of various election campaigns. Bowman's occupation appeared as secretary in the *Belfast Directory* for 1887, p.229, and he would give his occupation as 'secretary of the Irish Protestant Home Rule Association' on third son Hugh's birth certificate later that same year. Copy at General Register Office, Dublin.

43 *NW*, 30 July 1886.

44 *Freeman's Journal*, 14 September 1886. Loughlin also refers to hon. secretary William [or James] Hammond being attacked and beaten at Ballymacarrett, East Belfast, citing the *Wexford Express*, 12 June 1886.

45 Jonathan Bardon, *Belfast: An Illustrated History* (Belfast 1982), pp.147-150.

46 *Belfast Directory* for 1887, p.229. The rent figure was quoted by Bowman when he gave evidence to the parliamentary select committee later that year. He also told the MPs he had been warned that his former home was 'on the agenda to be looted' and that he had been advised to move his wife and family.

47 See PRONI, SCH/135/1/2.

48 Author's conclusion based on records of William Bowman. Rose Bowman's aunt, Margaret Boomer, had married Alexander Officer from Dundrod, Co. Antrim. A number of the Officers subsequently settled in Belfast.

49 *NW*, 10 September 1886. This was one of about 150 court attendances by Bowman during 1886-1887,

according to his evidence to the select committee in August 1887.

50 *Ibid.*, 13 September 1886.

51 *Ibid.*, 25 September 1886.

NATIONALISTS, NOT SEPARATISTS

1 While the Young Ireland Society, founded in 1883, primarily concerned itself with the promotion of Irish culture and Nationalist-orientated literature, it gradually developed into a debating forum covering the wider literary field and contemporary political events, particularly those affecting the Nationalist community. See Eamon Phoenix (ed.), *A Century of Northern Life* (Belfast 1995), pp.11-12.

2 *Morning News* (hereafter *MN*), *Northern Whig* (hereafter *NW*), 28 October 1886. For Francis Davis (1810-1885), see Robert Welch (ed.), *Oxford Companion to Irish Literature* (Oxford 1996), p.135.

3 P. J. O. McCann, 'The Protestant Home Rule Movement, 1885-95' (MA, UCD 1972), pp.33, 49, 55. He suggests that for Protestant Home Rulers like Bowman and Pinkerton, land agitation had become the 'most urgent and important business.'

4 *Banbridge Chronicle*, 3, 13 November 1886; also *MN*, 10 November 1886, and *NW*, 11 November 1886. Also see McCann, p.96.

5 Englishman Joseph Arch did more than any other man of his time to improve conditions for farm workers. There is a strong possibility that Bowman met him as both attended the 1883 Trades Union Congress in Nottingham.

6 *MN*, 14 December 1886.

7 *NW*, 21 December 1886.

8 According to McCann, p.93, these figures were given by hon. secretary James Johnston. Bowman would claim the Belfast branch had 800

members and many more sympathisers when giving evidence to the parliamentary select committee in August 1887.

9 *NW*, 28 January 1887.

10 Lord Castlereagh, also the 2nd Marquess of Londonderry, was Chief Secretary for Ireland from 1798-1801.

11 Letter to *MN*, 17 February 1887.

12 The *NW* reported on 29 October 1883, that Belfast businessman Forster Green was offering £5,000 towards the establishment of a hospital for the treatment of consumptive patients. His dream was realised when the Forster Green Hospital opened in 1896.

13 *MN*, 18 March 1887.

14 Land-grabbers took advantage of the eviction of tenant-farmers for their own gain.

15 *NW*, 16 April 1887.

16 *MN, BNL*, 28 January and 29 March 1887. Arthur Balfour would serve as British Prime Minister for three years following the resignation of Lord Salisbury, his uncle, in July 1902.

17 Liz Curtis, *The Cause of Ireland* (Belfast 1994), p.145. Also see Timothy Healy, *Letters and Leaders of My Day*, vol. 1 (London 1928), pp.272-273, in which he claimed the publication of a forged letter in *The Times* of 18 April 1887, implicating Parnell in the Phoenix Park murders of 1882, was timed to coincide with the bill's second reading at Westminster, thus ensuring the perpetual aspect won the support of Liberal Unionists as well as Conservatives.

18 For coverage of the meetings, see *MN* and *NW*, 14, 15 April 1887; also McCann, p.70.

19 The Plan of Campaign had been proclaimed in December 1886. See *NW*, 20, 21 December 1886. The subject is expanded upon by Sally Warwick-Haller in *William O'Brien and the Land War* (Dublin 1990), also by Laurence M. Geary in *The Plan of Campaign* (Cork 1986), and by Curtis, pp.144-145. McCann, p.55, suggests that the calls by Bowman, Pinkerton and others for the formation of tenants' defence associations represented a form of Plan of Campaign.

20 McCann, p.70; James Loughlin, 'The Irish Protestant Home Rule Association and Nationalist Politics,' in *Irish Historical Studies*, xxiv, no. 95 (May 1985), p.352.

21 *NW*, 14 April 1887. McCann, p.68, gives the attendance as 300.

22 *MN, NW*, 19 April 1887. Fr Convery, later Archdeacon, was a leading Catholic priest in West Belfast until his death aged 84 in 1931.

23 *NW*, 15 April 1887, for report of Ulster Loyalist Anti-Repeal Union meeting in the Ulster Hall, Belfast. For more about the Union, which included the Rev. Hugh Hanna among its membership, see Curtis, p.130.

24 *MN, NW*, 9 May 1887. See also McCann, pp.72-76, for references to the provincial meetings.

25 *MN, NW, Belfast News-Letter* (hereafter *BNL*), 10, 11 May 1887.

26 *MN, NW*, 12 May 1887.

27 Curtis, pp.146-147.

28 *MN*, 13 May 1887.

29 *Ibid., NW*, 14 May 1887.

30 *NW*, 16 May 1887; *MN*, 17 May 1887.

31 *MN*, 17 May 1887.

32 *NW*, 13, 20 May 1887.

33 *MN*, 24 May 1887.

34 *NW*, 20 May 1887.

35 *Ibid., MN, BNL*, 21 May 1887.

36 *NW, MN, BNL, Newry Reporter*, 26 May 1887.

37 George Henry Bassett, *Co. Down 100 Years Ago: a Guide and Directory* (Belfast 1988), p.157.

38 *NW*, 27 May 1887.
39 *Ibid.*, 30 May 1887.
40 *Ibid.*, 31 May 1887.
41 *Ibid.*, 4 June 1887.
42 *Ibid.*, 20 July 1887.
43 A series of Land Acts from the mid-1880s provided facilities for tenant purchase. See Phoenix, p.123.
44 *BNL*, 22 June 1887.

TESTIMONY AT WESTMINSTER; DEFIANCE IN ULSTER

1 Queen's University, Belfast, British Parliamentary Papers, Belfast Constabulary Bill (1887) x., pp.693-862. Reports of Bowman's appearance before the parliamentary select committee also appeared in *Northern Whig* (hereafter *NW*), *Morning News* (hereafter *MN*), and *Belfast News-Letter* (hereafter *BNL*), 15 August 1887. The town council had voted to take over the powers of the Police Commissioners and the Police Committee back in January 1843, thus giving the council authority over the police in Belfast. See W. A. Maguire, *Belfast: Site and City* (Keele 1993), pp.46-47.

2 Among the provisions of the 1887 Constabulary bill was the appointment by the Lord Lieutenant of magistrates with a yearly salary of £1,000. A clause proposing the establishment of a Police Watch Committee, an aspect the Nationalists opposed, was not pursued.

3 Dr. Alexander Dempsey (d.1920), brother of James Dempsey, was later knighted for public services.

4 *MN*, 16 August 1887. The by-election was at Northwich in Cheshire.

5 *MN*, 20 August 1887; P. J. O. McCann, 'The Protestant Home Rule Movement, 1885-95' (MA, UCD 1972), p.79.

6 *MN*, 23 August 1887.

7 *Ibid.*, 16 September 1887; McCann, pp.80, 96.

8 *MN*, 15 September 1887.

9 *Ibid.*, 16 September 1887.

10 *Ibid.*, 17 September 1887.

11 *Ibid.*, 22, 23 September 1887.

12 *Ibid.*, 24 September 1887.

13 *Ibid.*, 4 October 1887.

14 *Ibid.*, 3 March 1887.

15 *Ibid.*, 14 October 1887. In a series of proposals dubbed the *Unauthorised Programme*, Joseph Chamberlain had called for 'graduated taxation and the revision of taxation; the emancipation of the soil by the establishment of free trade in land and the establishment of a peasant proprietary; free education; and taxation of unoccupied land, sporting land rents and royalties.'

16 *MN*, 4, 5 November 1887.

17 For background to the jailing of MPs, see Curtis, *The Cause of Ireland* (Belfast 1994), p.149. Biographical details about Alex Blane are limited, a key source being the *Armagh Guardian*, 11 December 1885, which profiled successful election candidates. In Dublin's municipal elections of January 1899, Blane stood unsuccessfully under a Labour ticket in the city's Trinity ward. He polled 537 votes, just 54 short of the number polled by the fourth and final successful candidate. See *Freeman's Journal*, 18 January 1899.

18 *MN*, 6, 7 January 1888.

19 *MN*, 12 January 1888. James Dempsey was the sole Catholic candidate standing for election to the town council, the first to be held following the passing of the Municipal Corporation of Belfast Act. He polled 721 votes and finished bottom of a list of seven candidates seeking a total of six seats. He told the *MN*, 28 November 1887, that Belfast's population comprised 70,000 Catholics and 150,000

Protestants, and 'after Mr Sexton's efforts the Catholics of Belfast are still unable to claim any share of the municipal representation.' Maguire, p.99, indicates that the town council had not had a Catholic member since 1878.

20 A reference in *MN*, 28 November 1887, to an attempt to give two Liberal Unionists seats on the town council with the backing of the Conservatives. Dempsey said he had succeeded in having them disqualified.

21 *MN*, 23 January 1888.

22 *Ibid.*, 24 January 1888.

23 *Ibid.*, 27 January 1888.

24 *Ibid.*, 2 February 1888.

25 The full list appeared in *MN*, 25 January 1888.

26 *Ibid.*, 2 February 1888.

27 *Ibid.*, 31 January 1888, *Banbridge Chronicle*, 1 February 1888.

28 Author's assumption.

29 *MN*, 24 February 1888.

30 *MN*, 17 March 1888. By then Wallace was also the editor and publisher of the Limavady-based weekly newspaper *Brotherhood*.

31 *MN*, 19 March 1888.

32 *Ibid.*, 6 April 1888. The Sexton Debating Society was founded on 21 November 1885, under the patronage of future West Belfast MP Thomas Sexton. Its motto was: 'Educate that you might be free.' See *Irish News*, 19 January 1934.

33 Joseph Devlin was the future Belfast Nationalist leader who would serve as MP for North Kilkenny (1902-1906); West Belfast (1906-1918); the Falls division in Belfast (1918-1922), having defeated Eamon de Valera; and Fermanagh and South Tyrone (1929 until his death in 1934).

34 *MN*, 11 April 1888.

35 Patrick Dempsey (d.1922) was another brother of James Dempsey.

36 *MN*, 20 April 1888.

37 *Ibid.*, 23 March 1888.

38 *Ibid.*, 13 June 1888.

39 *Ibid.*, 16 June 1888.

40 *Ibid.*, 28 June 1888.

41 *Ibid.*, 30 June 1888.

42 *Ibid.*, 16 August 1888.

43 Three people were killed at Mitchelstown, Co. Cork, when police opened fire on a National League meeting on 9 September 1887. See Curtis, pp.148-149. During detention in Tullamore jail John Mandeville served a term of solitary confinement for refusing to do prison work or to associate with criminals. Released on Christmas Eve 1887, his death at the age of 39 the following July was attributed at an inquest to ill-treatment received in prison. See Curtis, pp.148-152.

44 *MN*, 27 June 1888. John Morley had served as Gladstone's Chief Secretary for Ireland.

THE BIRD OF PASSAGE'S TRANSITION FROM NATIONALISM TO SOCIALISM

1 Bowman inferred this in a speech at Annaclone, Co. Down, *Morning News* (hereafter *MN*), 27 January 1888.

2 *Walthamstow Guardian* (hereafter *WG*), 8 March 1895.

3 *MN, Banbridge Chronicle*, 8 September 1888.

4 A speaker at Annaclone in 1886 said of McClinchy that it was 'very proper that one who had learned the lesson of freedom under the stars and stripes should preside at this meeting in favour of the freedom of Ireland.' See *MN*, 10 November 1886.

5 While a relatively unimportant occasion, Gladstone was indicating how much store he continued to place in the views of the Irish Protestant Home Rule Association.

6 A profile of John Stewart Wallace,

with portrait, appeared in *MN*, 5 April 1888, with further details in *MN*, 10 October 1888.

7   Author's conclusion based on available information.

8   *MN*, 31 October 1888.

9   Brian M. Walker, *Ulster Politics, The Formative Years, 1868-86* (Belfast 1989), pp.238, 249. Robert McCalmont died aged 61 in 1890.

10 The equivalent of several thousand pounds in the 1990s. Nine years after the presentation Bowman would speak of a working man with a wife and family to support needing a pound a week to survive. See *Belfast Evening Telegraph* (hereafter *BET*), 23 November 1897.

11 *Belfast Directory*, 1892, p.374.

12 P. J. O. McCann, in 'The Protestant Home Rule Movement, 1885-95' (MA, UCD 1972), pp.91-92, is of the opinion that by 1889 the association had become 'minimal and unimpressive.' In his conclusion, p.144, McCann states: 'The historical contribution of the IPHRA was minimal; its presence and its effects, its importance and its influences, were immediate and contemporaneous; the Protestant Home Rulers of 1886-1895 left little for posterity to ponder. The one fact that it did understand was the one which it set out to disprove or obscure: that few Protestants in Ireland wanted Irish self-government.'

13 Members of the Belfast Radical Association included president Hugh Hyndman and vice-presidents Robert McCalmont, John Bruce Wallace and Thomas McClelland. Its aims included the promotion of radical principles in Belfast and district and their adoption in parliament; self-government for England, Ireland, Scotland and Wales, and an imperial parliament for imperial affairs; land nationalisation; abolition of the principle of hereditary government; payment of MPs and election expenses; regulation of conditions and hours of labour; and arbitration for international questions instead of war. See *Brotherhood*, 21 December 1889 (names); *Belfast Weekly Star*, 7 June 1890 (aims).

14 *Northern Whig* (hereafter *NW*), *Belfast News-Letter*, 23 January 1885; also *MN*, 25 October 1888, for report of meeting held in Glasgow under the auspices of the Northern branch of the Irish National League, at which James Simpson proposed resolutions endorsing Gladstone's Home Rule proposals and expressing 'unabated confidence' in Parnell and the Irish parliamentary leaders and the 'great Liberal Party.' John Shaw Maxwell would become founding secretary of the Independent Labour Party, a key element in the birth of the modern-day Labour Party.

15 James Morrison Davidson, a Scottish Nationalist and land reformer, echoing Bowman's activities, would become a socialist. See John W. Boyle, *The Irish Labour Movement* (Washington, D.C. 1988), p.345. See also Queen's University, Belfast, British Parliamentary Papers, Belfast Constabulary Bill (1887) x, pp.693-862: Bowman told the 1887 parliamentary select committee that he and Scottish-based Ulster radical John Ferguson had toured parts of the Falls and Shankill Roads affected by the 1886 riots.

16 Mitchell Library, Glasgow, for registers of Whiteinch Primary School.

17 Mitchell Library for 1891 Glasgow census report. Their rented accommodation included two rooms with one or more windows.

18 Bowman placed regular advertisements in *Brotherhood* from 31 August 1889. Describing itself as 'a weekly paper

designed to help the peaceful evolution of a juster and happier social order,' *Brotherhood* was edited and published by the Rev. Bruce Wallace in Limavady between April 1887 and October 1889, when it moved to Belfast. It was absorbed by the *Belfast Weekly Star* (hereafter *BWS*) from June 1890. A complete run of the two papers, from May 1889-July 1891, is on microfilm at the British Newpaper Library, Colindale, London. The National Library of Ireland, Dublin, has four volumes comprising monthly editions of *Brotherhood*.

19 Information courtesy of Dr Hamish Fraser, Department of History, University of Strathclyde, Scotland. Also see Eamon Phoenix (ed.), *A Century of Northern Life* (Belfast 1995), pp.196-200, for an analysis of the role played by Irish exiles in Scotland.

20 *Brotherhood*, 11 May 1889.

21 *Ibid*.

22 *Ibid*., 28 September 1889.

23 *Ibid*., 5 October 1889, for aims of Henry George Institute and list of speakers; *ibid*., 23 November 1889, for Bowman's talk.

24 Bowman and Davitt both attended the 1882 Trades Union Congress in Manchester. See J. D. Clarkson, *Labour and Nationalism in Ireland* (New York 1925), p.182.

25 *Brotherhood*, 1 March 1890.

26 Clive Behagg, *Labour and Reform, Working Class Movements, 1815-1914* (London 1991), pp.114-115, suggests that the shift from Liberalism to a commitment to independent working-class representation could best be seen in the personal development of Keir Hardie – a Liberal supporter until the mid-1880s, an independent when he stood for parliament in 1888, and independent labour MP for West Ham South by 1892.

27 *BWS*, 19 July 1890; *Brotherhood*, August 1890 (monthly edition).

28 *BWS*, 30 August 1890; *Brotherhood*, October 1890.

29 *BWS*, 13 September 1890; *Brotherhood*, October 1890.

30 *BWS*, 11 October 1890.

31 *Ibid*., 29 November 1890, for annual meeting. As an example of his presidential activities, Bowman would visit the Govan area of Glasgow the following February to help with the establishment of a land restoration branch. See *BWS*, 21 February 1891.

32 Book in author's possession.

33 *BWS*, 28 February 1891.

34 Records of William Bowman.

35 *Belfast Directory*, 1887, p.85.

36 Records of William Bowman.

37 *BWS*, 11 April 1891.

38 Whiteinch Primary School registers.

39 PRONI, SCH/3/1/various, for Argyle Place National School registers.

40 Records of William Bowman.

41 *Ibid*.

42 General Register Office, Dublin, for birth certificate.

43 *MN*, 24, 29 June 1892.

44 Stoker was a self-proclaimed 'philosophical Home Ruler.' See Barbara Belford, *Bram Stoker – A Biography of the Author of Dracula* (London 1996), p. 230.

45 *NW*, 2, 9 September 1893.

46 See Behagg, pp.103-106. Although it was reputedly the leading socialist organisation of the period and often achieved a high public profile, support was limited numerically and, as a result, its importance should not be exaggerated. Yet, few followers of early British socialism were not at some time linked to the Social Democratic Federation. Behagg states that its membership in 1885

was no more than 1,000 and when it put up two candidates in London constituencies in that year's general election they polled just 59 votes between them. The SDF's eight-point programme of action, published each week in *Justice*, called for: 1, All organisers or administrators to be elected by equal direct adult suffrage, and to be maintained by the community; 2, Legislation by the people to be such that no project of law shall become binding until accepted by the majority of the people; 3, The abolition of standing armies and the establishment of national citizens' forces; the people to decide on peace or war; 4, All education to be compulsory, secular, industrial and free; 5, The administration of justice to be free to all; 6, The means of production, distribution and exchange to be declared and treated as collective or common property; 7, The production and distribution of wealth to be regulated by the community in the common interests of all its members, and 8, The establishment of international courts of arbitration.

47 *Justice* carried a column detailing SDF public meetings in the main centres of population in Britain. While not every branch identified its guest speakers, between July 1893 and August 1895 Bowman was named as a Sunday lecturer on at least 30 occasions, although it is likely he fulfilled a Sunday speaking engagement almost every week.

48 Author's conclusion. The 10 March 1894 edition of *Justice* identified the secretary of the Clerkenwell branch as W. Bowman. According to the Local

Studies Department of Finsbury Library, London, a William Bowman resided at 234 Compton Street, Clerkenwell, in 1885 (from register of electors for parliamentary borough of Finsbury).

49 Vestry House Museum, Walthamstow, for Markhouse Road School records.

50 Boyle, p.346, claims that Bowman was an active member of the SDF's Brixton branch. This would appear to be based on Bowman's participation in the Brixton debate on temperance in June 1894. Since the branch was then newly-formed and Bowman had been attending SDF meetings for a year or more at that point, the author believes Boyle to have been mistaken. Furthermore, Bowman had certainly been living in Walthamstow from the beginning of 1894, as evidenced by his children's school enrolment dates. The launch of the Brixton branch was reported in the *Brixton Free Press* and *Justice*, both of 19 May 1894. For the temperance debate, see *Justice*, 16 June 1894. A further meeting at Brixton, covered by the *South London Press*, 30 June 1894, carried no reference to Bowman, supporting the conclusion that he had been a visiting speaker.

51 The family's first floor accommodation at 57 Warner Road was listed under the name of William Bowman in the 1894-1895 and 1895-1896 editions of the Walthamstow directory (at Vestry House Museum).

52 Records of William Bowman (son of Alexander Bowman), also school register at Vestry House Museum.

53 *Walthamstow Reporter* (hereafter

WR), 14 December 1894. The term 'Radical' in this context refers to those within the Liberal Party, following the resignation of William Gladstone, who favoured Joseph Chamberlain's line of thinking. Sammy Herbert was owner of the rival *WG*.

54 *WR*, 14 December 1894.

55 *WG*, 14 December 1894. The same edition gives details about the candidates and their occupations.

56 *Ibid.*, 21 December 1894.

57 Bearing in mind the 59 votes mentioned in note 46, it was a praiseworthy achievement for an Irishman living in a London suburb.

58 *WG*, 21 December 1894; *Justice*, 22 December 1894.

59 Information contained in letter written by his daughter, Monica Bruce Wallace, in 1970 and made available to the author by John W. Boyle.

60 *WG*, 22 February 1895.

61 This emphasises that Bowman's political allegiances lay no longer with the Liberals, particularly those who supported Joseph Chamberlain. Maude Terrace, Bowman's first address, was named after Courtenay Warner's wife, while Warner Road, the second, was named in honour of family members who had made the land available a few years earlier for housing.

62 *WR*, 1 March 1895.

63 *Ibid.*

64 *WG*, 1 March 1895.

65 Copy at Vestry House Museum.

66 *WR*, 8 March 1895, for election result and comment.

67 *WG*, 14 December 1894.

68 Records of William Bowman.

69 School registers at Vestry House Museum.

70 W. A. Maguire, *Belfast: Site and City* (Keele 1993), p.103, refers to the absence of serious rioting in Belfast – on the same scale as that experienced in 1886 – following the defeat of Gladstone's second Home Rule bill. That would have been a further factor in Bowman's decision to return home for good.

71 In February 1900 Keir Hardie put a resolution before a meeting of delegates from the Social Democratic Federation, the Fabian Society, the Independent Labour Party and 67 trade unions, to create an organisation that would support a 'distinct Labour group in parliament, who shall have their own whips and agree upon their own policy.' The resolution was accepted and Ramsay MacDonald became secretary of the new Labour Representation Committee – which marked the birth of the Labour Party in all but name. However, the SDF contended that the new body's manifesto was not overtly socialist and rapidly disaffiliated itself. See Henry Pelling, *The Origins of the Labour Party, 1880-1900* (Oxford 1965), also Behagg, pp.119-121.

BACK IN THE BELFAST FOLD AND ELECTION SUCCESS

1 For Agnes Street National Schools, see PRONI, SCH/197/1/1-6. Bowman attended his final Social Democratic Federation rally at London's Kingsland Green on 24 August 1895. See *Justice*, 23 August 1895. No further editions carried his name as a speaker. His departure was not mentioned in the SDF newspaper.

2 The children's address was given as 205 Tennent Street in the Agnes Street School register for 1895. William McHenry, Bowman's brother-in-law, was a commercial traveller in the linen trade.

3 John W. Boyle, *The Irish Labour Movement* (Washington, D.C. 1988), p.346.

4   He was employed at either the Falls Flax Spinning Co. in Conway Street or at the adjacent Forth River Spinning Mills, or, perhaps, both. At a Belfast Corporation meeting Bowman complained about a sickening smell coming from the dam at the east side of Conway Street which he passed each day on his way to work. See *NL*, 4 July 1898.

5   This address appears in the school registers and was the one he used on his 1897 election papers.

6   Bowman's name featured in a Belfast Trades Council report for the first time in more than a decade when he chaired a meeting on 30 January 1897. See *Northern Whig* (hereafter *NW*), 1 February 1897. This suggests that his membership, as a flaxdressers' delegate, had been renewed at that month's annual meeting.

7   David Bleakley, 'Trade Union Beginnings in Belfast and District with special reference to the period 1881-1900, and to the work of the Belfast and District United Trades Council during that period' (MA, QUB 1955), p.89.

8   Boyle, pp.183, 187; Ann McKee, *Belfast Trades Council: the first 100 years* (Belfast 1983), p.11. See also Clive Behagg, *Labour and Reform, Working Class Movements, 1815-1914* (London 1991), pp.116-121, on the birth of the ILP and its aims.

9   Meetings were often targeted by anti-socialist objectors who tended to link it with support for Home Rule, despite the presence in its ranks of a strong-minded Unionist like William Walker. For more about Walker's role in Belfast working-class politics, see W. A. Maguire, *Belfast: Site and City* (Keele 1993), p.104; Boyle, pp.186-187; Donal Nevin (ed.), *Trade Union Century* (Dublin 1994), pp.70, 166.

10 *Labour Leader*, 10 October, 17 October, 7 November 1896. Despite such praise for the efforts of speakers like Bowman, the Belfast ILP branch did not last past 1897, its place being taken by the Belfast Ethical Society. Subjects covered at the latter's meetings, with Bowman on the lecture rota, included literature, spiritualism, evolution and modern science. See Boyle, pp.187, 191. Bowman's renewed membership of the trades council coincided with the winding down of his role as lecture secretary with the local ILP.

11 *Belfast News-Letter* (hereafter *BNL*), 3 November 1896.

12 Boyle, p.186; Bleakley, pp.118-21.

13 *Labour Leader*, 7 November 1896.

14 *BNL, NW*, 4 May 1897.

15 The White Linen Hall was replaced by the new city hall in the centre of Belfast.

16 *BNL*, 2 November 1897.

17 Ian Budge and Cornelius O'Leary, *Belfast; Approach to Crisis: A Study of Belfast Politics* (London 1973), pp.117-119; Maguire, p.102. The Belfast Corporation Act of 1896 had extended the area of the borough from 6,800 to 16,500 acres (10sq. miles to 23sq. miles), with the electorate increasing from 39,603 to 47,294.

18 *BNL*, 27 November 1891, 28 November 1893.

19 *Ibid.*, 18, 27 November 1891. Thomas Harrison was a Liberal Unionist. Austen Morgan, *Labour and Partition; the Belfast Working Class* (London 1991), p.70, states that he had served as secretary of the Ulster Liberal Unionist Association. He was also a veteran of the Belfast Debating Society, denouncing Henry George's land nationalisation scheme as 'utterly impractical.' See *NW*, 27 January 1885.

20 *Irish News* (hereafter *IN*), 8

November 1897. The vote was 19-10.

21 Belfast Trades Council minutes (hereafter BTC minutes), 19 November 1897.

22 *Ibid.*, 4 December 1897; Peter Collins, 'The Belfast Trades Council' (Ph. D., University of Ulster 1988), pp.84-85; Boyle, p.166.

23 *BNL*, 11 October 1897. The strike, over a demand by the Amalgamated Society of Engineers for an eight-hour day, lasted from June 1897 until the end of January 1898. It ended in defeat for the union, with the Engineering Employers' Federation imposing a settlement on the ASE which established that the union would not 'interfere' with 'the management of business.' See Behagg, p.111; also *BNL*, 17-31 January 1898, for the ending of the dispute.

24 *BNL*, 17 November 1897.

25 *Ibid.*, 26 November 1897.

26 *Belfast Evening Telegraph* (hereafter *BET*), 17 November 1897.

27 *Ibid.*, 18 November 1897.

28 In the non-transferable balloting system Bowman and the other labour candidates stood a better chance of electoral success if the 'plumping' method was used – in other words, a vote for labour and no other candidate.

29 *BET*, 19 November 1897. David Carlisle, a renowned speaker on political platforms, died aged 75 in 1921. The challenge to Bowman over allegedly atheistic views perhaps stemmed from some of the lectures given at meetings of the Belfast Ethical Society and his known socialist sympathies.

30 *BET*, 23 November 1897.

31 *Ibid.*, 26 November 1897. Sir William McCammond died suddenly on 2 March 1898.

32 Boyle, p.167.

33 Bleakley, p.46.

34 *BNL*, 24 November 1897.

35 *Ibid.*, 26 November 1897.

36 Budge and O'Leary, p.121. The 60 aldermen and councillors elected to Belfast Corporation were profiled in *BNL*, 27 November 1897.

37 Its first year of activities was noted by *IN*, 26 November 1897. Maguire notes, p.102, that three Catholics had been elected to the local authority in 50 years.

38 *IN*, 25 November 1897. The alderman for Smithfield was James Dempsey, who had contested North Belfast in 1886 and had failed in his bid the following year to win a council seat. He died in 1909.

39 E. L. (Effingham) Richardson was secretary of the Irish TUC between 1901 and 1909, served as president of the Dublin Trades Council in 1903, and became the first manager of the Board of Trade labour exchange in Dublin in 1910. Irish trade unionists had won council seats prior to 1898, including, for example, Eugene Crean, leader of Cork Trades Council, in 1886. However, such victories were due in no small part to Parnellite support, as indeed was Richardson's unopposed election.

40 BTC minutes, 4 December 1897. The increased franchise Richardson hoped for would be created through the Local Government (Ireland) Act, 1898. It finally saw the full assimilation of the Irish parliamentary and local government franchises. Property requirements were abolished for candidates who were required only to be registered local government electors. See Boyle, p.164.

41 Belfast City Hall, Belfast Corporation minutes (hereafter Corporation minutes), 1 December 1897; *BNL*, 2 December 1897.

42 Corporation minutes, 1, 3 January 1898; *BNL*, 2, 4 January 1898.

43 Bowman would serve on the same committees throughout his entire term of office, chairing the police committee between June and September 1898, in the absence of its chairman.

44 *BNL*, 2 February 1898.

45 *Ibid.*, 24 January 1898.

46 Corporation minutes, 15 February 1898.

47 BTC minutes, 1 January 1898. At the trades council's meeting on 29 July 1898, it was announced that Richard Wortley had stepped down due to ill-health (he died the following year). Bowman was proposed for the presidency but he sought leave to withdraw after John Murphy's name was put forward. Murphy was thus the unanimous choice for president, with Bowman serving as his vice-president.

48 BTC minutes, 26 March 1898; *BNL*, 28 March 1898.

49 BTC minutes, 7 May 1898; *BNL*, 9 May 1898.

50 BTC minutes, 21 May 1898; *BNL*, 23 May 1898.

51 *BNL*, 2 July 1898. Matches made from white or yellow phosphorus became illegal under the White Phosphorus Matches Prohibition Act of 1908, which took effect from 31 December 1910. See *IN*, 8 January 1909.

52 *BNL*, 16, 21 July 1898.

53 Boyle, p.168; BTC minutes, 9, 16, 29 July 1898.

54 *BNL*, 25 July 1898.

55 *Ibid.*, 19 October 1898. While Bowman would attend the laying of the foundation stone for the new Belfast City Hall in 1898, he was no longer a member when it was opened officially on 1 August 1906. See *BET* of that date.

56 *BNL*, 3 December 1898.

57 *Ibid.*, 21 December 1898.

58 *Ibid.*, 7 January 1899; also 10 January 1899, for explanatory letter by Gageby.

59 See Budge and O'Leary, p.192; also Maguire, p.136. Triennial elections for all councillors would be introduced in 1947, while a proportional representation system, introduced by Lloyd George in 1919, would be abolished by 1923.

60 *BNL*, 17 January 1899.

61 *Ibid.*, 2 March 1899, for confirmation of ruling; 4 March 1899, for special trades council meeting.

62 *Ibid.*, 2 February 1899.

63 The practice would in time be adopted. Belfast's Central Library has 1904-1905 editions of Belfast daily newspapers with the racing news painted out.

64 *BNL*, 10 April 1899. According to Boyle, p.276, the trades council organised Christmas treats and summer excursions between 1899 and 1910. Robert McClung, 'Recollections of the Belfast Labour Movement' (1929), noted that Walker remained a Poor Law Guardian for nine years.

65 *BET*, 27 April 1899.

66 *BNL*, 4 May 1899.

67 *Ibid.*, 23-25 May 1899.

68 *Ibid.*, 8 May 1899. William Hill stood in a number of corporation elections, including six wards simultaneously in January 1901, quite likely because he had been prosecuted by the authority for allegedly using substandard materials and workmanship during the construction of houses at Strandtown, Belfast. The charges were dismissed. See court report in *NW*, 1 January 1898.

69 *BNL*, 9, 16, 18, 19 May 1899.

70 *Ibid.*, 20 May 1899.

71 *Ibid.*, 20 June 1899.

72 *Ibid.*, 22 June 1899.

73 *Ibid.*, 6 July 1899.

OLD WOUNDS REOPENED FOR THE APOSTLE OF SOCIALISM

1 *Belfast News-Letter* (hereafter *BNL*), 7 July 1899, for court report.

2 *BNL*, 11, 14 July 1899.

3 *BNL*, 20 July 1899. Gerald Balfour was brother of former Irish Chief Secretary Arthur Balfour.

4 *BNL*, 21 July 1899.

5 *Ibid.*, 3 August 1899. Alexander Hopkins (d. 1940) rode out the scandal, continuing his work with the Salvation Army (for almost 60 years in total), being linked with the Ulster Volunteer Force during the post-1912 Home Rule crisis, and winning a seat on Belfast Corporation.

6 *BNL*, 5 October 1899.

7 Sir Samuel Black retired in 1909 and died the following year.

8 *BNL*, 14 November 1899. The councillors' plea fell on deaf ears. Robert McClung, 'Recollections of the Belfast Labour Movement' (1929), also refers to the subject as a key issue in Labour's 1910 general election campaign in North Belfast. To this day vacant land remains free from taxation through the rates.

9 *BNL*, 4, 10 January 1900.

10 *Ibid.*, 11 January 1900.

11 *Ibid.*, 14 January 1900; Linen Hall Library, Belfast, Belfast Trades Council minutes (hereafter BTC minutes), 13 January 1900.

12 *BNL*, 17 January 1900. Dr James Williamson served on the corporation for 44 years until his death in 1944.

13 *Ibid.*, 29 January 1900; BTC minutes, 27 January 1900.

14 A reference to the town in Macedonia, near where Antony and the future Emperor Augustus decisively defeated Brutus and Cassius in 42BC.

15 *BNL*, 17 March 1900. Queen Victoria's only visit to Belfast occurred in 1849, with further visits to Ireland in 1853 and 1861.

16 *Ibid.*, 27 April 1900.

17 *Ibid.*, 2 May 1900.

18 *Ibid.*, 2 August 1900.

19 *Ibid.*, 29 September 1900.

20 Letters in *BNL*, 2 October 1900; Alan Carr, *The Early Belfast Labour Movement, part 1, 1885-1893* (Belfast 1974), p.29.

21 *BNL*, 29 September 1900.

22 *Ibid.*

23 *Ibid.*, 1 October 1900.

24 *Ibid.*, 2 October 1900.

25 *Ibid.*

26 There was strong opposition to the Boer War among socialist groups in Britain and Ireland, including the SDF, ILP and, in the early stages, the British TUC. See John W. Boyle, *The Irish Labour Movement* (Washington, D.C. 1988), pp.199-200. See also *MN*, 12 May 1887.

27 *BNL*, 3 October 1900.

28 *Ibid.*, 4 October 1900.

29 The Conservatives and Unionists won 402 seats, the Liberals 186 and the Nationalists 82. In Ireland the results were as follows: 76 Nationalists, five independent Nationalists, 17 Conservatives, four Liberal Unionists and one Liberal.

30 Boyle, pp.169-170.

31 This is achieved by adding together the attendance figures given for Bowman (and other councillors) at each quarterly meeting of Belfast Corporation and published in the press.

32 BTC minutes, 11 February 1898.

33 *Ibid.*, 25 February 1898.

34 Boyle, pp.169-170.

35 BTC minutes, 9 November 1900. Walker received 23s. 6d. a week from the trades council in 1900-1901 after losing his job for writing a critical letter to the War Office in his

capacity as the body's secretary. See Boyle, p.169.

36 Belfast City Hall, Belfast Corporation minutes, 1 January 1901; *BNL*, 3 January 1901.

37 *BNL*, 8 January 1901.

38 Thomas Adair (1838-1909) had chaired meetings of the Irish Land Restoration Society and was one of the prime movers at the inaugural meeting of the Irish Protestant Home Rule Association in May 1886. Joseph Cairns, a member of the Painters' Union, was one of the Belfast delegates in the opening parade for the Cork exhibition on 3 July 1883.

39 BTC minutes, 12 January 1901; *BNL*, 14 January 1901.

40 Boyle, p.285.

41 For nominations, see *BNL*, 7 January 1901.

42 *Ibid.*, 26 January 1901.

43 The introduction of proportional representation in 1919 led to the election to the corporation of 10 members of the Belfast Labour Party, the official Labour group, three independent Labour candidates, and six Labour Unionists. Labour's representation was cut to just two after the voting system was abolished. See W. A. Maguire, *Belfast: Site and City* (Keele 1993), p.136.

THE IRISH TRADE UNION CONGRESS YEARS

1 The Belfast Congress was held on 30, 31 May and 1 June 1898, the city having replaced Clonmel as the venue at short notice. See QUB, Irish Trade Union Congress (hereafter ITUC), *Reports*, 1898; also extensive reports can be found in the local daily newspapers for the period 31 May-2 June 1898.

2 The annual reports of the ITUC indicate the union or trades council represented by each delegate. Bowman represented both bodies in 1898, the municipal employees only in 1899 and 1901, and the flaxdressers only in 1900. On occasions in the 1899 and 1901 annual reports Bowman is referred to as a flaxdresser.

3 For standing orders committee, see ITUC, *Reports,* 1898, p.27.

4 *Ibid.*, pp.44-45.

5 *Ibid.*, pp.33-34.

6 *Belfast Evening Telegraph* (hereafter BET), 2 June 1898.

7 Congress took place from 22-24 May 1899. References are mainly from ITUC, *Reports,* 1899. Extensive coverage can also be found in the *Derry Journal*, 24, 26 May 1899. Congress was also covered by the *Londonderry Sentinel*, 23, 25 May, and the *Derry Standard*, 26 May 1899.

8 ITUC, *Reports*, 1899, p.41.

9 *Derry Journal*, 26 May 1899.

10 ITUC, *Reports*, 1899, p.57. The report sidestepped much of the political division, whereas the *Derry Journal*, 26 May 1899, provided a detailed account.

11 *Belfast News-Letter* (hereafter *BNL*), 25 May, 18 June 1899.

12 ITUC, *Reports*, 1900. Reports can also be found in the Belfast daily newspapers and the *Irish Times*, 5-7 June 1900; also John W. Boyle, *The Irish Labour Movement* (Washington, D.C. 1988), pp.216-217.

13 ITUC, *Reports*, 1900, p.45. The committee usually met four times a year. According to the 1899 ITUC report it had met just twice during the year, both times in Belfast. The day after the Derry Congress ended the committee met in the Guildhall and Bowman was elected vice-chairman, pp.54, 58-59. The 1900 ITUC report, p.24, indicated that it

had met in the trades hall library, Dublin, on 7 August 1899, 14 April, 31 May and 1/2 June 1900.

14 ITUC, *Reports*, 1900, pp.24-26. Also see ITUC, *Reports*, 1899, pp.31-33.

15 Andrew Boyd, in *The Rise of the Irish Trade Unions* (Tralee 1985), p.71, explains the Quinn v. Leathem case thus: The North of Ireland Operative Butchers' Society was involved in a lawsuit that has become world-famous and has been studied by generations of lawyers in many countries. The case arose out of an attempt by Joseph Quinn and other officials of the union to compel Henry Leathem, a [Lisburn] flesher operating in the Belfast Abattoir, to employ only union labour. Leathem refused to dismiss some of his workmen who had been expelled from the union for not paying their contributions. He tried, however, to encourage them to rejoin the union and even offered to pay their arrears of contributions. But the union rejected this offer and in the course of the dispute that followed Quinn and his colleagues persuaded Andrew [Munce], a meat retailer [of Cornmarket, Belfast], not to take supplies from Leathem. When [Munce] stopped buying meat, Leathem brought an action against the union officials on the grounds that they had conspired together to injure him and that, as a result, he had suffered material damage. The case was tried by a judge and jury who found for Leathem and awarded him £250 damages [later reduced to £200]. The union appealed against the decision and took the appeal to the House of Lords which upheld the jury's decision. 'The Quinn v. Leathem case established,' adds Boyd, 'that if two or more persons combined together, without legal justification, to injure another and by doing so caused him damage, they were liable in an action for conspiracy.' Additional information from substantial reports of the House of Lords hearing from *BNL* and *Northern Whig*, 12, 14 June 1901; also Boyle, pp.225-226. The contemporary reports refer to Munce, whereas Boyd uses Munroe.

16 ITUC, *Reports*, 1900, pp.30, 43.

17 *Ibid.*, pp.45-46.

18 Linen Hall Library, Belfast, Belfast Trades Council minutes (hereafter BTC minutes), 8 June 1900.

19 *Ibid.*, 30 July 1900.

20 British TUC Library, London, British Trades Union Congress, *Reports*, 1900, p.5. The report incorrectly stated that Ratcliffe Street was in Hull.

21 *BNL*, 22 September 1900.

22 *Ibid.*, 24 January 1901; ITUC, *Reports*, 1901, pp.25-31.

23 Bowman became the first outgoing chairman of the parliamentary committee to serve as Congress president who was not also president of the host trades council (for example, James McCarron of Derry in 1899). The practice would be adopted by Congress from 1903 onwards. Boyle states, p.353, that Sligo had no trades council, implying that was the reason for Bowman's election. In fact, it was the president of Sligo Trades Council who proposed him.

24 Bowman had struck up a useful relationship with the local trades council, having visited Sligo with E. L. Richardson and Hugh McManus, from the parliamentary committee, that March to deliver a lecture on preparing for Congress. See ITUC, *Reports*, 1901, p.33. Other sources for the Sligo Congress are the *BNL*, 28-30 May 1901, and the *Sligo Champion*, 1 June 1901.

25 ITUC, *Reports*, 1901, pp.7-12.

26 Philip James Bailey lived from 1816-1902.

27 Sir Josselyn Gore-Booth's sister Constance, as the Countess Constance Markievicz, would become the first woman ever elected to Westminster.

28 ITUC, *Reports*, 1901, p.53. Walker also sought unsuccessfully to bar any delegates from attending Congress who were not '*bona fide* workers' for the union they represented. A motion clearly aimed at trade unionists like Bowman, delegate of the municipal workers, it was defeated by 31 votes to five. *Ibid.*, p.57.

29 *Ibid.*, p.58. The order bell is in the possession of Ivan Bowman, great-grandson of Alexander Bowman.

30 BTC minutes, 8 August 1901.

A NEW LIFE ON THE FALLS ROAD

1 Author's conclusion based on a succession of addresses in close proximity to the Crumlin Road.

2 The inference that Bowman's decision to apply for the position at Falls Road was 'against his will,' is contained in the records of son William.

3 Information about Hugh Bowman from his descendants, also *Belfast Directory*, various years.

4 Linen Hall Library, Belfast, Belfast Trades Council minutes (hereafter BTC minutes), 13 June 1901. According to John W. Boyle, *The Irish Labour Movement* (Washington, D. C. 1988), p.278, Joseph Mitchell (d. 1901) and Samuel Monro (d. 1925) both severed their links with the trades council in 1894 in a row over the method used to select delegates to attend that year's British Trades Union Congress in Norwich. At the time Monro was president and Mitchell was vice-president. Mitchell was appointed superintendent when

the Falls Road baths opened in 1896.

5 Belfast City Hall, Belfast Corporation Baths and Lodging House Committee minutes (hereafter Baths minutes), 26 June 1901.

6 *Ibid.*, 17 July 1901.

7 *Ibid.*, 14 August 1901.

8 This was the same Thomas Johnston who had confronted Bowman back in 1884-1886 over his Liberal politics. Prominently identified with the Orange Order – he had served as secretary of the Co. Grand Lodge of Belfast – Johnston (1850-1931) was also a member of the Masonic Order.

9 Baths minutes, 11 September 1901. In 1902 Robert Gageby (d. 1934), grandfather of noted *Irish Times* editor Douglas Gageby, was appointed a Justice of the Peace for Belfast. Belfast Trades Council, of which he remained a member as a representative of the Flaxdressers' Union, referred to him as the 'first *bona fide* working man to be placed in that onerous and responsible position.' See BTC minutes for 6 November 1902.

10 BTC minutes, 19 January 1902. The roll call indicating attendances can be found at the back of the same minute book.

11 QUB, Irish Trade Union Congress, *Reports*, 1902, pp.24, 32. Boyle, pp.222-223, states that most parliamentary work on behalf of the ITUC in the first decade of the twentieth century was done by Nationalist MPs.

12 Bowman's name was one of four put forward in 1903 as potential Belfast Labour Representation Committee candidates in North Belfast, the seat ultimately contested by William Walker. Walker was nominated by nine unions affiliated to Belfast Trades Council, Robert Gageby also by nine, with one nomination each for Bowman and Alex Taylor.

Bowman's name was probably suggested by the Belfast Municipal Employees' and Other Workers' Association. See *BNL*, *Northern Whig* (hereafter *NW*), *Irish News* (hereafter *IN*), 29 June 1903, also Boyle, p.293. It would be fanciful, however, to suggest that Bowman might have won where Walker would fail. Standing for parliament would not only have cost Bowman his corporation position, as it had borough cashier Edward de Cobain in 1885, he would also have lost the home which accompanied the job at Falls Road. Furthermore, there is every likelihood that his Home Rule past would have been used against him by the Conservatives. There is little doubt, however, that Bowman retained an enthusiasm for socialism. In Robert McClung, 'Recollections of the Belfast Labour Movement' (1929), there is a reference to Bowman 'debating Socialism' at Bethany Presbyterian Church, Agnes Street, in 1906. According to McClung it was a time when 'we found the churches and clergy were taking a keen interest in Labour and Socialist questions.' There is also a reference by Boyle, p.205, note 137, to Bowman [misnamed as Alexander Brown], William Walker and Alex Taylor having been leaders of the Christian Socialist Brotherhood in Belfast. It was a loose fellowship of committed Christians within the city's trades union movement.

13 The Bowman family's 1911 Census return (National Archives, Dublin) indicates that the house, 2a North Howard Street, comprised nine rooms and had a total of eight windows to the front. By that time the two eldest Bowman children, William and Robert, had moved out, but the family had a boarder, 18-year-old apprentice fitter John Watt

Knox, from North Antrim. Knox, who later returned to the family farm at Magherahoney, died aged 70 in 1963.

14 There is likely to have been at least one further address since Bowman's 1901 Census return cannot be traced to any of the named streets.

15 Baths minutes, 25 September 1901.

16 It was agreed that the Falls Road baths should stay open each Sunday following an approach to the corporation by the Belfast Catholic Association. See baths minutes, 3 June 1903. There was a further debate on the issue five years later when it was confirmed that the baths should remain open on Sunday mornings for three months a year. See *Belfast News-Letter* (hereafter *BNL*), 23 July 1908. The practice ceased after the First World War.

17 Baths minutes, 24 September 1902.

18 *Ibid.*, 30 September 1902.

19 *BNL*, 22 November 1902; Baths minutes, 3 December 1902.

20 *Ireland's Saturday Night*, 8 October 1904.

21 Baths minutes, 2 May 1906.

22 *Ibid.*, 18 October 1904.

23 *Ibid.*, 16 October, 13 November, 11 December 1907.

24 He had initially put forward the idea at a baths committee meeting on 2 October 1907.

25 Baths minutes, 4 September 1907.

26 *Ibid.*, 24 December 1907, 8 January 1908.

27 *Ibid.*, 5 February 1908 (for Lassar baths); 26 August 1907 (for creche).

28 *Ibid.*, 5 August 1908.

29 *Ibid.*, 16 September 1908. Reports in *IN* and *Belfast Evening Telegraph*, 24 September 1908, explained that the Lassar type of bath was the invention of a Berlin professor of skin diseases. 'Its general adoption, by reason of its greater cleanliness in use, should be

of distinct advantage in furthering the cause of public health,' stated the *IN* report. 'The bath utilises an elaborate series of overhead and side sprays which ensures a continuous stream of fresh water, thus obviating any chance of contagion or infection, in addition to a much greater economy in working as compared to the old plan.' By November they had been used by 235 people and the first year produced an income of £32. 18s. 0d. See Baths minutes of 25 November 1908.

30 *Ibid.*, 6 August 1908.

31 *Ibid.*, 12 May 1909.

32 Confirmed from records held by the swimming section of the Sports Council for Northern Ireland.

33 Baths minutes, 23 June 1909.

34 *Ibid.*, 19 January, 2 February, 2 March 1910.

35 *Ibid.*, 10 February 1910.

36 *Ibid.*, 30 August 1910.

37 *Ibid.*, 14 August, 4 September 1912.

38 *Ibid.*, 21 May 1912.

39 *Ibid.*, 19 November 1913.

40 *Ibid.*, 19 May 1915.

41 *Ibid.*, 5 May 1915.

42 *Ibid.*, 3, 17, 31 October, 14 November 1917.

43 *Ibid.*, 16 April 1919, 23 February 1920.

44 *Ibid.*, 15 December 1920.

45 *Ibid.*, 23 June 1921.

46 See Joe Baker, *The McMahon Family Murders and the Belfast Troubles* (Belfast 1991), for contemporary reports of the violence in the early 1920s; also W. A. Maguire, *Belfast: Site and City* (Keele 1993), pp.135-136.

47 Baths minutes, 6 July 1921.

48 *Ibid.*, 30 January 1922.

49 *Ibid.*, 13 March 1922.

50 *Ibid.*, 27 March 1922.

51 Belfast City Hall, Belfast Corporation minutes, 3 April 1922; Baths minutes, 23 June 1922.

52 *Ibid.*, 18 December 1922. Richard Ferguson was appointed acting superintendent to replace Bowman and moved into the accommodation at North Howard Street. He died in 1932, having worked for the corporation for 38 years.

THE CHURCH CONNECTION

1 *History of Congregations in the Presbyterian Church in Ireland*, no author cited, Presbyterian Historical Society of Ireland (Belfast 1982), pp.144-145.

2 Alex Boyd had co-represented Belfast's municipal employees with Bowman at the 1901 Irish Trade Union Congress held in Sligo.

3 Donegall Road Presbyterian Church (now Richview), committee minutes (hereafter Donegall Road minutes).

4 Donegall Road minutes, 24 August 1903.

5 *Ibid.*, 9 May 1904. See also *History of Congregations in the Presbyterian Church in Ireland*, pp.195-197.

6 *Belfast News-Letter* (hereafter *BNL*), 16, 17, 18, 20 November 1905.

7 *Ibid.*, 16 November 1905.

8 Some additional details from Jessie C. Barbour, *The Rock on the Plain, Cregagh Presbyterian Church 1900-1993* (Belfast 1994).

9 Courtesy of Presbyterian Historical Society of Ireland, Belfast.

10 Robert McClung, 'Recollections of the Belfast Labour Movement' (1929).

11 *History of Congregations in the Presbyterian Church in Ireland*, pp.133-134. Bethany and Agnes Street Presbyterian Churches became a united charge known as Immanuel in 1971.

12 Donegall Road minutes, 31 May 1909.

13 *BNL*, 28 March 1912.

14 The figure of 500 families in 1912

is given in *History of Congregations in the Presbyterian Church in Ireland*, p.196.

15 Donegall Road minutes, 5 May 1913.

16 The significance of the May 1913 anti-Home Rule memorial at Donegall Road Presbyterian Church, was that it coincided with the launch by Carson of renewed opposition in Ulster.

17 Donegall Road minutes, 8 March 1920. See also Fountainville entry in *History of Congregations in the Presbyterian Church in Ireland*, pp.169-170.

18 Richview Presbyterian Church, committee minutes, 11 May 1920.

19 Argyle Place Presbyterian Church records, courtesy of West Kirk Presbyterian Church.

FINAL DAYS AND THE NEXT GENERATION

1 Belfast City Hall, Baths and Lodging House Committee minutes (hereafter Baths minutes), 6, 22 June 1922.

2 *Ibid.*, 31 July 1922.

3 *Ibid.*, 14 August 1922. Bowman was 68 when he retired. His superannuation was mentioned at the next full meeting of Belfast Corporation. See *Irish News* (hereafter *IN*), 2 September 1922.

4 Family information drawn from the records of William Bowman, unless otherwise stated. Also see obituary reports for Alexander's children as follows: Hugh, *Co. Down Spectator*, 13 August 1965, *Belfast Telegraph* (hereafter *BT*), 9 August 1965; Robert, *BT*, 5 October 1970.

5 Belfast City Hall, Register of Births, Marriages and Deaths.

6 *Northern Whig* (hereafter *NW*), 4 November 1924.

7 Information courtesy of Cooke Centenary Church, Belfast.

8 *BT*, 3 November 1924; *BNL, NW*, 4 November 1924. The obituary did not appear in *IN*, although a death notice was published on 4 November 1924. While the author of the report, most likely second son Robert, might not have submitted it to the paper lest it encouraged memories of Bowman's Home Rule past, it is equally possible that the editor chose not to publish it because of the reference to Bowman becoming a Unionist.

9 *Ireland's Saturday Night*, 8 November 1924.

10 Richview Presbyterian Church, committee minutes, 4 November 1924; Baths minutes, 5 November 1924.

11 Baths minutes, 26 November 1924.

12 Will at PRONI.

13 Copy of souvenir booklet at National Library of Ireland, Dublin.

14 *BNL*, 5 November 1924.

15 Additional information from Dr John A. Howard (son).

16 Probably Harland and Wolff, where aircraft construction commenced during the latter part of the First World War.

17 Sons Eric and Geoffrey, both RAF pilots, lost their lives during the Second World War. For Eric, see *Co. Down Spectator*, 3 January 1942 (obituary); for Geoffrey, *ibid.*, 2, 16 June 1945 (obituary). Hugh's distinguished legal career, which included being appointed a QC at the age of 45 in 1967, was cut short with his death four years later. He and his wife Jean had two sons, Geoffrey and Terence. Their middle names, Alexander and Hugh respectively, maintain a family tradition. For Hugh Bowman (jnr.), see *Co. Down Spectator*, 12 March 1971 (obituary); Jean Bowman, *ibid.*, 30 May 1991 (obituary); also for Edgar Bowman, *ibid.*, 12 December 1980 (obituary).

18 Additional research by Joseph McGiverin (sen.), of Holyoke, Massachusetts.

BIBLIOGRAPHY

CONTENTS
A. Newspapers
B. Recollections
C. Private papers
D. Manuscript and printed primary sources
E. Books, articles and pamphlets
F. Theses

A. NEWSPAPERS

Armagh Guardian
Banbridge Chronicle
Belfast (Evening) Telegraph
Belfast Morning News
Belfast News-Letter
Brixton Free Press
Brotherhood/ Belfast Weekly Star
County Down Spectator
Derry Journal
Derry Standard
Freeman's Journal
Ireland's Saturday Night

Irish News
Irish Times
Justice
Labour Leader
Leinster Leader
Londonderry Sentinel
Lurgan Times
Northern Whig
Portadown News
Sligo Champion
South London Press
The Times
Walthamstow Guardian
Walthamstow Reporter
Weekly Northern Whig

B. RECOLLECTIONS

Robert Bowman

Helen Burland (née Bowman)

Rosemary Graham (née Howard)

Dr. John A. Howard

Rosaleen Wood (née Bowman)

The above-named, all grandchildren of Alexander Bowman, were interviewed on various dates and at various locations about Bowman family history.

Stuart Kelly (great-grandson), on Hugh Bowman's family background, various dates.

Margaret McLain (née Bowman, grand-daughter), on Hugh Bowman's family background, various dates.

C. PRIVATE PAPERS

William Bowman (eldest son of Alexander Bowman), family details in an account written in the 1940s for his own son Alexander.

Minnie Grimmett Howard (née Bowman), diary relating family events.

Robert McClung, recollections of the Belfast labour movement, written in 1929, and supplied to the author by John W. Boyle.

D. MANUSCRIPT AND PRINTED PRIMARY SOURCES

Argyle Place Presbyterian Church (now West Kirk), Belfast, records (in local custody).

Belfast Constabulary Bill (1887), British Parliamentary Papers, at Queen's University, Belfast.

Belfast Corporation, minutes of Corporation and Baths and Lodging House Committee meetings, 1897-1924, at Belfast City Hall.

Belfast and Province of Ulster Directory, Belfast, various years.

Belfast Trades Council, minute books for various years, at Linen Hall Library, Belfast.

British Trades Union Congress, *Reports*, 1882, 1883 and 1900, at TUC Library, London.

British Trades Union Congress, souvenir brochure published to mark Congress in Belfast, 1929, at National Library of Ireland.

Census details for Belfast, 1911, at National Archives, Dublin.

Census details for Glasgow, 1891, at Mitchell Library, Glasgow.

Census of Ireland for the Year 1861, HMSO, Dublin, 1863.

Clifton Street Presbyterian Church, Belfast, records (in local custody).

Cliftonville Presbyterian Church, Belfast, records, at Public Record Office of Northern Ireland.

Cooke Centenary Presbyterian Church, Belfast, records (in local custody).

Donegall Road Presbyterian Church (now Richview), Belfast, committee minutes and other church records, 1903-1924 (in local custody).

Dundonald Presbyterian Church, records (in local custody).

Eglinton Street Presbyterian Church, Belfast, marriage records, at General Register Office, Dublin, and PRONI.

Ekenhead Presbyterian Church, Belfast, records, at PRONI.

Election address by Alexander Bowman when standing for Essex County Council in 1895, at Vestry House Museum, Walthamstow, London.

Irish Protestant Home Rule Association, Dublin executive minute book, at National Library of Ireland.

Irish Trade Union Congress, *Reports*, 1898-1904, at QUB.

Loughaghery Presbyterian Church, Co. Down, births and

marriages records, at PRONI.

Ordnance Survey maps for Co. Down, 1832 and 1931, at PRONI.

Primary Valuation of Ireland (Griffith), Dublin, 1863, at PRONI.

School records for Markhouse Road School, Walthamstow, at Vestry House Museum.

School records for St. Paul's, Argyle Place, and Agnes Street National Schools, Belfast, at PRONI.

School records for Whiteinch Primary School, Glasgow, at Mitchell Library, Glasgow.

St. Michael's Church, Dromara, Co. Down, births and marriages records, at PRONI.

Thom's Irish Who's Who, Dublin, 1923.

Thom's Official Directory of the United Kingdom of Great Britain and Ireland for the Year... , Dublin, various years.

Tithe applotment books dated 1826, at PRONI.

E. BOOKS, ARTICLES AND PAMPHLETS

American Biographies, Harper and Brothers, New York and London, 1974.

Baker, Joe, *The McMahon Family Murders and the Belfast Troubles*, revised edition, Glenravel Publications, Belfast, 1991.

Barbour, Jessie C., *The Rock on the Plain, Cregagh Presbyterian Church 1900-1993*, Presbyterian Church in Ireland, Belfast, 1994.

Bardon, Jonathan, *Belfast: An Illustrated History*, Blackstaff Press, Belfast, 1982.

Bassett, George Henry, *Co. Down 100 Years Ago: a Guide and Directory* (1886), Friar's Bush Press, Belfast, 1988.

Behagg, Clive, *Labour and Reform, Working Class Movements, 1815-1914*, Hodder and Stoughton, London, 1991.

Belford, Barbara, *Bram Stoker – A Biography of the Author of Dracula*, Weidenfeld and Nicolson, London, 1996.

Boyd, Andrew, *The Rise of the Irish Trade Unions*, Anvil, Tralee, 1985.

Boylan, Henry, *Dictionary of Irish Biography*, Gill and Macmillan, Dublin, 1988.

Boyle, John W., *The Irish Labour Movement*, Catholic University of America Press, 1988, Washington, D.C., 1988.

Budge, Ian and O'Leary, Cornelius, *Belfast; Approach to Crisis:*

A Study of Belfast Politics, 1613-1970, Macmillan, London, 1973.

Carr, Alan, *The Early Belfast Labour Movement*, part 1, 1885-1893, Athol Books, 1974.

Clarkson, Jesse Dunsmore, *Labour and Nationalism in Ireland*, Columbia University Press, 1925.

Colles, Ramsay, *History of Ulster*, vol. 4, London, 1920.

Collins, Peter (ed.), *Nationalism and Unionism, Conflict in Ireland, 1885-1921*, Institute of Irish Studies, QUB, 1994.

Crealey, Aidan H., *An Irish Almanac*, Mercier Press, Cork and Dublin, 1993.

Curtis, Liz, *The Cause of Ireland*, Beyond the Pale Publications, Belfast, 1994.

Day, Angelique, McWilliams, Patrick (eds.), *O.S. Memoirs (Mid Down)*, vol. 12, Institute of Irish Studies, QUB, 1992.

Dictionary of National Biography, various volumes, Oxford.

Doherty, J. E. and Hickey, D. J., *Chronology of Irish History since 1850*, Gill and Macmillan, Dublin, 1989.

Geary, Laurence M., *The Plan of Campaign*, Cork University Press, 1986.

Hamilton, Paul, *Up the Shankill*, Blackstaff, 1979.

Healy, T. M., *Letters and Leaders of My Day*, vol. 1, London, 1928.

History of Congregations in the Presbyterian Church in Ireland, various authors, Presbyterian Historical Society of Ireland, Belfast, 1982.

Irish Linen – A History of William Ewart and Son Ltd., no author cited, company publication, Belfast, 1964.

Jenkins, Roy, *Gladstone*, Macmillan, London, 1995.

Liggett, Michael, *A District Called Ardoyne*, Glenravel Publications, Belfast, 1994.

Loughlin, James, 'The Irish Protestant Home Rule Association and Nationalist Politics, 1886-93,' *Irish Historical Studies*, xxiv, no. 95 (May 1985).

Lyttle, Wesley G., *Betsy Gray*, reprint of the original book with other stories and pictures of '98, Mourne Observer Press, Newcastle, Co. Down, 1997.

McKee, Ann, *Belfast Trades Council: the first 100 years (1881-1981)*, Belfast, 1983.

Maguire, W. A., *Belfast: Site and City*, Keele University Press, 1993.

Marsh, Arthur, Ryan, Victoria and Smethurst, John B., *Historical Directory of Trades Unions*, vol. 4, Scolar Press, Aldershot, 1994.

Messenger, Betty, *Picking up the Linen Threads – Life in Ulster's Mills*, Blackstaff, 1978.

Milford, the Rev. Robert, *The Shankill Road*, Sabbath School Society, Belfast, 1971.

Mitchell, Arthur, *Labour in Irish Politics, 1890-1930*, Irish University Press, Dublin, 1974.

Morgan, Austen, *Labour and Partition; the Belfast Working Class, 1905-1923*, Pluto Press, London, 1991.

Nevin, Donal (ed.), *Trade Union Century*, Mercier, Dublin, 1994.

Newmann, Kate, *Dictionary of Ulster Biography*, Institute of Irish Studies, QUB, 1993.

O'Connor, Emmet, *A Labour History of Ireland 1824-1860*, Gill and Macmillan, Dublin, 1992.

Pelling, Henry, *The Origins of the Labour Party, 1880-1900*, second edition, Clarendon Press, Oxford, 1965.

Phoenix, Eamon (ed.), *A Century of Northern Life, The Irish News and 100 years of Ulster history, 1890s to 1990s*, Ulster Historical Foundation, Belfast, 1995.

Pike, W. T. (ed.), *Ulster Contemporary Biographies*, Brighton, 1909.

Rutherford, George, *Old Families of Carrickfergus and Ballynure*, ed. Richard Clarke, Ulster Historical Foundation, 1995.

Scottish Biographical Dictionary, Chambers, Edinburgh, 1992.

Scottish National Dictionary, vol. 2, Edinburgh, 1941.

Shanks, the Rev. George Hay, Boardmills, *Bible Temperance: Containing an examination of Rev. Dr Murphy's tract on Wine in the Bible*, Belfast, 1869.

Ulster Liberal Unionist Association, *A Sketch of its History, 1885-1914*, with introduction by J. R. Fisher, Belfast, 1913.

Vincent, J. and Stenton, M. (eds.), *McCalmont's Parliamentary Poll Book of all Elections, 1832-1918*, Harvester Press, Brighton, 1971.

Walker, Brian M., *Parliamentary Election Results in Ireland, 1801-1922*, Royal Irish Academy, Dublin, 1978.

Walker, Brian M., *Ulster Politics, The Formative Years, 1868-86*, Ulster Historical Foundation and the Institute of Irish Studies, QUB, 1989.

Warwick-Haller, Sally, *William O'Brien and the Irish Land War*, Irish Academic Press, Dublin, 1990.

Welch, Robert (ed.), *Oxford Companion to Irish Literature*, Oxford, 1996.

Wheeler, Gordon, 'A History of Belfast Central Library,' *Linen Hall Review*, 5:2, 1988.

Who's Who of British Members of Parliament, vols. 1-3, ed. Stenton and Lees, Harvester Press, 1976-1978.

Who Was Who, various volumes, A. & C. Black, London.

Wright, Frank, *Two Lands On One Soil, Ulster politics before Home Rule*, Gill and Macmillan, Dublin, 1996.

F. THESES

Bleakley, David, 'Trade Union beginnings in Belfast and District with special reference to the period 1881-1900, and to the work of the Belfast and District United Trades Council during that period,' QUB, MA, 1955.

Collins, Peter, 'The Belfast Trades Council,' University of Ulster, Ph. D., 1988.

McCann, P. J. O., 'The Protestant Home Rule Movement, 1885-95,' UCD, MA, 1972.

INDEX